T0244562

Caring Ca.

'Across the world, welfare systems are being remade in the image of "basic income". Tom Neumark powerfully intervenes in this debate by showing how Nairobi's grant recipients experience care and violence, freedom and bureaucracy. It has implications far beyond Kenya.'
—Dr Kevin P. Donovan, University of Edinburgh

'Tom Neumark approaches a key laboratory of twenty-first-century African experimentality, Unconditional Cash Transfers, from the recipients' end, attending to relations of care and, notably, care for relations, among Nairobi's urban poor. Instead of simply critiquing the obvious limitations of such programmes, *Caring Cash* explores their "poetics of care" and fragile "ethics of solidarity", against the backdrop of a violently strained social fabric.'
—Paul Wenzel Geissler, Professor of Social Anthropology, University of Oslo

'*Caring Cash* grapples with a contentious intervention in international development – cash grant programmes – in a caring yet critical way, rehabilitating this often-critiqued approach to poverty alleviation while unpacking its relative limited sustainability. Neumark's monograph interrogates both the discourse and its practitioners' ethics. It is a must read for policy-makers and analysts; development workers and critics; Non-Governmental Organisation (NGO) employees and activists; and scholars of development studies and economic anthropology.'
—Chambi Chachage, Assistant Professor, Institute of African Studies, Carleton University

'This rich ethnography sees the care economy from multiple stances of Neumark's research participants – programme bureaucrats, engaged social workers mediating a caring relationship between beneficiaries and NGOs, and recipients themselves, revealing a multifaceted set of understandings and motives. This book would be a great introduction to the cash grant literature for students and practitioners, so much of it being programmatic and policy oriented, and removed from describing the work that cash grants actually do.'
—Sibel Kusimba, Associate Professor of Anthropology, University of South Florida

Anthropology, Culture and Society

Series Editors:
Holly High, Deakin University
and
Joshua O. Reno, Binghamton University

Recent titles:

The Limits to Citizen Power:
Participatory Democracy and the
Entanglements of the State
VICTOR ALBERT

The Heritage Machine:
Fetishism and Domination
in Maragateria, Spain
PABLO ALONSO GONZÁLEZ

Vicious Games:
Capitalism and Gambling
REBECCA CASSIDY

Anthropologies of Value
EDITED BY LUIS FERNANDO ANGOSTO-
FERRANDEZ AND GEIR HENNING
PRESTERUDSTUEN

Ethnicity and Nationalism:
Anthropological Perspectives
Third Edition
THOMAS HYLLAND ERIKSEN

Small Places, Large Issues:
An Introduction to Social
and Cultural Anthropology
Fourth Edition
THOMAS HYLLAND ERIKSEN

What is Anthropology?
Second Edition
THOMAS HYLLAND ERIKSEN

Anthropology and Development:
Challenges for the Twenty-first Century
KATY GARDNER AND DAVID LEWIS

Seeing like a Smuggler:
Borders from Below
EDITED BY MAHMOUD KESHAVARZ
AND SHAHRAM KHOSRAVI

How We Struggle:
A Political Anthropology of Labour
SIAN LAZAR

Private Oceans:
The Enclosure and Marketisation of the Seas
FIONA MCCORMACK

Grassroots Economies:
Living with Austerity in Southern Europe
EDITED BY SUSANA NAROTZKY

Rubbish Belongs to the Poor:
Hygienic Enclosure and the Waste Commons
PATRICK O'HARE

The Rise of Nerd Politics:
Digital Activism and Political Change
JOHN POSTILL

Base Encounters:
The US Armed Forces in South Korea
ELISABETH SCHOBER

Ground Down by Growth:
Tribe, Caste, Class and Inequality in
Twenty-First-Century India
ALPA SHAH, JENS LERCHE, ET AL

Watershed Politics and Climate Change
in Peru
ASTRID B. STENSRUD

When Protest Becomes Crime:
Politics and Law in Liberal Democracies
CAROLIJN TERWINDT

Race and Ethnicity in Latin America
Second Edition
PETER WADE

Caring Cash

Free Money and the Ethics of Solidarity in Kenya

Tom Neumark

PLUTO PRESS

First published 2023 by Pluto Press
New Wing, Somerset House, Strand, London WC2R 1LA
and Pluto Press Inc.
1930 Village Center Circle, 3-834, Las Vegas, NV 89134

www.plutobooks.com

Copyright © Tom Neumark 2023

The right of the author to be identified as the author of this work has been
asserted in accordance with the Copyright, Designs and Patents Act 1988.

British Library Cataloguing in Publication Data
A catalogue record for this book is available from the British Library

ISBN   978 0 7453 4014 2   Paperback
ISBN   978 1 786807 83 0   PDF
ISBN   978 1 786807 84 7   EPUB

This book is printed on paper suitable for recycling and made from fully
managed and sustained forest sources. Logging, pulping and manufacturing
processes are expected to conform to the environmental standards of the
country of origin.

Typeset by Stanford DTP Services, Northampton, England
Simultaneously printed in the United Kingdom and United States of America

Contents

Series Preface		vi
Acknowledgements		vii
Prologue		x
Introduction: Grants and the Care for Relationships		1

PART I

1	The Ghetto: A Place of Refuge and Charity	35
2	Scoring the Poor	68

PART II

3	Under the Aegis of Mistrust	105
4	Detaching from Others, Surviving with Others	131
5	A Mother's Care	150
Conclusion		177
Notes		184
References		192
Index		206

Series Preface

As people around the world confront the inequality and injustice of new forms of oppression, as well as the impacts of human life on planetary ecosystems, this book series asks what anthropology can contribute to the crises and challenges of the twenty-first century. Our goal is to establish a distinctive anthropological contribution to debates and discussions that are often dominated by politics and economics. What is sorely lacking, and what anthropological methods can provide, is an appreciation of the human condition.

We publish works that draw inspiration from traditions of ethnographic research and anthropological analysis to address power and social change while keeping the struggles and stories of human beings centre stage. We welcome books that set out to make anthropology matter, bringing classic anthropological concerns with exchange, difference, belief, kinship and the material world into engagement with contemporary environmental change, capitalist economy and forms of inequality. We publish work from all traditions of anthropology, combining theoretical debate with empirical evidence to demonstrate the unique contribution anthropology can make to understanding the contemporary world.

Holly High and Joshua O. Reno

Acknowledgements

This book has taken many years to finish and along the way I have incurred numerous debts. The first is to those in Korogocho. The book contains only a fraction of what they taught me and yet it could not have been written without them. They dared to share with a stranger their lives, marked by anguish and sadness, but also by wisdom and a cautious determination. While they remain anonymous in the book, they and I know who they are. In particular, I am indebted to Kamau, Jude and John – the best guides I could have hoped for, and who got me out of countless pickles.

The residents of Korogocho are accustomed to being surveyed and surveilled by a changeable cast of organisations. They were understandably wary when asked to open their lives, once again, to the gaze of a curious outsider, not least that of a white, male student from Britain who inexplicably arrived without a *mradi* (project). They would sometimes ask how my research would help them escape from their often harrowing circumstances. I have never found a satisfying answer to that question. I certainly cannot see how this book will help. But contained within me is a quiet hope: that the caring, ethical efforts my interlocutors showed me and taught me about, presented in this book through the bushy layer of my own interpretation, will offer a modest addition to our collective understanding of life. It is an unsatisfying response for sure, but then any other would be disingenuous. And so, an acknowledgement of my debt to them goes hand in hand with a deep-felt apology for my inability to repay even a part of it.

The remaining people I am also in arrears to, but I hope they will be more easily mollified by some straightforward appreciation.

For much of my time in Nairobi, I was hosted and sustained by Baba and Mama Maina, and their children Koi, Mwangi and Maina. I thank them deeply for welcoming me into their home with such unguarded hearts. I am also immensely grateful to John Gitau Kariuki, my Kiswahili guide and Wallace 'Jackababa' Oyugi, my Sheng one.

The research would not have been possible without the support of various international and Kenyan NGOs and their representatives. I also owe a debt to the government of Kenya and its civil servants for facilitating the research and for sharing their perspectives. I acknowledge the British Institute in Eastern Africa for providing me with an institutional home during my fieldwork. There I met Lys Alcayna Stevens, John Arum, Margarita Dimova, Hannah Elliot, Kerry Kyaa, John Perkins, Hannah Waddilove, and Sam Wilkins who all played their part in keeping my head above water.

Quite conventionally, this book is a conversation between the world 'out there' and the academic community that I have been inculturated into. Much of this took place in the Department of Social Anthropology at the University of Cambridge, where this book began its life as a doctoral dissertation. Two anthropologists there, Harri Englund and Henrietta Moore, deserve my greatest appreciation. They offered me reassurance, pushed me to think harder, urged me to stay close to my material, and showed me, in their own inimitable style, the value this has. I may have sometimes strayed from their sound advice, but I could not have written this book without them.

My thanks to my fellow doctoral candidates of the writing-up group and to its facilitator James Laidlaw, all of whom helped shape my ideas. During my time at Cambridge, both during my studies and when I took up a teaching position, I was able to able to rely upon a supportive group of friends and colleagues with whom to share ideas and companionship. Thank you Paolo Heywood, Nick Evans, Jess Johnson, Jonney Taae, Ross Porter, Fred Ikanda, Viesturs Celmins, Fiona Wright, Rachel Wyatt, and Laura Chinnery.

The book travelled with me, often weighing down on me more heavily than my luggage, as I took up a series of academic positions. After studying then teaching at Cambridge, I lived in Tanzania for two years, during which time I was employed as a Research Fellow in the Department of Social Anthropology at the University of Edinburgh. I am grateful to Jamie Cross for the opportunity to work remotely back before it was considered acceptable, for enthusing me with his own devoted work, and for encouraging me to write this book. From Tanzania I moved to the Institute of Health and Society (HELSAM) and the Centre for Development and the Environment (SUM) at the University of Oslo. At SUM, Katerini Storeng and Sidsel Roalkvam showed me what a nurturing academic environment looks like, and demonstrated through their work and collegiality the good that comes from it. At HELSAM, Ruth Prince graciously gave me the freedom to develop my ideas, set an example with her scholarship and, by extending her warm friendship, made it all fun.

I am thankful to the fellow anthropologists, colleagues, and friends who have challenged and supported me in equal measure. They have offered enriching conversations, feedback on my writing, as well as perceptive comments which – while they may well have forgotten them – have nonetheless made their mark on this book. These people include Edwin Ameso, David Bannister, Matei Candea, Kevin Donovan, Wenzel Geissler, Maia Green, Ben Jones, Sian Lazar, Bill Maurer, Vickie Muinde, Samwel Ntapanta, David Parkin, David Pratten and Jamie Wintrup.

At Pluto Press, I am grateful to David Castle for his backing and the anonymous reviewers who pushed me to write a better book. I thank Wesley Osoro for the cover illustration and Melanie Patrick for its design.

Financial assistance was provided by the University of Cambridge's Domestic Research Studentship; a Research Fellowship at the University of Edinburgh funded by the UK's Engineering and Physical Research Council; and a Postdoctoral Fellowship funded by the European Research Council and SUM. Two chapters, somewhat revised, have been published previously. Chapter 3 is based on 'Trusting the Poor: Cash Grants and the Caring Bureaucrat in Kenya', *Anthropological Quarterly* 93(2), 2020: 119–49. Chapter 4 appeared originally as '"A Good Neighbour Is Not One That Gives": Detachment, Ethics and the Relational Self in Kenya', *Journal of the Royal Anthropological Institute* 23(4), 2017: 748–64.

That this book has made it this far is because of my family and friends. With my parents, Ann and Jim, and my brother, Ben, I calibrate my sometimes errant moral compass and receive unconditional reassurance. Hugo Madden, a close friend and intellectual companion, has, through countless conversations over the last two decades, sympathetically scrutinised many of my ideas. And I have always felt the hands of my friends on my back. Thank you Luke Buxton, Chris Hollins, Vaishnavee Madden, Chris Marshall, Ross Pepper, Linzey Ryan, Simon Whitley, and Will Hodson.

Finally, I thank Aurelia, whose wisdom and wit is matched only by her patience and positivity in the bleaker moments. She has taught me that it's just a book, and it's how we treat one another that matters the most.

Note on translation and naming

Most of the quotes that appear in this book were originally in Kiswahili and Sheng, and all translations are my own. Unless otherwise stated, all organisations and interlocutors are referred to by pseudonyms.

Prologue

Recently having gone blind – she still did not know why – Beatrice was not able to see the diarrhoea on the packed-dirt floor in her concrete one-roomed home. Reflexively, and without saying anything, Kamau wiped it up with a cloth that was lying by the *jiko* (charcoal stove) on the floor between us. Beatrice was well aware that her newborn grandson, Lorenzo, was unwell. The two of us had dropped by to see her that morning, but we had met many times previously, after she had been introduced to us as a beneficiary of a particular humanitarian non-governmental organisation (NGO) programme. Each month, over an eight-month period, a message to her phone would signal the arrival of a small cash grant payment deposited into her mobile money account. That day, after chatting a little while in her home – a bedroom really, that doubled up through the strategic placement of a curtain, as a kitchen-cum-living room – we bade farewell with promises we would visit her again soon.

Kamau, who was assisting me with my research, had been born and raised there in Korogocho, one of the largest of Nairobi's ghettos, as the slums in this sprawling city are known locally.[1] While he had moved to just outside the ghetto, his mother and sister still lived in the same small compound, with shacks constructed out of mud and corrugated iron, wedged between the rest of the slum and the Nairobi River. There they made some income running a small business raising and selling chickens.[2] But it was not just his family, nor the modest and temporary employment that I offered him as my research assistant, that drew Kamau back into Korogocho. As a youth activist and community worker, he was working with young people there, and trying to tap into the tributaries of foreign, charitable money of which he himself had been a beneficiary – sponsoring some of his education – to see how he might help them escape from the some of the worst criminal temptations the ghetto offered. He had already managed to bring into the centre of Korogocho a shipping container, hoping to fill it with books and connect it to the grid for lighting. But even in its current state, children could still meet and study there in some peace.

Given Kamau's intimate familiarity with Korogocho, it was not surprising that when we left Beatrice's home that day, he instantly recognised the noises coming from somewhere nearby. 'Those are gunshots', he stated in his typically calm and understated manner. I did not immediately hear them myself. I was still unaccustomed to the cacophony of noises that formed the ghetto's soundscape. Many of Korogocho's sounds come from the *jua kali*, the Kenyan Kiswahili term for the informal economy, which translates as 'fierce sun', a reference to the way that workers labour throughout the day under the sun's often piercing rays. The sounds of this economy reverberate in the ghetto, as wood is chopped, bicycles and motorcycles repaired, metal doors and gates welded, and the food staple maize is ground. I had begun to recognise some of these sounds, but the noises of gunshots were still unfamiliar to me.

The gunshots were far enough away for Kamau not to be alarmed, despite not being entirely sure where they were coming from. We walked hesitantly to the crossroads between the two neighbourhoods where the tarmac road began, the recent result of a slum upgrading programme funded by Italian government sovereign debt relief. A crowd had gathered there. A fistfight erupted, unconnected to the gunshots, but quickly fizzled out. The gunshots, though, continued. A young man in the crossroads crowd told us they were coming from Grogan, a neighbourhood of Korogocho only a few hundred metres away. It was the neighbourhood most feared by my friends and interlocutors, and which was once described by the journalist and scholar Mike Davis as 'the most wretched' one in the slum (Davis 2006, 44). The gunshots were closer than Kamau had thought. A middle-aged man ambled alongside us with reassurances that they were only warning shots fired up into the air by the police. No doubt they were also a show of force by the authorities. Over the course of a few days, we were able to piece together a fuller picture of the events.

The previous week, a *boda* (motorcycle taxi) driver had been summoned at around 5 a.m., over an hour before sunrise, to collect a man at his shack in Highridge, another neighbourhood in Korogocho. The time was not unusual; the day starts early for men, many of whom regularly walk the hour and a half journey south along the city's streets and busy highways towards the Industrial Area. Yet the driver, upon arriving at the shack, was murdered and his motorbike stolen.

Reacting to the typical failure of the police to investigate crimes in the ghetto, some of his fellow *boda* drivers had, on the day that Kamau and I visited Beatrice, decided to investigate themselves. After receiving a tip-off, they were eventually able to locate his motorbike, with the new owner agreeing to lead them to the man he had bought it from. Travelling on foot together as a group they ended up in Grogan. There they found the man and apprehended him before he could disappear into the lattice-work of small alleyways that criss-cross Korogocho. Before long, a larger group of residents had gathered to watch and intervene. At this point it had seemed certain to the bystanders that the man the drivers had been led to, whom they believed was the murderer, would be lynched. However, although the police, who are experienced by Korogocho's residents more as a violent threat than a form of protection from violence, were initially absent, they did arrive in time to rescue the suspect. Firing their assault rifles into the air, they hauled the man the few hundred metres to the Chief's Camp, the centre of the Provincial Administration, a part of the governmental structure that extended the power of the president down to the ground (Branch and Cheeseman 2006).[3]

Dissatisfied with the police's chosen method of addressing the murder, the large group of a few dozen mostly young men descended upon the camp to make their case and, they hoped, get the man back into their possession. It was then that the police fired first tear gas and then more gunshots to dispel the gathering crowd. But this time the shots were not only warning ones. Two men in the crowd were hit and were rushed bleeding on the back of *bodas* to the nearest hospital; fortunately, as I later found out, surviving their injuries.

As we stood at the crossroads listening to the early version of the story – that the police were firing warning shots – two men nearby continued to chop through a pile of firewood. It seemed inexplicable in light of what was happening, and I pointed it out to Kamau. He made a polite grunt of acknowledgement. It was not the right time for observations, so I shut up, and we stood there without talking. It was only a few months after the murder of an activist named Nyash, who was one of the first people I had met when I had arrived in Korogocho.[4] He was shot and killed outside his shack in Grogan. I did not know him well, but Kamau and he were friends. I learned that he had left behind his elderly mother, Mary, who had already lived through the death of six of her children, either from illness or at the hands of the police (Mwangi 2018). Rumours abounded about Nyash's murder, but many people at the time believed he was killed by the police in response to his tireless work to expose police brutality in the ghetto.

After a few moments of silence between us, Kamau spoke. 'People seem so dehumanised now in Koch', he said, using the shortened nickname for the ghetto, 'Now it only surprises you if it's someone close to you who is killed.' Other friends afterwards worried aloud that if someone so high profile as Nyash could be killed, it meant that even ordinary residents could be, too. Insecurity in the ghetto was a constant worry for everyone, and the only item that seemed to have a permanent place on the agenda of the *baraza* (public meetings) when they took place.

The murder of Nyash and the *boda* driver happened on the street. As did the fights, muggings and armed robberies that many of my interlocutors, along with their partners, children and friends, had been the victim of. Women I knew had seen their children or their husbands injured and sometimes killed. Violence happens quickly in Korogocho, but word also travels fast. After bumping into different people I knew when I was out doing my fieldwork, conversation would invariably turn to the most recent violent incident. Gunfights on the street the day before and even bodies found the next morning. These events and others intimately experienced built, in people's minds and bodies, a particular backdrop to life in the slum.

Talk about the largely male violence that I have described spun about the ghetto. But the women with whom I spent most of my time also spoke to me of less visible forms of violence. Some spoke of their experience of domestic violence that remained hidden behind the closed corrugated metal door of their shacks, its physical effects concealed by layers of clothing. Others talked of break-ins into their homes, masked sometimes by the noise of rain on a tin roof, which others in more privileged positions – myself included – often find soothing. The outcome of such forms of violence and suffering is never an angry mob to be dispersed by police gunshots or tear gas.

Nor is this the outcome for the violence of poverty, disease and exclusion that disproportionately affects those women situated on the margins of both a state-managed capitalist economy and the everyday networks of care in Kenya. Women I knew in the ghetto would be as likely to talk about the street violence of the ghetto as they would their own, often desperate, attempts to feed their children, get them to school, and keep them out of trouble. In fact, as the murder of Nyash showed, the violence of the street enveloped everybody, intruding insistently into the lives of the women with whom I spent time and jeopardising their hopes of keeping a family alive and together in the midst of it.

One, always hopeful and never certain, outcome for the women ensnared within these violent unfoldings was to be incorporated into some institutionalised form of care. There was very little in the way of a comprehensive state welfare system in Kenya during my fieldwork, or even today; rather, there were disjointed, time-limited and uncertain charitable projects that floated in and around the ghetto. One such programme was the one that Beatrice had begun to receive and the purpose of us visiting her: a cash grant. It was partly an interest in the cash grant that brought me into the ghetto, but as I was immersed in its workings through my ethnographic fieldwork both there and across Nairobi, I was drawn deeper into the struggles, ambitions and hopes of differently situated actors, from grant recipients to civil servants to NGO workers.

Introduction: Grants and the Care for Relationships

Caring Cash is a story about care and relationships. On the one hand, it is about the globally networked charitable relationships of care and their experiments with cash grants. In the parlance of policy, the grants that had recently arrived in Korogocho during my fieldwork were known as 'unconditional cash transfers'. Backed by aid money, in partnerships and sometimes independently, the government and NGOs in Kenya began to offer this 'free money' to the poor and vulnerable across the country in the 2000s. On the other hand, the care I talk about during the course of this book refers to the ways in which people like Beatrice, whose home we had emerged from before hearing the gunshots in the prologue, but also others like neighbours, lovers and bureaucrats, engaged in acts of care that sought to keep intact the persons and relationships that constituted their lives. Acts and words of care such as that expressed by Beatrice, when she told me 'I'm just trying to be a good mother', after we had been talking about her teenage daughter, the mother of the sick baby Lorenzo.

At the time of our visit that day, like on most days, Beatrice's husband Jacob was hustling away from home. In previous years he had found piecemeal work with NGO projects back in the area of his natal home, and once, when I was visiting Beatrice, he pulled out certificates evidencing his attendance at various workshops.[1] But aid budgets, particularly those routed towards HIV/AIDS that had created a surge in foreign aid funding from the 1990s, had now dwindled and meant this work, at least for Jacob, had begun to dry up. This work had been part of the larger charitable economy that extends across the globe and reaches into places like Korogocho. It was comprised of both governmental and non-governmental efforts; and understood by most people I knew in Korogocho, and often elsewhere in Kenya, as a voluntary gift to the poor rather than an entitlement of citizens. While once having worked on charitable projects, Jacob now found that he and his family had become recipients of charity themselves. Or at least, his wife had; Jacob was always reluctant to talk to me about the cash grant the family was receiving.

One late afternoon, after taking a break from the dust and exertion of sanding what would eventually become a school table, James, a carpenter I passed often as I went about my fieldwork, asked me what exactly it was that I was doing in the ghetto each day. I tried, as best I could at the time, to explain my interest in the cash grant programmes that were coming into Korogocho. I also expressed how I was interested in writing something that showed others, including the government, what the circumstances of life were like in the ghetto. Ignoring my interest in the cash grants, James sighed: 'There is so much research here, everything is already known about us. No, the problem is not that the government doesn't know about our suffering, it is just that the government doesn't care.' While anthropologists have routinely found themselves as witnesses for another's culture (Metcalf 2001) or suffering (Englund 2011), in Korogocho this was not something that James thought I should waste my time on. He had grown understandably weary, and cynical, of the persistent representations of Korogocho's suffering, not because they were necessarily inaccurate but because they had shown themselves to be impotent in the face of an apathetic and neglectful government. As with most people I met in Korogocho, James wanted much less research and a lot more action.

Caring Cash takes the reader to a moment in time in the early twenty-first century when there seemed to be in the cash grant what many of my interlocutors, particularly women, thought resembled something like real material and significant action.[2] Unlike many other forms of intervention that residents had seen through their time living in the ghetto and elsewhere, these cash grants appeared to them as actually rather useful. Of course, not without reservation, women, with whom, as I've said, I spent most of my time, welcomed the potentially life-saving capacity of these grants that gave them 'free money' and, because they were what was termed 'unconditional', ostensibly expected nothing in return. This meant that people receiving them were not required to jump through the burdensome, bureaucratic hoops that typify the more common conditional cash transfers that have been described as one of the most popular forms of welfare in and for the twenty-first century (Lavinas 2013), nor the 'empowerment money' in which debt stands as the privileged form of poverty alleviation (Elyachar 2002).[3]

For institutions that designed and advocated for unconditional cash grants, as well as many who received them, the grants represented a step-change from other forms of charitable interventions, such as the sacks of food or medical aid that have typified humanitarianism particularly, or the education as well as the microloans that have, for decades now, charac-terised development interventions in Kenya. One of the more appealing aspects of these cash grants, for many of their advocates, is the opportunity they purportedly provide to treat the poor in a far less paternalistic way. Cash grants are understood as a more ethical intervention, offering the poor greater dignity and freedom to exercise their own choices.

Of course, the view of a paradigmatic shift around assistance is far from unequivocal. Some, including my interlocutors, have drawn attention to the way in which grants understood as charitable giving retain some of charity's most vexing features. 'It looks like a refugee camp here,' Kamau said to me one day, shaking his head with disgust, as I sat on the ground with him in a local church compound watching people being enrolled onto one of the cash grants programmes. There have been other criticisms too. Some people have pointed to the apparently meagre financial value of cash grants, while others lament that grants merely perpetuate charity's focus on the very poorest in a manner which does little to stem the growing and more entrenched socioeconomic inequality that scars the world.

Similarly, for James, the carpenter, the introduction of cash grants was far from capable of remedying the years of neglect that slum dwellers had experienced, and neither would they challenge the insecurity produced by both the state's police and the ghetto's criminal gangs. They would certainly not provide the proper paying jobs that men wanted. In fact, James likely ignored my interest in cash grants because, as was the case for Jacob, Beatrice's husband, he understood them not only as what some called *pesa ya wazungu*, foreign, charitable money, but also *pesa ya wanawake*, women's money. For many men the charitable grants were not a salvation but a painful sign of what they perceived as their own failure to look after their own families, and the role of foreign charity in remedying that.

Caring Cash

A number of journalists and activists have described, as I have chosen to do in the prologue of this book, the textures and eruptions of violence and suffering that envelop Nairobi's slums. 'Here the end of the world is not a prophecy but a condition,' wrote the British comedian-cum-activist, Russell Brand (2013), after visiting Nairobi's sprawling rubbish dump, Dandora, which borders Korogocho and serves as a source of employment for some of its residents. Such apocalyptic descriptions have often been bolstered by a sombre statistical picture. Since 2002, the African Population and Health Research Center has carried out a so-called Demographic Surveillance Survey in Korogocho, producing an avalanche of statistics that largely portrays the slum as a nexus of social breakdown and ill health.[4]

These representations of slum life have often been accused of dehumanising slum dwellers, resembling a sort of poverty porn, which has fed upon and nourished the impulse, particularly among foreign individuals and institutions, to do good. Those anthropologists also producing descriptions that draw attention to overt and hidden violence in urban neighbourhoods across the world have also faced such accusations. Perhaps most famous were Nancy Scheper-Hughes' (1993, 1995) accounts of chronic hunger and 'maternal neglect' in Brazil, which, as she reported, were dismissed by some of her colleagues as a form of political activism that abandoned the discipline's more dispassionate attempts to understand, rather than judge, human realities.

Joel Robbins (2013) is similarly concerned by anthropology's turn away from a description and exegesis of the varied cultures that constitute our shared world and towards efforts, instead, to witness and account for the universality of human suffering. He has argued that anthropologists should also be prepared to explore how people, even in the most abject of conditions, strive towards their own particular conceptions of a 'good life'. Yet the circumstances that he himself witnessed in his own fieldwork were different from those I encountered in the ghetto of Korogocho (Robbins 2004). He saw a community in Papua New Guinea that had apparently lost their traditional culture to the incursion of Christianity, but he did not witness the ways in which people struggled with even the most fundamental task of staying alive.

I am particularly curious, however, about how the premise of the unconditional cash grants in Kenya resonated with both perspectives. That is, with what the anthropologist Sherry Ortner (2016) has summarised as 'dark anthropology' and what she calls 'anthropologies of the good'. Meaning, both the exploration of social relationships that produce misery and impoverishment, and the approach to explore, as Robbins and others argue, how people pursue their own value-rich projects of the 'good life'. The grant programmes in Kenya, still at a nascent and experimental stage, and nothing like the scale of state grant-based redistribution observed in other parts of Africa (Bähre 2011), nevertheless sought to be part of building something like a national social assistance system. They sought to reduce widescale impoverishment in the country while at the same time allowing the poor spaces of freedom through which to pursue their own values, goals and strategies, always within a market economy.

This book draws from one and a half years spent living in Nairobi, carrying out fieldwork with NGOs, civil servants and in the city's slums. Around seven months of this time was spent more or less every day in Korogocho. This became what George Marcus terms a 'strategically situated single site' (Marcus 1995, 111), through which I explored the cash grants and the care that was woven through, around and as a result of them. This methodology meant that during my fieldwork I encountered and interacted with both ordinary residents of the slum, some selected to receive grants, and with what I call, as I explain later, a ghetto-level bureaucracy, many of whom were also residents as well as occasionally recipients themselves of the charitable economy. The book therefore endeavours, as will be clear through its argument and structure, to keep both within its scope.

In Korogocho, at the time of my research, a quarter of the households received a cash grant payment of KSh2,000 (£13.54) each month in one, or sometimes, both, of two cash grant programmes. The scale of these grants, however, should not be overstated. One of the grants, what I call the *urban grant*, was a short-term eight-month programme that was funded and managed by a transnational humanitarian NGO. This NGO was part of a larger consortium. Together they were offering cash to slum dwellers, in Korogocho and another slum, as well as in a similar programme preceding the ones which took place during my fieldwork. They were also attempting to persuade the government to incorporate this grant, officially called the Urban Food Subsidy Cash Transfer, into its embryonic social assistance system. The other was what I call the *child grant*, officially known as the Orphans and Vulnerable Children Cash Transfer, funded largely by the World Bank, and managed by the government. This began life in 2004 as a UNICEF (United Nations Children's Fund) pilot project, and the institution's stickers still adorned the filing cabinets and computers in the offices of its secretariat. By the time of my fieldwork, it had been further scaled up, with funding mostly from the World Bank. A few years after my fieldwork had finished, the government, together with the World Bank, consolidated the grants into one overarching system called *Inua Jamii*, meaning 'raise the family' but otherwise known by its more technical moniker, the National Safety Net Programme.[5]

The grants – the urban grant and the child grant – were very different, both in their temporality and social and geographical scope, and I refer to both throughout this book. Sometimes I dwell more on one than the other as, during my ethnographic fieldwork, I was brought into the action as it unfolded. At other times in the book, however, the distinctions are not so important. The people I knew on each type of grant had experiences that were of course dissimilar as a result of variations around the grants, but they also had many experiences that were shared.

Uncaring Care

The aim to build such a system of institutionalised care emerged, as I will show later, from a partial recognition of, on the one hand, the fissures and failures of a state-managed capitalist political economy and, on the other hand, a sense that the more informal, sometimes but not exclusively kin-based solidarities, no longer kept people in the cities alive. Neither my interlocutors nor I would dispute that there is a lack of care, even disregard, for Korogocho's poorest and most vulnerable, but my interlocutors would also complain that people in everyday life no longer cared for each other. They would often explain to me how their appeals to others for assistance would be refused and met with a common refrain: 'Why should I help? I didn't ask you to Nairobi.' In short, Korogocho's residents, like those of others in the urban peripheries of the world, commonly felt that not only had they been abandoned by the state, but also by other people around them (Ross 2010).

In a certain sense, then, a failure to care for and among the poor in Korogocho is self-evident. However, it is this book's contention that focusing on this failure of care ignores the way it endures. But what *Caring Cash* proposes is something different from just the persistance of care amidst violence, impoverishment and insecurity: it contains a recognition that care cannot be understood simply, or only, as the continuation of caring *within* relationships. I will chart another course in this book that offers a different, wider interpretation of care that reveals a tentative and hesitant ethics of solidarity in the ghetto.

My argument, simply put, is that care can be productively understood as a practice that is not only directed towards persons but also the attachments that connect them. That is, a care *for* relationships as well as *within* relationships. In other words, I do not just look at caring relationships but how the relationships, and relational units such as the household, often became objects of care themselves. To explore this, I build upon a wide-ranging, but especially anthropological, literature including on care, ethics and morality, kinship, violence and hunger, and bureaucracy, some of which is introduced within each specific chapter but some of which is discussed further in this introduction.

Caring Cash explores this different conceptualisation of care through the cash grants programmes that came into Korogocho offering a new form of institutionalised care for the poor. It imagines the cash grant programmes as akin to laboratories in which one can encounter and be exposed to people's caring practices and forms of solidarity. By this I do not mean what Cheryl Mattingly (2014) has called 'moral laboratories', which are the everyday spaces in which people encounter, debate and critique issues of a moral nature. Nor is it my intention to perpetuate the idea of particular places as useful laboratories for scientific, technological or human development, which, as others have shown, for instance in the field of global health, is a powerful one producing troubling effects on political processes and local populations (Fejerskov 2017).

Instead, when I call the cash grants programmes laboratories through which I encountered and began to make sense of care, I mean it more in an imaginative rather than a methodological or practical sense. Imaginatively treating the programmes like laboratories means thinking about how particular perspectives concerning my interlocutors' logics and poetics of care were revealed, facilitated, and sometimes provoked by the programmes which had as their aim to give money to the poor while minimising the technocratic knowledge practices of bureaucracy and surveillance.

Working through particular puzzles that I encountered during my fieldwork, as women, many of whom lived in extreme poverty, were identified to receive and then began receiving cash grants, I show how these forms of care manifested themselves in Korogocho across a range of domains, from bureaucracy to neighbourliness to motherhood. There, I suggest, it was not that the cash grants simply allowed people the material means through which to pursue their own ethical projects (Sen 2001; Laidlaw 2013). They were hardly substantial enough in themselves for this. But rather the grants revealed and sometimes facilitated particular sorts of caring efforts that sought to attend to a frayed relational fabric that constituted the grounds of hope for such a life in an undefined and uncertain future.

This also means that this book does not propose an argument that involves contrasting individualising humanitarian and poverty-alleviating policies to the 'relational' people and lives they seek to affect. Anthropological critiques of humanitarianism and development often counterpose the ideologies of individualism, for instance embodied in the market-based approaches of these programmes, with the relational lives and values of those people in whose lives they seek to intervene (for a good example of this approach see Elyachar 2005). Often these tend to emphasise the ways in which people's everyday lives reveal explicit, as well as more under-stated, quieter, forms of care that look conventionally caring. Instead, I propose that if relationships were not only important to, but to some extent constituted the survival of my interlocutors' biological and social selves, then a task for scholars is to understand how people worked to keep themselves, each other, and the relationships that connect them alive. This has also meant that I have looked at acts that may appear to many of us, at least on the surface, as *uncaring*. Both detaching from others and watching people too closely, for example, may sometimes come across as uncaring but they are an aspect of the repertoire of my interlocutors' acts of caring that constitute the tentative ethics of solidarity that I explore in this book.

To put it another way, solidarities are not failing – but neither are they simply enduring while either rubbing up against the individualism of mar-ket-based approaches to poverty alleviation or being nourished through things like cash grants. Instead, I believe it is productive, and possible, to look at them by examining the work of care – not in order to describe the entirety of what care is nor to suggest discrete bounded 'cultures' of care but rather, as I have said, as puzzles to be grappled with.

This also means I do not say with any finality what 'care' is for my inter-locutors. Care, as others have shown (Ross 2010; Biehl 2012; Han 2012), and as I have witnessed in Korogocho, is a multifaceted and complex phenomenon experienced differently and transformed through particu-lar historically situated political and economic relationships, and shifting norms and values. My aim in this book is not to try to capture its textures in their entirety, but rather to show how my interlocutors' actions and reflections challenged me to think about a different, perhaps less noted, but – I believe – vitally important form of care.

In the rest of this introduction, I develop this proposal in more detail, beginning first with the cash grants themselves, which, as I have said, I imagine both as a form of care itself but also as quasi-laboratories through which to analyse other modalities of everyday care.

A Brief History of Cash Grants

Cash grants have drawn significant attention from journalists and academ-ics in recent years. This is largely due to the rise in the 1990s and 2000s, as a result of economic crises, of the expansion of large-scale cash grant programmes in countries such as Mexico, Brazil and South Africa. For example, South Africa, through the 1990s and especially after the end of apartheid, rapidly grew its own cash grant programmes, resulting in the situation today in which roughly 61 per cent of citizens are in receipt of a grant. But the interest in cash grants has also been engendered by more recent attempts to build related forms of social assistance in other parts of the world, including in Africa.

Along with the other Washington-based institutions, the World Bank's enforcement of neoliberal policies focusing on economic growth is well documented, but these have often existed alongside a muted acknowledgement of their limitations. For instance, as early as 1990, in its World Development Report that year, the World Bank signalled the importance of, albeit extremely minimal, forms of material redistribution. While much of the World Bank's interest rested on food aid and workfare, in a specific chapter on 'transfers and safety nets' there were glimmers of recognition concerning the viability and desirability of cash-based aid in its explanation: 'Cash transfers are often more effective than food rations: cash is faster to move and easier to administer, and it does little or no harm to producers and hence to future food security' (World Bank 1990, 97). It would not, however, be until the early 2000s that countries in Africa outside of South Africa began to look seriously at the viability of cash grants.

A great degree of the early interest in cash grants was led, significantly, not by African governments, but by foreign institutions, particularly multilaterals, including the World Bank but also the African Development Bank, the World Food Programme and UNICEF, bilateral aid agencies, such as the then British Department for International Development (DFID), the Swedish International Development Cooperation Agency (SIDA), and Germany's Deutsche Gesellschaft für Internationale Zusammenarbeit (GIZ), as well as numerous transnational development and humanitarian NGOs. From the very beginning these actors were keen to see how they might encourage governments in Africa to build national state social assistance systems, although those same actors often nevertheless took over responsibility either for providing the resources for, or for running the operations of, the cash grant programmes. During my fieldwork, the pilot and experimental grant programmes heavily funded by foreign philanthropic and development aid institutions could be seen across rural and urban Kenya. Many of these are also present today through institutions like the New York-headquartered GiveDirectly and as a result of humanitarian NGOs responding to the economic impacts of the Covid-19 crisis.

In Nairobi's ghettos the grant programmes have joined other forms of charitable interventions in constituting a diverse, multifaceted economy that, in its simplest terms, seeks to intervene in and transform people's lives (Bornstein 2003; Mosse 2005; Englund 2006; Bornstein and Redfield 2011b; Venkatesan and Yarrow 2012). Rather than involving the transference of state responsibilities to non-state institutions (Ferguson and Gupta 2002, 989) it is an economy that has not only incorporated both state and non-state actors, but it is also one that is characterised by shifting ideas about who is responsible for the poor.

Finally, it is necessary to make clear the relationship between cash grants and the diverse fields of charitable and other forms of intervention that seek to assist. The anthropologists Erica Bornstein and Peter Redfield (2011a) have created a neat and helpful distinction between some of the most prominent of these fields, namely, human rights, development and humanitarianism. They suggest that human rights and development can be characterised as falling, respectively, on the political and economic poles of what we understand as the political economy, while humanitarianism is concerned with physical (and psychological) suffering. But the grants, whether they are stand-alone or have been incorporated into the government's *Inua Jamii*, cannot easily be confined to these fields. As I show in chapter 2, the cash grants in Korogocho, as an attempt to form a state social assistance system, have always been concerned with both the political economy, or what we might call the social body, and the biological body. But I do not consider what exists in regard to the cash grants as an instance of a Polanyian double movement as some have speculated (for instance Hickey 2008). This is because neoliberal capitalism is not inherently against any form of social protection or welfare (Collier 2011) but also because, to date, the grants remain squarely in the charitable realm.

Failure

Behind the cash grants globally was an understanding of a two-fold failure of care. One is perhaps the more familiar sense of the failure of the nation-state to care for and protect its citizens. As I have said, this resulted in efforts by an architecture of globally distributed and networked institutions to encourage and build new forms of state social assistance in countries like Kenya. This architecture encompasses a diverse set of actors and initiatives, including the ones I have already mentioned but also others: the International Labour Organization's 'social protection floor'; governments in Latin America that have implemented large-scale cash grant programmes; and, of course, crucially, the Kenyan government, particularly through the 'Social' pillar of the government's long-term developmental programme, Vision 2030.

The other idea of the failure of care though is perhaps less familiar, and here I wish to explore it in greater depth. This sense of failure is concerned with how informal forms of support and solidarity, long lauded by both government administrators and anthropologists, were no longer working for those on the margins of society. The recognition of the informal in Africa, and more widely in the global South, had, interestingly, emerged not only from the discipline of anthropology but also had its origins in Kenya.

In the 1970s, the anthropologist Keith Hart coined the term 'informal economy' to describe all those economic activities he had observed in Ghana that were not being captured by official statistics that were fixed only on the health or otherwise of wage-labour. The term was popularised when the International Labour Office in Kenya adopted it for their mission report in 1972 (ILO 1972; Hart 1973). Since that time, these informal economic practices have increasingly been viewed as an integral part of anti-poverty interventions (Ferguson 2010), accompanied by the argument that policy makers and practitioners must work 'with the grain' (Kelsall 2011).

Within the social sciences, the concept of the informal economy has undergone a similar process of deconstruction as that performed by anthropologists upon the concept of culture. Perhaps most critical of the concept has been Keith Hart (2009) himself, yet, as he has shown, the idea of the informal economy has taken on a new and rich life outside of the discipline of anthropology, despite being subject to intense critique within it. Part of this life has involved institutions applying the label of informality to the very objects that anthropologists have made their stock and trade. Take the World Bank's first strategy paper for social protection in Africa. The excerpt below follows a section that outlines the range of challenges, from the global economic situation to the context of rural agriculture, that Africa now faces (World Bank 2012, 3):

> Africa's reliance on informal support networks increasingly is ill-suited for these challenges. African societies have long-standing informal solidarity networks that give households a level of protection in times of shocks. These traditional systems include intra-family transfers, gift

giving, labour-sharing arrangements, burial and funeral societies, and informal credit and savings schemes. While informal solidarity has been an important part of social risk management strategies for African households, these informal safety nets are ineffective in times of covariate shocks and exclude the very poorest households.

The World Bank now offers us informal support networks, informal solidarity networks and informal safety nets. What the report describes, however, has close family resemblances to objects of anthropological study that far pre-date this categorisation of activities as informal. These more nuanced anthropological accounts also steer away from the romantic, rose-tinted views of these, often kinship-based, forms of solidarity, which, as John Iliffe wrote many years ago, are hardly 'universal providers of limitless generosity' (Iliffe 1987, 7).

But from the perspective of this particular World Bank report, it is not merely that informal forms of support are not limitless in their generosity, but that they are no longer even viable. The informal economy was once, and in many cases still is, considered a vibrant aspect of economic life in Africa, to such an extent that financial and development institutions have sought to incorporate it into the formal economy (Elyachar 2005). But informal, everyday solidarities are cast as 'ill-suited' and 'ineffective' in confronting the contemporary challenges facing the continent. Furthermore, they are deemed as working only for certain sections of the population, excluding the poorest who need support the most.

The argument that traditional mechanisms of solidarity are ill-suited to contemporary challenges facing the African continent is, of course, a subset of a more long-standing one concerning tradition and modernity. As we saw with the concept of the informal economy, the conventional argument that tradition acts as a brake on modernity is uprooted by development agencies and banks to show how traditional forms of economic activity can be tapped into as part of the long march to modernisation. But informal solidarities are not granted the same status. They are neither seen as brakes on, nor accelerators to, modernity, but as bundles of practices, norms and values that have very little to offer to challenges brought about, it could be argued, by a history of economic policies that have had ideals of modernity firmly in sight. Of course, as anthropologists have routinely argued, many so-called 'traditional' aspects, from kinship to ritual, are an integral part not only of modern societies but of the way they create both tremendous wealth and entrenched inequality. That is, the very realities that cash grants and other forms of redistribution sought to address. Furthermore, African governments, including the Kenyan government, saw social assistance not as an alternative to an ill-suited or ineffective informal solidarity, but as a way of supporting and nourishing it. Yet, despite these aspirations, as we shall see in this book, the more negative appraisal of the informal often prevailed, and had far-reaching consequences in the cash grants that arrived in Korogocho.

Freedom in Money and Redistribution

As I have noted, cash grants represent a shift away from privileged forms of social and humanitarian assistance, particularly in the global South. The movement towards cash grants in Kenya was part of a globally distributed one that sought to convince sceptical others not only that the poor were knowledgeable, skilful and virtuous, but that these qualities could be best put to use within, rather than outside, the market. The act of giving cash is therefore pervaded by sentiments of a moral nature, invoking ideas of dignity, character, responsibility but also – crucially – freedom.

Markets and money have long been equated with the idea of freedom. In money's origin myth, the problem of the 'coincidence of wants' led to the invention of the concept and phenomenon of money that gave people the freedom through which to trade (Graeber 2011). This association of money with freedom was also extended influentially by Simmel, who wrote that money 'is really that form of property that most effectively liberates the individual from the unifying bonds that extend from other objects of possession' (Simmel 2011, 383). Of course, social scientists have worked particularly hard in questioning some of the myths and the prevailing views that surround money. As Bill Maurer (2006) argued, money very rarely acts as an 'acid' dissolving existing social relationships to leave only the individual and her freedom.

In my discussions with NGO workers and civil servants around cash grant programmes in Kenya, as well as in the initiatives like the International Labour Organization's Social Protection Floor, I have noticed two distinct ways in which money retains its strong connotations of freedom, particularly around redistribution. The first focuses on individual freedom and is borne from the recognition that while money might ostensibly have the capacity to free, its unequal distribution on a global scale means that many, including in places like Korogocho, remain essentially unfree, enslaved by the forces of the free market. Cash grants might be understood as one way through which to begin remedying this situation.

The second idea of freedom that surrounds the concept of grants is considered at a collective level. Here, humanitarian institutions, usually concerned with the basics of life and death, find themselves drawing from arguments about free markets being providers of collective welfare. Take, for instance, the European Commission's funding guidelines on 'The Use of Cash and Vouchers in Humanitarian Crises', where they write: 'the recognition that local markets may be able to respond to increases in demand for a variety of commodities and services together with the fluctuating availability and costs of cereals on the world market encourages the further consideration of cash-based programming' (European Commission 2013, 11). In situations of hunger or other crises, they are arguing, a supply of food is available, or could be available, locally but is not matched by a 'demand', understood in the classical economic sense not of a *desire* to purchase food but a will combined with the *capacity* to do so. Giving cash grants is considered as a way through which to generate the necessary demand that the market then tends to automatically match with supply. Cash grants, they conclude, both benefit and nourish free markets to the advantage of the poor.

I mentioned earlier that some proponents of cash grants considered existing informal solidarities as inadequate and even exclusionary, but into their mistrust they also brought other concepts that had somehow got in the way of the poor's individual freedom to pursue their own strategies. In their view, a key barrier to individual freedom – that, is the ability of the poor to exercise their own choices – and collective freedom – in other words, the market responding to those people's choices – was expert knowledge imparted to the poor.

Given the focus on redistribution and cash grants, it is therefore unsurprising, although somewhat disconcerting, that discussions surrounding cash grants often seem to echo the sentiments of the economist Friedrich Hayek. It is worth quoting him at length when he wrote:

> if government uses its coercive powers to ensure that men are given what some experts think they need; if people thus no longer exercise any choice in some of the most important matters of their lives ... [and] must accept the decisions made for them by appointed authority on the basis of its evaluation of their need ... it will no longer be competitive experimentation but solely the decisions of authority that will determine what men shall get. (Hayek 2011 [1944], 377)

But while Hayek advocated for redistribution *through* the market, those behind cash grants instead propose for redistribution *within* the market. The former famously argued for the market as a mechanism of redistribution, whereas the latter group incorporate the market into existing and new forms of, still largely charitable, redistribution.

Unconditionality

The cash grant programmes that unfolded in Korogocho were claimed by their designers to possess a particular novelty, not only in the way they gave money but also in what they saw as their unconditionality. This sets them apart from other, often more politically palatable and widespread forms of assistance, including particularly well-known cash grant programmes that are strongly conditional. Recipients of these types of schemes continue to receive the money only if they seek to become the sorts of persons that institutions expected them to become. Here payments are imagined both as a resource and an incentive for behavioural change for the poor. To give an example, in Brazil's famous Bolsa Família (Family Allowance) scheme, recipients are required to demonstrate their capacities and virtues of caregiving by ensuring they immunise their children, register them with authorities, and ensure their regular attendance at school.[6] In these grants, then, conditionality is concerned not with ploughing the furrows through which charitable money flows, such as the transformation of cash into in-kind items such as food aid or medicine, but about moulding the people to whom the currents are directed.

In considering the poor as lacking the necessary knowledge, skills and virtues to improve their own lives, these conditional types of cash grants also have similarities to other programmes of assistance and personal transformation. Most notably those widespread 'financial empowerment' efforts, such as microcredit, extensively explored by anthropologists, to assist and 'empower' the poor to escape the poverty and thereby become, it is hoped, detached and independent from that very assistance (Elyachar 2005; Moodie 2008; Welker 2012; Guérin 2014).[7] While these schemes have sought to recognise the industriousness of the poor, they have also been criticised for their singular pro-market focus on indebtedness as a poverty alleviation strategy and their emphasis on income generation in the informal economy.

In contrast to other dominant forms of assistance, the unconditional grants that reached Korogocho, and which have become popular across

Africa, aspired neither to indebt people nor to burden them with the demands of the bureaucratic will. While this does not involve a wholesale abandonment of technocratic knowledge, as we shall see in chapter 2 when we explore the identification of recipients, these epistemologies of technocracy concerned with shaping, poking and cajoling the recipients play a more diminutive role than in the schemes that I have discussed above. Individual recipients are rarely monitored or expected to attend training sessions, meetings or capacity-building exercises that anthropologists and others have routinely encountered in development and humanitarian programmes. The unconditional grants seem, then, to represent a divergence from traditional and contemporary charitable and state social assistance, which has its origins in the application of regulation and expert knowledge (Sealander 2003).

I interviewed the Nairobi chair of the Cash Transfer Learning Partnership – a global partnership of humanitarian actors engaged in the policy, practice and research of cash transfers – who put it like this: 'Cash transfers are a big part of the solution.... It's good to give cash, it's flexible, and it's treating poor people not as stupid.'[8] The poor, according to this American NGO worker, as well as others I met, are knowledgeable, have the wisdom to make good judgements, and can use this knowledge and wisdom gained throughout their lives to make appropriate decisions. What I find particularly interesting is the way that the NGO worker's views respond to the concerns that anthropologists have had for many years.

I have earlier mentioned how these types of views resonated with calls for anthropologists to study the good, as well as to study the social relations that structure exclusion and impoverishment, but they also related even more closely to scholars who have been concerned about 'expert' knowledge and paternalism, having documented its many adverse effects (Goodell 1985). Most recently, writing about behavioural psychological theories of paternalism, for instance, Veena Das has worried that paternalism 'ends up in a distrust of the poor and their ability to take responsibility for themselves' (2015, 198). Das's concern echoes earlier work in anthropology that critiqued how the development apparatus portrayed the poor as 'ignorant' (Hobart 1993); that is, as subjects whose particular (lack of) knowledge rendered them sufficiently untrustworthy to secure their own well-being, and which justified the use of paternalistic policies.

While a minimal amount of bureaucratic rules and regulations in unconditional grants is sometimes a result of practical necessities, such as the lack of capacity to enforce them, there are other sorts of more moral-inflected reasonings around trust (Hanlon et al. 2010, 136).[9] As James Ferguson has written, drawing from his study of government welfare in Southern Africa, unconditional grants involve 'a recognition that "the poor" may be trusted to look after their own best interests' (2015, 194). Regulation and expert knowledge are reduced because they are seen as enacting violence upon the poor's very freedom to apply their knowledge and skills, which have now been recognised as superior to the experts' (here, an inversion of hierarchy), to their own lives and ambitions. In this way, the grants seem to be part of a larger anti-bureaucratic impulse, imbued with what Paul du Gay has argued to be a 'thoroughly romantic belief that the principle of a full and free exercise of personal capacities is akin to a moral absolute for human conduct' (du Gay 2000, 3). This also accords with the reference to flexibility made by the chair of the Cash Learning Transfer Partnership. Through the grants, traditional charitable gifts and state welfare transfers have been transformed into the more flexible unmediated gift of money.

In fact, the grants also resemble Foucault's more prescriptive suggestions for social security in France, which he argued should offer 'maximum independence' (Foucault 1990, 165). Foucault himself gave Milton Friedman's negative income tax proposal as an example of a policy that would offer assistance, in 'a very liberal and much less bureaucratic and disciplinary way' (Foucault 2008, 207). Understandably then, for certain commentators, these grants should be celebrated for treating the poor with a dignity that comes about from trusting them to make their own decisions without the heavy hand and the penetrating eye of the technocratic expert. But they also challenge some of the more simplified dichotomies between liberalism and those social formations that are considered as illiberal. Grants, as a form of social assistance as well as humanitarianism, combine ideas around dependency and material support with those concerning autonomy and self-realisation.

What Do Cash Grants Do?

Scholars intrigued by cash grants and the recent enthusiasm for them, approach them in different ways, motivated by their divergent interests. But to some extent uniting them is a central question: what happens when you transfer money directly to poor and vulnerable people? The answers depend very much upon what is meant by *happens*.

One answer is that people spend the money wisely and, correspondingly, often their health improves, their children's educational outcomes get better, and their income grows (for a helpful overview of some of these impacts see Hanlon et al. 2010). Studies have also shown how the grants can reduce both poverty and income inequality (for instance Lloyd-Sherlock et al. 2012). These are crucial insights that have contributed to the popularity of cash grants. They have also served as important insights for those advocating for grants, including Basic Income, who face people hostile to the need for new forms of economic redistribution. Despite the usefulness of these findings, however, many cash grant designers, either worried themselves about the idea of just giving people money, with the attendant fears of welfare dependency, or about the reaction of important political constituencies, have often redesigned them by attempting to 'graduate' people out of grants. This was also the case for what I am calling the urban grant, which at the end of this short-term grant offered recipients larger lump-sum payments or vocational opportunities designed to help them start a business or gain employment.

Another answer to what happens when you simply give money to the poor is that cash grants exacerbate existing inequalities. Maxine Molyneux (2007) has pointed out, in relation to social assistance in Latin America, that the programmes, while possibly empowering women within particular accepted gender roles and relationships, might, in some cases, end up reinforcing the very social divisions that create inequalities between genders. Therefore, while criticisms might be levelled at the lack of welfare services for women (for example Lewis 2000), the introduction of a cash grant form of welfare might be short-sighted in its inability to tackle inequality between the sexes. Transferring money to a woman reinforces the recipient's category as a responsible mother, ignoring the possibility of shared responsibilities, or any recognition that the recipient is likely to view themselves in many other ways than as a mother. Again, then, we see here the important argument that social assistance fails to address some of the fundamental relations that contribute to and exacerbate suffering. But grants might also transform relationships, as Erik Bähre (2011) has shown in South Africa, where, in the face of vast unemployment, young people are often dependent on their parents as recipients of grants, such as pensions.

Yet another answer is related to the previous one, but is less about what cash grants do than what they represent and what political possibilities they might enable or inhibit. Richard Ballard has argued that the growing cash grant movement does not 'signal an epochal shift to a post neoliberal era', but rather combines liberalised economic growth with 'bolder biopolitical interventions for the poor' (Ballard 2013, 1). This attention to the poor, for instance in moral philosopher Thomas Pogge's (2007) efforts to extend a Rawlsian contractarian approach to a global scale, ignores inequality.[10] From the Marxian tradition, then, scholars argue that what is happening when people are given money is merely a failure in political imagination. Göran Therborn (2007), for example, has dismissed calls for Universal Basic Income, which constitutes an even more politically radical proposal than the grants I have studied, as a 'curious utopia of resignation'. That is, an idea that masquerades as utopian but merely continues to acquiesce to the current, dystopian, capitalistic world (see also Prince and Neumark 2022).

Such calls from this tradition mirror arguments that even a presence of significant state welfare represents a failure of a given political economy to deliver equality. Of course, it must be noted that in Kenya state welfare remains still limited. There, cash grants have not, to date, developed into the sort of grant-based forms of economic redistribution that we have seen in countries such as South Africa. In the years since the first pilot of the child grant in 2004, still only around 1.2 million, or about 2.4 per cent, of Kenyans received any kind of, largely aid-funded, government grant. Even if we were to include the sporadic grants offered by the NGO sector across the country, which are difficult to calculate, I do not believe this would change the numbers in a dramatic way – although they *would* emphasise some Kenyans' continued reliance on foreign-funded NGOs. The new cash grant schemes in the country, then, might represent a paradigmatic shift around the way assistance, whether social or humanitarian, is delivered, but they do not yet constitute a substantial rethinking of economic redistribution in Kenya, in comparison again to South Africa (Bähre 2011). Even experiments taking place in the country around Basic Income, which are different from the cash grants I studied, carried out for instance by Give-Directly, are highly selective towards particular geographies in Western Kenya, and thus do not constitute anything resembling a national *universal* system of assistance.[11]

Others, however, argue that we should be open to different political possibilities, retaining a particular sort of political curiosity, and perhaps optimism, about what else is generated in the wake of these schemes. James Ferguson, for instance, has noticed how in South Africa, the government has expanded its grant programmes to more and more of the population, beyond just the 'weak and afflicted'. In this way, he writes, the 'institutional ambitions of the social grant bureaucracy gradually creep toward a kind of universalistic, citizenship-based entitlement' (Ferguson 2015: 204–5). This is certainly an interesting, even encouraging, change in South Africa. But, for some, what is crucial is the ways in which people might understand themselves as having such entitlements. Gregory Duff Morton (2015), for example, has shown that Brazil's Bolsa Família, perhaps the largest cash grant programme in the world, has not generated feelings of entitlement among its beneficiaries, and neither has it produced social movements that support it. In fact, cash grant designers who are cognisant of the political limitations that surround the scaling-up of grants have sometimes argued that the grants should be redesigned in a way that helps to foster relationships not only between people in communities receiving the grants, but between those people and the state or other institutions. These positions stem from the larger argument that a more relational approach should be taken to policy design and implementation, which, some argue, would lead to more 'transformative' grants that combine giving money with inculcating in their recipients an understanding of themselves as rights-bearing citizens. While these might be laudable goals, it is not very clear that it is the design of the grant programmes that will enact the necessary transformation of wider social relationships within which they are embedded. As I discuss in chapter 3, in Kenya, state and non-state actors were wary of the very possibility that the grants might generate new entitlements and, as a result, actively attempted to mitigate against this hazardous prospect.

Relationality and Care

My own approach in this book recognises but is somewhat divergent from much of the literature on cash grants, and this is because ethnographic fieldwork, as it is wont to do, led me in a different direction. As I observed the arrival of the grants, the way they were absorbed into households, and their wider afterlives in Korogocho, I was drawn to what it means 'to care' in the ghetto. But in doing so, I was confronted with things that confused me about what care was. Over time I have realised that I cannot make sense of these puzzles if I only look at how people cared for each other *in* relationships. In the rest of this introduction, then, I turn to what constitutes *Caring Cash*'s central argument concerning care both *in* and *for* relationships, by taking the book's first steps in constructing the framework that will be completed over its course. To do so means first looking briefly at the idea of relationality, and its connection to care.

Despite its contemporary reputation, it has not always been the case that my own discipline of anthropology has fully acknowledged the significance and depth of social relationships across the world's full spectrum of societies. As economic anthropologists Chris Hann and Keith Hart have said, the field of economic anthropology was able for a long time to ignore the 'substantivists' who considered the economy as embedded in the relations of society because they conceded the debate with the 'formalists' by admitting their methods could only be applied to 'traditional' worlds (Hart and Hann 2011, 70). Since then, however, most scholars in the social sciences would concur that real persons in all societies are never the economically rational, maximising individuals conceptualised in classical economics, but instead are enmeshed in rich and diverse relational worlds that shape people's decisions and values (for instance Gudeman 2001).[12] This means examining varied objects and practices as relational, whether concerning humans or, in recent decades with the post-humanist turn, including non-humans. The importance of attending to the textures of particular social relations has therefore been productively extended to the more technical domains often seen as operating on more abstract and universalist principles (for instance Bear 2015; Harvey and Knox 2015), something I will also turn to in due course.[13]

This book is predominantly concerned with caring relationships other than those that have been perhaps more widely discussed, with some exceptions, by social scientists. Medical spaces such as clinics and hospitals have, for obvious reasons, been privileged ones for social scientists and others thinking about care (Mol 2008; Garcia 2010). I am more interested, however, in the care that takes place in non-clinical spaces. Part of the reason for my interest in these spaces is because the grants themselves sought, to some extent, to keep people *out* of the clinical ones, tackling issues of ill health before they escalated. In Africanist anthropology, forms of care outside of the formal healthcare system have often been discussed in the context of child and elderly care (Levine 2008; Simon 2015). Care of the sick outside of the clinic has also been explored extensively, for instance, in relation to HIV/AIDS (Geissler and Prince 2010) and Ebola (Parker et al. 2019). The economic aspect of care has also been discussed by anthropologists through discussions of informal mutualities and self-help (Rodima-Taylor 2014; Shipton 2014); indeed, the very initiatives that the World Bank and others consider to be failing.

The anthropological literature is certainly more nuanced than the World Bank's when it comes to the ways in which forms of care, solidarity and mutuality are transforming. Anthropologists and their colleagues in allied disciplines have described how forms of mutuality are transforming, and often straining, because of the play of political and economic forces and relationships that result in violent, predatory, and even neglectful policies and practices. As we shall see, my contribution in this book is to show how some people live in a context in which these and other sorts of relationships are marked by fragility, and what they do about it. This means similarly looking for care that takes place outside the clinical space; in the home, between neighbours and others, and even in local forms of bureaucracy.

Looking at what people do to care for fragile lives and relationships means arguing neither simply for the erosion nor the continuation of caring relationships but how the fragility and care of both are intertwined. One good place to start considering this is to turn to discussions about personhood.

Personhood and Relations

Anthropologists have long argued that the liberal conception of the individual person is an impoverished one that does not take into account the expansive spectrum of persons, and ideologies about them, in societies across the world (Carrithers et al. 1985). Perhaps most influential in anthropology has been Marilyn Strathern's (1990) popularisation of the concept of the *dividual*, which she uses to describe Melanesian personhood. Unlike Westerners, she argues, Melanesians do not think of people as having a unitary core attached to which are a range of external roles, for instance, mother, wife, child. Instead, they see their personhood very much made up of their relationships with others, so that one's role depends upon the relationships that are being enacted at any given moment. Strathern's arguments, of course, are not intended to describe either Melanesian or Western persons, but rather to explicate how people within these societies *think* about personhood. Yet they have also been helpful to anthropologists, and others, who have found the individualism inherent in liberal politics particularly problematic (Englund 2008).

Unconnected to the anthropological literature on personhood has been an interest in this topic within the fields of moral and political philosophy. Like anthropologists, these philosophers have been dissatisfied with the dominance of liberal models of the individual. But unlike anthropologists, they have largely directed their ire inwards, at their own discipline. They argue that many of their own theories of moral and political life have been built up from a flawed assumption of the moral actor as an autonomous and rational individual. Take as an example Michael Sandel, who criticises John Rawls' starting point for his theory of justice, which Sandel says is based on the idea that 'We are distinct individuals first, and then (circumstances permitting) we form relationships and engage in co-operative arrangements with others' (Sandel 1982, 53). Moral and political philosophers have instead argued that we as persons are in some ways constituted by our relationships rather than being simply prior to them.

This philosophical work to connect morality with relationality has perhaps received the most elaboration within feminist moral thinking. The pioneering work of Carol Gilligan (1982) and Joan Tronto (1993), has generated an impressive literature on what has been called the 'ethics of care' that has brought a greater recognition to the importance of care and relationships. Carol Gilligan (1982), in particular, challenged the patriarchal views of moral experience, showing how women's moral reasoning rested to a greater extent on responsibilities and relationships than the rights and rules that tended to dominate men's reasoning.

Despite many similarities, the model of a relational person in feminist moral philosophy has some differences from some of the more radical ideas of personhood posited in anthropological texts, for instance, with Strathernian ideas of the dividual I have just discussed. The philosopher Virginia Held, for instance, has written that 'The ethics of care values the ties we have with particular other persons and the actual relationships that partly constitute our identity' (2006, 14). For Melanesians, the relationships engaged with at a particular moment *fully* constitute not an identity – that is, an outward representation of a person – but the person itself.

This book is not concerned with the issue of whether persons or their identities in Korogocho are fully or partly constituted by relationships. Those are empirical questions that I intentionally did not pursue. Instead, my interest is to begin with the basic starting point that relationships are vital for people's selves; their moral experience, economic well-being, as well as biological survival. This means that taking inspiration from, and building upon, feminist moral philosophy as well as anthropological studies of care, I am interested in the care for relationships. This also means my approach's starting point is similar to that implied by Jarrett Zigon and Jason Throop when they talked of 'relational-being'. They write:

'If moral experience arises out of a concern for the constituting relationships that bring our and others' being into existence, then a significant aspect of this moral experience must be to care for those relations' (Zigon and Throop 2014, 9). If we recognise both that we are all relational beings, but also that being relational is not just a moral but also an economic and biological experience, then it means beginning to explore how we remain connected to others. In other words, it is not enough to point out that we are *all* relational, but we must also strive to understand how *different* people care for those constitutive relationships.

In *Caring Cash*, I argue for the need to expand our appreciation of what care is by including the care of both persons and the relationships that constitute persons. This means incorporating, but also going further than the idea that care is directed only at persons within relationships. In this argument, a relationship, for example one between a mother and a child, is a caring relationship. In the ghetto, a mother will endeavour to feed her infant when she is hungry, she might stop her child from walking into a busy road, and she might put money aside for the child's school fees. In turn, a child may care for her mother through fetching water for the household, looking after siblings, sending remittances when older or attending to the mother when she is sick or infirm. These are all *acts* of care that take place within a *relationship* of care.

To say that relationships are objects that can be cared for means, at the outset, recognising that people desire for many of their relationships to survive and that they want them to be of a sufficient and particular quality. They will also work to make this happen. But this view can also, I argue, open up new ways of interpreting people's behaviour. As I shall show, norms, values or practices that might appear as antithetical to care if we pay attention solely to the person as an object of care, can be shown to be synonymous with care when we include relationships as their objects. I am therefore interested in the intertwinement of not only care, but also certain forms of disregard towards persons and the relationships that connect persons in different ways. Solidarity, in this way, is not necessarily built out of kindness and munificence. This is perhaps intuitive to the reader. When Shakespeare's Hamlet declared 'I must be cruel only to be kind' to prevent his mother from betraying her deceased husband with her new husband, King Claudius, his reasoning was directed not simply to a person, whether his mother, his father, or the new king, but also more widely to the relationships that pertained between them.

It is also apparent, though, that caring for relationships necessitates varied forms of caring for the persons that they connect. This means caring for their physical bodies, but also for that person's future, hopes, dreams and ambitions. Without this care, the desirable form of a relationship can be harmed, potentially irreparably. In the extreme case, a lack of care can lead to the physical death of the other.[14] One might also withhold care for the other, not necessarily always out of a clear choice, but nonetheless in a way that leads to relational transformation where parties become estranged from each other. As we shall see in chapter 5, this was a common concern for mothers living in extreme poverty in Korogocho. In this same chapter we shall also see how care for persons, and therefore the relationships too, must be distributed in order to care for the relational unit of the household. This distribution does not always follow the logic of a rational acting individual, deciding where to care and where not to care, but involves attending to others in whatever way possible where needs impinge themselves. But this is not to say, however, that people do not sometimes rationalise their actions.

An Ethnography of Grants

At the outset of my fieldwork, in mid-2010, I had a broad research interest in the sorts of interventions, including cash grants, that aimed to alleviate both poverty and other forms of suffering in Kenya's urban slums. After visiting a number of these slums, and meeting and getting to know many of their residents, I eventually began spending most of my time in just Korogocho. One reason for spending so much time in Korogocho was the presence there of the cash grant programmes through the lens of which I came to view care and relationships. In the early preparatory stages of my fieldwork, I had come across the evaluation of the first pilot of the urban cash grant programmes that had taken place in Korogocho following the post-election violence of 2007–8. I soon got wind of another that would be taking place, designed and managed by a consortium of transnational NGOs. I also became aware that Korogocho had been chosen to be among one of the original pilot sites of the child grant in 2003.[15]

Much of my fieldwork in Korogocho coincided with the introduction and unfolding of the urban cash grant. I spent most of my time during the early part of that period with the local implementing NGO and with their social workers, as well as the community workers and community health workers they recruited, as they travelled across the ghetto carrying out a survey designed to identify recipients. This way of doing fieldwork is familiar to anthropologists who have studied how institutions aspire to intervene in the lives of the poor. For instance, Vinh-Kim Nyugen has written how 'workshops gave him a privileged glimpse into how international consultants and local workers interacted, shedding light onto how differences in opinion, goals, or strategies were reconciled or elided' (Nguyen 2010, 58). This type of fieldwork, including mine, has involved observing and participating in surveys, meetings, training sessions, and in research and planning exercises. In the Foucauldian (1979, 1991) turn in anthropology over the last few decades, scholars have also found these sorts of sites important for the formation of new types of subjectivities. For instance, when an outside agency carries out a training session for young women and men designed to unleash their inner entrepreneurial spirit. Linked to this, too, is the culture of audit and the bureaucratic forms that have been extensively examined and theorised (Strathern 2000; Gupta 2012; Hull 2012; Bierschenk and Olivier de Sardan 2014; Mathur 2015). But because of the unconditional nature of the urban grant programme, as well as that of the child grant, after the initial identification stage had been completed official bureaucracy was minimised, if not removed entirely.

James Ferguson has described the state's role in unconditional grants in South Africa as both universally engaged, because it directly provides for each and every citizen, and maximally disengaged, because it is 'taking no real interest in shaping the conduct of those under its care, who are seen as knowing their own needs better than the state does' (Ferguson 2010, 177). It was, of course, not the case in Kenya that the state was universally engaged, given that it only provided, and even then largely through aid funding, small payments to only a small proportion of its citizens. But as we shall see in chapter 3, the idea that even unconditional cash grants in Kenya are maximally disengaged also requires more scrutiny. But it was the case that unconditional cash grants in Korogocho minimised the opportunity to engage in 'traditional' sites of fieldwork concerned with tracing the textures of policies and programmes, such as training sessions or close monitoring of recipients. Annelise Riles (2004) has described this sort of situation in another very different context – central bankers in Japan – as the unwinding of technocratic knowledge. While I was interested in thinking about what she calls the unwinding of technocratic knowledge in relation to my own subject of cash grants in Kenya, I was equally interested in the fruits of that labour. I was interested in what happened when expert and bureaucratic knowledge was unwound in a specific locale. In short, what happens when NGO and government workers seek to prioritise the knowledge of those they seek to help, and give them an amount, and type, of resource and freedom to turn that knowledge into action? This question guided much of my research but also my fieldwork. In fact, it raised methodological questions about how to do fieldwork on a policy idea that inadvertently reduced many of the traditional opportunities for fieldwork itself. During some of my fieldwork, I sought out opportunities through which I could encounter what did remain in regard to bureaucratic activity; for instance, visiting national and local governmental and non-governmental offices associated with both grants, or attending the rare meeting. Sometimes I looked for, and participated in, comparative examples in Korogocho that represented more traditional paradigms of assistance such as nutrition clinics and youth entrepreneurship workshops. But this, I realised, merely sidestepped the methodological question, and ignored the very phenomena I was interested in. Therefore, I tried instead to experience the winding back of bureaucracy in ways similar to how residents and others working in Korogocho experienced it themselves. This meant spending time with these people, at their homes, their 'offices', and on the street, gradually building up my understanding of their lives and histories, their important relationships, their priorities and their values. It also meant accompanying people, and visiting them, in hospital, spending time at the Chief's Camp, attending funerals, and even participating in political protests.

It is still of something of a disappointment that I never lived in Korogocho itself, although I did sometimes stay over. I regularly asked those to whom I was becoming close to help me find a place to stay. Whenever I asked, the answer was always 'Not yet.' Korogocho, they would often tell me, and as the reader will have already got a sense of, was not at that point safe enough.[16] My fieldwork, therefore, would involve travelling into the slum at first light each day, packed into one of the city's *matatus* (shared minibus taxis), and returning to my apartment, and my partner who had moved with me from the UK, in the evening. There is no doubt I missed certain things and missed out on experiencing an important dimension of life by not experiencing night-time in Korogocho. But with lasting and deep gratitude I note that some of these shortcomings could be compensated for by three particular people in Korogocho. They appear, as with everyone else in this book, under pseudonyms, but are clearly distinguished because I call them research assistants. My research would not have been possible without them. Kamau, Jude and John introduced me to

Korogocho, showed me around, and at the beginning helped to translate. But they were also more than research assistants. They were key interlocutors, teaching me and correcting me when I frequently got things wrong, while constantly keeping me safe.[17] Moreover, through them, as well as other community workers, I was also able to meet the cash grant recipients whose stories of care feature prominently in this book, and particularly in chapters one, four and five.

Most of these recipients were women, and it soon became clear that as a white male researcher I would be confronted with particular challenges – but also opportunities. To a large extent, with some important and impressive exceptions (for instance Ross 2010), contemporary social scientific descriptions of urban life in Africa have tended to pay most attention to men, particularly young men (Simone 2004a; Elyachar 2005; Mains 2007; Weiss 2009; Di Nunzio 2019). As in other parts of Africa, men in Nairobi are often highly visible and widely heard. As I alluded to in the prologue, in the mornings in east Nairobi, men can be seen on the pavements and streets striding quickly to cover the long distances to the Industrial Area, wandering the streets selling consumer goods or toiling in the roadside *jua kali* industries, and squeezed in the back of trucks as they are taken to work on construction sites. It is not that women are not visible. Far from it: they congregate on street corners in anticipation of domestic work, operate food and other stalls at markets and on the roadside, and work shifts at bars and restaurants, selling food, drinks and sometimes sex. But space is always gendered, and these sorts of public spaces have different social dynamics for women, and especially so for their interactions and encounters with men.

The home, as both my male and female interlocutors regularly reminded me, was a space for women and their children. It was generally easier for me to meet women in their homes during the day than outside in more public spaces where they often felt constrained talking to men for fear of *mjadala* (gossip). For that reason, I spent a lot of my time inside the shacks of Korogocho hearing women's stories and meeting their children. Many, but not all, of the women I knew lived much of the time alone with their children, either widowed, often as a result of their husband contracting HIV/AIDS; as single parents who no longer had any contact with the father of their children; or as second wives.

I am not a parent and I therefore have no direct experience of parenthood. To study lives that are different than one's own is, of course, the hallmark of anthropology. But it might be argued that parenthood is a sort of difference that remains uniquely inaccessible. Moral philosopher Laurie Ann Paul (2014) has suggested, for instance, that parenthood is an example of a 'transformative experience' that produces radically new selves.[18] While her argument concerns the ability to make rational decisions about whether to participate in such experiences, I think it also points to methodological difficulties in a non-parent's ability to access the experience of parenthood. Of course, having experienced parenthood does not mean a problem-free entry into the experience of parenthood in different circumstances, such as for the mothers in Korogocho. Parenthood is shaped by, among other things, gender, class, race, ethnicity, and nationality. But, as a white, British man, it would cross the threshold of the absurd to claim any more than a limited understanding of the exigencies and turmoil of motherhood as experienced by impoverished, black, Kenyan women living in a slum.

When I draw upon the lives and reflections of my interlocutors, including the women who received cash grants, but also the many others in and outside the slum, including young men hustling in the city, community health workers in the charitable economy, government workers and NGOs in offices, and of course my research assistants, I recognise that only certain aspects of their experience were made available to me, partially and incrementally, over a too-short period of time.[19] Their lives, experiences and thoughts are far richer and more varied than I could grasp through the period I spent with them and, therefore, than I can offer the reader. In lieu of the sort of depth and richness that can be captured through longer-term longitudinal studies of urban life (for example Ross 2010), I have focused instead, in this book, on some of the things my interlocutors taught me about how they kept themselves, others and the threads of the delicate, often ragged, relational fabric intact.

Chapter Outline

By treating the grants as laboratories through which to comprehend the complex and often seemingly contradictory modalities of care in Korogocho, this book is structured as interpretations of a series of intertwined events, acts and spaces. These knit together my observations with perspectives of my differently situated interlocutors, from local NGO workers to community health workers to those receiving, or hoping to receive, assistance from either of the two cash grants.

Part I introduces the reader to the fragile lives and relational fabric of Korogocho, the charitable economy that enveloped it, and the cash grants that emerged to identify those that were considered most deserving of support.

Chapter 1 explores how Korogocho as a place has been produced through processes of stratification and differentiation from the colonial through to the postcolonial period. By following the case of one of its residents, Lucy, the chapter explores how wider factors have shaped the lives of those migrating to Nairobi and who end up in ghettos such as Korogocho. I attempt in this chapter to give the reader a sense of what life was like in Korogocho, beyond the vignettes I have provided in the prologue and in this introduction. This chapter also introduces the ways in which Kenyans have, over the last few decades, become enveloped by a partial, uneven, and fragmented series of development, global health, humanitarian and human rights interventions that constitute the charitable economy. This politically complex and fraught economy has brought into the ghetto multiple actors, from the government to local and transnational NGOs and multilaterals such as the World Bank, all offering new, usually time-limited, opportunities for both residents and local precariously employed community workers, or what I call ghetto-level bureaucrats, as various attempts are made to know, shape and save the lives of the marginalised.

Chapter 2 has two interlinked aims. First, to show how the two grant programmes – the urban grant and child grant – that unfolded in Korogocho were premised on a consideration of both the biological and the social body. While they had emerged from a history of global health and humanitarian norms, relationships and values, the creators of these grants began to recognise wider social relationships. Not only were the grants considered by a varied set of actors as the building blocks of state social assistance system, they were also interwoven with a recognition of social relationships as both an outcome and a determinant of the diseased biological body.

Connected to this, the second aim of the chapter is to show how the grant programmes aimed to reach the poorest citizens by sidestepping the grounded and concrete relational persons and knowledge that were part of an always tension-laden fabric of sociality in the ghetto. This, I argue, meant that while the impulse to assist individual lives as part of a nascent social assistance programme recognised the social body at a more abstract level, it ignored how it actually existed as a historically embodied fact on the ground. Drawing on situated critiques of this process, I show

how ghetto-level bureaucrats interpreted this as a way through which the humanitarian NGO that sought to bring institutionalised care into the slum endeavoured to cut them out and evade specific responsibility to people in the ghetto. By drawing attention to the relational entanglements and disentanglements as they were experienced, disputed and negotiated, this particular part of the chapter seeks to lay the foundation for Part II of the book.

If Part I is about Korogocho, its history and people, and the way in which the poor recipients of the grant and their benefactors were cut from the wider relational fabric, Part II is about how this reveals something new, I believe, about the ways in which the loops of this fabric are woven and kept intact. This part constitutes the core of the book's argument, and if necessary, a reader who is pressed for time may go directly to it. In the three chapters of this second part, I show, in different ways, how people cared for the relationships that were integral to the lives of Korogocho, and how this care for relationships interacted with the care for other persons, constituting a stuttering, even faltering, ethics of solidarity.

Chapter 3 continues the focus on bureaucracy around the cash grant programmes, but particularly the ways in which technocratic knowledge was unwound. Ghetto-level bureaucrats and their situated knowledge and labour around the charitable economy were once again, and even more profoundly, sidestepped in an effort to trust the poor. When the demand for monitoring and surveillance in the cash grant programmes was relaxed, these slum bureaucrats did not simply acquiesce. Instead, they sought to reinsert themselves by continuing to surveil the poor. I show how their conscious reinsertion can be interpreted by seeing them as bureaucrats who endeavoured to care for a relationship between the charitable benefactors and the poor. This is the first example within the book of how a form of uncaring, in this case in revitalised forms of paternalism, can be understood as caring when the object of care is the relationship itself, in this case, a fragile relationship that connected the charitable economy to the people of Korogocho.

Chapters 4 and 5 turn towards those matrifocal households that the grant programmes had identified as particularly vulnerable, and therefore eligible for inclusion on the schemes. In chapter 4, I explore how integral to efforts to survive for these households were relationships with those outside it, including with neighbours and lovers. I aim to show how *not* giving, as well as acts of detachment and distancing, can be understood as a deeply moral economic act that attempts to care for the intimate and interpersonal relationships. Through these sorts of uncaring acts, women worked to ensure that relationships of solidarity endured into an always indeterminate future.

Chapter 5 moves more deeply into the households themselves, exploring the relationships between mothers and their children. This final chapter explores how mothers strived to care for their children, allocating care, which included attempts to move children away from them, in ways that sought to preserve the relational unit of the household into the future. While the earlier chapters in this second part of the book pay attention mostly to the care for relationships, this chapter shows how the care for persons is always intimately involved in this relational care. Moreover, it is involved in hopeful and uncertain attempts to attend to the quality of relationships and their concomitant obligations.

Throughout this book, my aim is to build upon and contribute towards our understanding of caring relationships and forms of solidarity, particularly in Africa. Urban contexts, however, often present us with a challenge when thinking about such matters. While rural contexts are hardly spaces unmarked by disregard and exclusion, urban ones are often seen as paradigmatic of it. Indeed, my interlocutors themselves regularly remarked on the limits of care among those living in poverty in the urban ghetto. This does not mean though that care does not unfold in the midst of this poverty, as I often observed. Others have recognised this too, showing how, despite people's protestations to the contrary, care and solidarity continue to take place but often in quieter, unacknowledged, and more understated registers. However, the approach I take in this book is a little different. My aim is to show how acts that might be expressed loudly and explicitly but which appear *uncaring* could also be understand as a way of attending to the fragile threads that constitute the ghetto's social cloth. In this way, my own, often naïve thoughts about solidarity and care, were challenged by my friends and interlocutors who, despite expressing the disregard that existed, both from the state, as well as NGOs and from each other, nevertheless showed me both the importance of relationships and their fragility. They showed me that relationships, spanning from intimate neighbourly ones to more abstract charitable ones, can be like human bodies: fragile, vulnerable, and even sometimes burdensome, yet absolutely integral to life, and things that need to be carefully attended to.

PART I

1

The Ghetto: A Place of Refuge and Charity

On the freshly swept concrete steps in the compound of the local Catholic church, I found myself sitting with some new friends. Because there was no match being played on the football field behind us, our sole source of entertainment was to watch another group of young men unroll a large piece of paper. While not exactly the crowd puller of a football match, it was sufficiently out of the ordinary to pique our interest. As I was once told by John, my research assistant, if you walk around Korogocho with a paper in your hand, it will be taken as a sign by residents that something, most likely a development or humanitarian intervention, is imminent. Craning our necks to look properly, we saw printed on the paper a series of lines and squares, constituting a digitally generated map of Korogocho. At that time, smartphones were uncommon in the ghetto, but if my new friends and I had visited one of the many cyber cafés dotted around its perimeter we would have been able to have seen the same details online.[1]

Today, several years later, it is possible to take a virtual tour through Korogocho using Google Maps' 'Street View' feature. I invite the reader to take it and recommend starting at these coordinates: -1.2532, 36.8850. From there, travel north-west up the Kamunde Road. This was my usual path into and through Korogocho. The tour will take you along some of the ghetto's tarmac roads, offering a glimpse of the many *vibanda* that constitute the informal economy: semi-permanent shacks selling school uniforms, shoes, plastic and metal homeware, hardware and construction materials, fruit, vegetables and meat. You will see the *Mpesa* mobile money kiosks, as well as the stalls and 'warehouses' where men attend to broken electronic equipment, recycle plastic bottles and weld metal gates, and where women sell vegetables and freshly fried, delicious chapattis. Taking a right on Kamunde Road onto Community Lane will take you to what is still today called the Chief's Camp. This dirt compound, shaded by tall trees, is separated from the rest of the ghetto by a chain-link fence.

Inside is a collection of one-storey concrete buildings and shipping containers which house the Provincial Administration, its police, and the slum upgrading Residents Committee. Also there you will find a health clinic, a community hall, a church, and Koch FM, a community radio station.

The compound itself, the buildings and the different actors are the spaces and conduits through which the charitable economy's uneven and often politically fraught flows of resources, norms and values reach the ghetto. It would be there that I would also encounter, during my fieldwork, further materialisations of these flows. I would see lorries ferrying sacks of maize from the World Food Programme and distributing it at the church to those affected by HIV/AIDS. Cars belonging to a range of transnational humanitarian and development NGOs, from Médecins Sans Frontières (MSF) to World Vision, carrying representatives for meetings with Korogocho's authorities. Sometimes the Kenyan legal centre, *Kituo cha Sheria*, would arrive to conduct legal aid and human rights education camps. The walls inside the health centre were covered with more evidence of foreign, global health interventions: health education posters, emblazoned with the branding of organisations from MSF to the World Health Organization (WHO), jostled for space.

Through both NGO and government schemes, and often partnerships between the two, Korogocho's slum dwellers were variously taught how to save their money, start a business, feed their children, stave off alcohol or drug addiction and, in perhaps one of the more outlandish schemes, to use self-defence to fend off attackers. Occasionally people were offered more than just the opportunity to acquire new knowledge or skills. For instance, attendees of training sessions might occasionally receive a small *per diem*, a lunch, or sometimes a t-shirt emblazoned with a public health message. At times, recipients of charity were also able to forge further connections within the charitable economy, leading to subsequent invitations to activities, such as workshops with their concomitant *per diems*, and some could even manage to secure access to food aid or a loan.

The virtual tour will be interesting to those who have never visited Korogocho, or even a slum in Kenya, even though it will only offer a static representation of ghetto life captured from a Google Street View car as it drove through the ghetto on a sunny day in February 2018. It will not squeeze you down the often plastic-bag-strewn, packed-dirt alleyways through which not only people but wastewater flow. Nor will it take you through the jagged and warped, painted corrugated-iron doors that separate the streets and alleyways from the compounds. Neither will it give you a sense of the congestion. Estimates of Korogocho's population vary, but it is likely to be somewhere just shy of 100,000 people. It is hard to estimate the population; people move regularly and many do not consider it a home. With most shacks just one storey high, and with Korogocho occupying just one and half square kilometres of land, it has a population density two and a half times that of Manhattan. And yet these crowded conditions are not unusual for Nairobi. Korogocho is just one slum of hundreds with similar housing conditions, and which according to the human rights organisation Amnesty International (2009), shelter half of the city's population while occupying only 5 per cent of its land.

For a very long time, slums in Kenya had been literal blank spots on the maps of national and municipality administrators. Authorities had not recorded the shacks – designated as informal forms of housing – nor the services and amenities that served their inhabitants. In Korogocho this began to change in the early 2000s as various initiatives were instigated to develop the slum's housing, transport, sanitation and water infrastructures. To transform the slum's infrastructure required the production of technocratic, including cartographic, knowledge concerning what already existed. Yet this knowledge remained largely out of the public domain until the young men with the map on the football field endeavoured to change the situation. The men were part of a recent initiative, beginning around 2010, that had begun with both foreign and Kenyan technologists and activists attempting to transform local residents into digital, open-access, cartographers (Poggiali 2016). This initiative had begun, predictably, in Kibera in the west, and thereafter moved to others in the city. Predictably, because Kibera had, over recent decades, become a magnet for NGOs, social enterprises, artists and individual philanthropists motivated by and perpetuating the popular discourses that claimed it was Africa's largest slum.

When the cartographic efforts reached Korogocho, they joined other, more long-standing, efforts at documenting life and living conditions there. As I mentioned in the introduction, in 2002, almost a decade before these different mapping exercises began, the African Population and Health Research Center had been carrying out a Demographic Surveillance Survey in Korogocho. During my fieldwork, the institution's field researchers, carrying branded rucksacks and measurement tools, could regularly be seen traversing the streets and alleyways of the slum. Surveying the same people regularly over years, the institution and its researchers had generated vast bodies of data that drew attention to socio-demographic and health-related trends concerning the births, deaths, migration, pregnancy, vaccinations, marriage, education, livelihood and housing characteristics of the residents.

Beyond sheer population density, the statistical picture of Korogocho produced by the African Population and Health Research Center and others, can shock. The HIV/AIDS rate in Korogocho has been estimated to be as high as 14 per cent (Madise et al. 2012; NACC and NASCOP 2012). The slum's maternal mortality rate has been estimated at 706 per 100,000 live births, much higher than average in Kenya of 560 (which in turn compares to 2 in Norway, where I now live and work). If Korogocho was a country, it would have the seventh worst maternal mortality rate in the world. It would fare about as well (or badly) with its child mortality, which has been estimated at 92.5 deaths per 1,000 live births (Emina et al. 2011). Over three-quarters of the children who died during the time these surveys took place did so as a result of common communicable diseases, particularly pneumonia and diarrhoeal disease.

Such a statistical picture joins the often harrowing textual and visual representations produced by journalists, NGOs and artists who have been photographing and filming in ghettos like Korogocho for many years, documenting the shootouts, cholera outbreaks, and fires. Many of the videos, in English and Kiswahili or the Sheng street language, are also available to the reader on YouTube. But these actors' representational labour is regularly interwoven with their interventional efforts: videos are also available showing, among other things, the distribution of food aid, the slum tours, roller-skating projects, handwashing campaigns and biogas initiatives. In an attempt to take over ownership of the narrative of their lives and their fellow slum dwellers, musicians born and brought up in Korogocho, as well as in other ghettos in Nairobi, have filmed their own music videos for original tracks as they look to document their life in their own words and through their own eyes.

An online, interactive experience of Korogocho is likely to be of interest to the reader. But such an encounter is, of course, strikingly different from the experience of the Kenyans who arrive in Nairobi and end up living in Korogocho. To them, the ghetto is an initial, and what usually turns out to be lasting, disappointment. For the many migrants who arrive from Kenya's more rural areas, Korogocho's shacks, erected from an amalgam of mud, wood, plastic and corrugated iron, are far too reminiscent of the village houses they had left when attempting to establish a better, more modern life in the city. There is something, therefore, quite apt in the government's administrative term for the neighbourhoods that make up Korogocho: *vijiji* (villages).

But after this first disappointment, what awaits the new arrivals is, in truth, much worse. Most people rent their shacks from landlords who expend little effort in ensuring they are habitable. The constructions are rarely sufficiently weatherproof; they let in the chill of Nairobi's winters, and leak during the long rains that occur from around the end of March to May. Residents still remember the El Niño in the late 1990s that caused the Nairobi River to swell and flood those shacks situated on its river-banks, and which subsequently led to devastating outbreaks of cholera.

Today, the spread of water-borne diseases is made worse by poor water and sanitation facilities. Long-drops are not always regularly emptied and simply having piped water in your compound places you in the very upper echelons of Korogocho society. Residents, in fact, pay more for the water they queue for than the middle classes in other parts of the city who enjoy the benefits of piped water. Electricity is never reliable. Just a year before my fieldwork, one neighbourhood in Korogocho had been without elec-tricity for many months after thieves had stolen the transformer. Acts of transformer oil theft had in fact taken place across the country around the time of my fieldwork, sometimes for human food production, despite the oil clearly not being intended for human consumption (Oriedo 2010). One resident once recounted the story with a chuckle, 'But that oil, it made really good chips!' It was the sort of black humour that was not uncommon in Korogocho, nor in other urban spaces on the margins across the world (Goldstein 2003).

I hope to have given the reader a glimpse into the material conditions of life in Korogocho. But, of course, this initial, surface-level description is in no way sufficient to understand either the ghetto or those people who have been forced to seek shelter within it. The task of this chapter is there-fore to show in more detail how Korogocho has been produced and its residents shaped through a long process of differentiation and stratifica-tion. It joins the efforts by others to show the lived, historical situatedness and particularities of urban life in Africa (for example, Weiss 2009; Ross 2010; Di Nunzio 2019).

These processes of differentiation and stratification began with the establishment of Nairobi by the British at the turn of the twentieth century. While such processes changed upon independence, I show how they did not produce the equity that many Kenyans had anticipated. I first chart this history before rooting it in how it has been lived. To do so, I follow the life history of one of my interlocutors, Lucy, who will also appear at various points throughout this book.

Despite Lucy's identification by both state and non-state institutions as a generic, quantifiable object of social or humanitarian intervention, her life should be understood in its particular positioning within a long history that I will explore, of space, movement and vulnerability, scored deeply with class, race, ethnicity and gender (Malkki 1996). Lucy's life history, which I will unpack in more detail later in this chapter, offers a glimpse into the experiences of a woman who occupies a position at the lowest rung of urban Kenyan society in the twenty-first century. Lucy joined others as part of a 'landless proletariat', a population which Kenyans argue has grown more significant in a society divided between these landless and the 'rich landowners' (Hornsby 2013, 367). Lucy, and many other landless like her, was often excluded from, or precariously and minimally connected to, forms of assistance from kith and kin, church, NGOs and the government. It was precisely due to the fact that she was in this vulnerable position that Lucy was brought into the urban grant programme that I investigated.

Lucy's history is intended not to be representative but rather illustrative of certain dimensions and aspects of urban life experienced by many of the others I knew in Korogocho who, like her, had been identified as a recipient of one of the two grant programmes, the urban grant, operated by a humanitarian NGO, and the government's World Bank-funded child grant, that had come to Korogocho. Both, as I show in the chapter's concluding section emerged out of a charitable economy that has enveloped Kenya and Korogocho over recent decades.

Nairobi under British Rule

Korogocho is a product of processes of stratification and differentiation in Nairobi that began over half a century before the slum appeared in the 1960s. Nairobi was first established by the British only a little over hundred years ago, in 1899, on land acquired by the Kikuyu through land transactions from the indigenous hunter-gatherer Ogiek (Ndorobo) and the pastoralist Maasai. Beginning life as a small outpost known only as Mile 329, the halfway point where workers building the British railway that was to link the East African coast to Uganda stopped to set up camp, Nairobi would come to play a crucial political, economic and moral role for the country, as Britain set about consolidating its colonial power in the region.[2] Yet although the actual original site of the camp was sparsely populated, largely because it was built on unsuitable, swampy land, the wider region it had been established within was marked by historical political and economic relations, including trading ones, between its various groups, but particularly Kikuyu and Europeans. In fact, by the time Nairobi was established, the Imperial British East African Company, originally responsible for the construction of the railway, had already for some years been depending upon Kikuyu and other trading systems for its food supply.

By 1902, Nairobi had grown to a small town of 6,000 people and by 1907, had been designated the capital of Britain's East African Protectorate. While the city now had transport, electrical and water and sanitation infrastructure, as well as amenities including banks and clubs (Robertson 1997, 12), these were only available for the European workers and families, in the western, more elevated, part of the city. The lower, swampier, east, which would eventually become known as Eastlands within which the Korogocho ghetto is situated today, was designated for the African and Indian railway workers who were provided with none of the amenities available to the Europeans. In a principle of urban planning for Nairobi that would last officially until the 1940s, non-European male workers were required to live alone, without their families, in the east, close to the river and in poor-quality clay-and-iron housing.[3] While women and children, whose agricultural and trading work was integral to Nairobi's food supply, were permitted to travel to the city during the day, they were expected to remain overnight in their rural areas. In reality, female traders, selling foodstuffs, beer and sex, would join these male railway workers, as well as both African and Asian male traders, as residents in the growing city. For women, landlessness, divorce, widowhood, domestic abuse, and even unwanted marriage were leading to migration to the city that often became more or less permanent. For some Kikuyu women, trade and prostitution had become intertwined, something which would increasingly pose a threat to, and become the subject of attempts at control by both the British authorities and the Kikuyu Elders (White 1990; Robertson 1997, 86).

Importantly, it was the initial difficulties that the British colonial government faced in securing an African labour force for the railway that had led not only to the importation of indentured Indian workers but also the crucial realisation that the coercion of African workers into the wage economy would be required in order to consolidate colonial rule

(Ruchman 2017) and feed its burgeoning centre of control. Over time, a range of measures, including hut and consumer-goods taxes and identification cards, were introduced as a way of turning previous subsistence farmers into labourers on the now European-owned farms as well as traders in Nairobi.

As a result of these political and economic transformations, Nairobi grew quickly, and with stark differentiations along lines of class, race and gender, as well as to some extent ethnicity lines, through the beginning of the twentieth century, and particularly from the 1930s. Railway workers were joined by others in creating a more diverse and informal workforce. New migrants included the Kikuyu men and women from the colonial reserves who, as a result of political, economic and legal factors, were now feeding the city through the Big Men-centred trading networks (Robertson 1997, 80), but Kamba and Luo migrants also came, from further afield. In the face of the growing migration, the British authorities' policies of racial spatial segregation did not abate. Legislation ensured that it would be the eastern area of the city close to the river, which historian David Anderson has argued the British viewed as being comprised of 'havens of disease and criminality', where population growth would be centred (Anderson 2001, 142).

The four years preceding the 1952 declaration of the Emergency that sought to quell the Mau Mau resistance, had seen significant periods of hunger, as well as cycles of displacement and 'repatriation' to the Kikuyu reserves established by the British rulers (Anderson 2006). These combined to increase the numbers of people migrating to Nairobi, and produced more formal housing estates, such as Kariobangi and Dandora, that border present-day Korogocho (Anderson 2001, 207). It was these settlements that housed many of those who took the oath of the Mau Mau freedom fighters. By the time of the Emergency, the Mau Mau independence fighters and their supporters had become deeply embedded into Eastlands' material and social fabric. As a result, the colonial authorities made concerted efforts to control migration to Nairobi. The Kikuyu population dropped by 50 per cent as a result of the mandate by the colonial powers that forced Kikuyus to carry special permits, aas well as the infamous Operation Anvil, which resulted in the deportation of many back to the reserves. Many Kikuyu hawkers and shop owners had their licences revoked and were replaced by non-Kikuyus, including Luos, who established their own neighbourhoods (Parkin 1978). Yet the wisdom of such repressive measures is questionable given that it was precisely these controls around movement that had helped to foster Kikuyu resistance in the first place. Moreover, the restrictions would have adversely impacted the economy of a city dependent on Kikuyu trade. It was therefore almost inevitable that, by the late 1950s, the colonial authorities would be forced to ease them, allowing many of those traders and others to return to Nairobi.

A recognition, both before and during the Emergency, that more needed to be done to house the traders and other workers now residing in Nairobi, was matched by a series of Acts passed in Britain that sought to increase development and welfare investment in its colonies. The increase in Britain's investment in Kenya, which was first justified and bolstered by evidence from the economist Maynard Keynes that it would help to reduce unemployment in Britain by improving export trade, was thereafter deemed necessary to head off the growing resistance to colonial rule. The increased colonial investment, aided by money raised on the stock market in London, allowed for a new programme of urban planning for Nairobi, encapsulated in the *Master Plan for a Colonial Capital* (Thornton White et al. 1948). This plan included not only a range of new public spaces, administrative buildings, and industrial areas and transport infrastructure, but also new housing estates for African workers and their families. Yet, the official recognition of Nairobi as a place for families to reside merely reflected what had already been happening unofficially for decades.

Although the plan and investment was able to produce some new housing estates in Eastlands, the construction was insufficient to meet demands, partly as a result of financial mismanagement (Anderson 2001). But also because, foreshadowing a feature of a future aid regime in the latter half of the twentieth century, the British colonial investment in welfare and development that was approved was invariably many times higher than the funds actually issued. Housing in Nairobi had continued to be built between 1952 and 1960, but slowly and without any real impact on the growing population in the city. By 1957, housing to accommodate 30,000 people had been created, but this ran far short of what was required, and the funding invested paled into insignificance compared to what was being invested in the housing for the settlers and other wealthy foreigners to the west of Nairobi.

Eastlands after Independence

Independence in Kenya in 1963 put an end to the explicitly racial differentiation of resources and services in Kenya. But the newly inaugurated

President Kenyatta did not set off on a path that would result in more equitable economic or welfare policies for Nairobi's African population as a whole. With regard to welfare, his new government continued to direct resources to the already well-resourced settler areas of the city in the west, but which were now populated by a growing group of elite Africans as well as Indians. The settlements, particularly in the east of the city, multiplied and grew at an unprecedented rate when Kenyatta lifted the last of the colonial-era restrictions on movement, yet the government failed to seriously address the fundamentals of land use and the now more economically segregated residential dynamics. As under British rule, the plans that were drawn up and the resources assigned were woefully unambitious and insufficient. They offered little to the newly arriving migrants from the rural areas who saw in the city an opportunity to be included in the rising national economic growth of the period.

In a cruel and unjust irony, Korogocho, with its feebly and hastily built shacks, was established by the quarry workers who built the rest of Nairobi with hard stone. Those workers, in the 1960s, extracted the rock that ended up as the ashlar, cut-stone blocks, that today have been estimated to house around 40 per cent of residents in Nairobi (K'Akumu 2013). It is an even crueller irony that the quarry the original workers toiled in, adjacent to Korogocho, has now become the city's sprawling landfill. Today fires burn on Dandora dump, or what residents refer to as *boma*, sometimes set by the rubbish pickers themselves to create space for more rubbish; other times erupting spontaneously from the methane. When the dump grows large, the grey and acrid smoke it emits quickly reaches Korogocho, increasing lead levels in the blood and causing respiratory problems in its population (Kimani 2007). Running between the dump and Korogocho is the Nairobi River that passes through on its way, via the Athi and then Galana rivers, to the Indian Ocean. With Korogocho being in the east of Nairobi, this means it has already travelled through much of the rest of the city. The river is full of both domestic and industrial waste, and has been so for decades, with dangerously high mercury levels, as well as of other metals, including lead, copper, chromium, zinc and manganese (Mbui et al. 2016). Even when Kamau, my research assistant, was a little boy twenty years previously, and waded and swam in the river to collect discarded fruit from the market upstream, it was already badly polluted. And yet despite its pollution, during my fieldwork, I often found it a welcome respite from the heat and the congestion of Korogocho. Of course, as a newcomer and without any real experience of the river, my perspective was different from that of the residents. The riverbank, for many of them, was a dangerous place, where illegal alcohol was brewed and where gangs would gather at night to stay away from the police.

Although the immediate post-independence period of the 1960s meant the lifting of restrictions on countrywide movement, the new government continued and developed further restrictions in the city which would shape its population's mobility. Squatter settlements were banned in the Central Business District, in order to make room for other sorts of infrastructure, such as offices and transport hubs, mainly for short- and long-distance buses. This led to the forcible eviction of thousands of people from where they had established what were, even then, exceptionally precarious livelihoods. Many of those evicted were expected to relocate and somehow re-establish their lives and livelihoods in Kariobangi estate, but many ended up in Korogocho, where they joined the original quarry worker inhabitants.

It is likely that some of the first residents of Korogocho came as a result of the demolition of a squatter settlement originally on the grounds of what is now Machakos Bus Station, a demolition which was designed to clear the city centre before Independence Day (Hake 1977). Into the 1970s, Korogocho continued to grow unabated and unplanned. New ghetto neighbourhoods emerged, with Highridge (where I spent much of my time during my fieldwork) and Gitathuru forming in the early 1970s. In 1978, Grogan emerged and grew following the election the following year, when squatter settlements were again cleared in the city centre in a joint operation between the government and Nairobi City Council, this time on Grogan Road (now Kirinyaga Road), and when prospective MPs were busy allocating land in return for potential voter support (Loeckx and Githua 2010).

With the realisation among an array of actors that urban areas of a newly independent Kenya would continue growing rapidly, more attention was paid to how the burgeoning formal and informal workforce could be accommodated. Especially as it had become clearer that the benefits of the economic growth of the time were unevenly distributed. As early as the 1970s, the International Labour Organization was warning that Kenya's economic growth was marked significantly by both regional and class inequality (Branch 2011, 110). Around the same time, the World Bank, which had only recently turned its attention to 'developing' countries like Kenya, was able to persuade Kenyatta's government of the benefits of its 'sites-and-services' housing schemes, initiating them in the rapidly growing

Eastlands in Nairobi, in locales surrounding present-day Korogocho, including the aforementioned Kariobangi, Ruaraka, Dandora and some of the Kayole estate, where they were expected to house up to 300,000 by 1985 (Lee-Smith 1990). This scheme involved the division of particular responsibilities. The government's role was to provide secure tenure to residents and some very basic utilities and services. Those individuals allotted land were then expected to build their homes out of whatever local materials they had, including *matope* (mud), with the requirement to upgrade them with more durable materials within 10 years.

The World Bank's support for these schemes was underpinned by its belief that the governments of 'developing' countries could ill afford to subsidise conventional large-scale housing, as had been the case in 'developed' countries, and that self-help was a viable and cost-effective alternative. While its ideological emphasis on self-help in housing was to turn out to be a precursor to its subsequent focus on individual economic empowerment into the 1990s and beyond (Elyachar 2002), this approach was not simply externally imposed on Kenya. As early as 1963, newly inaugurated President Kenyatta had begun emphasising self-help through his idea of *harambee*, which I will elaborate upon later. But in this case, not only would it amount to the government essentially divesting themselves of any responsibility for the basic needs of the very people who were integral to the country's impressive economic growth, but it would also end in failure as, in practice, large profit-oriented housing corporations, such as Mutiso Menezes International, took over the process in the much larger scale development of housing. Moreover, the attempt to offer some form of secure land tenure in the 'sites-and-services' locations was also, in reality, motivated by a concomitant and violent denial of land tenure elsewhere in the city.

An attempted military coup d'état in Kenya in 1982 led to a period of confrontation in the 1980s and 1990s between citizens and the state in the struggle for multi-party democracy (Fox 1996). But the 1990s were also a period of local municipal struggles across the city. In Eastlands, including Korogocho, the predominantly Kikuyu earlier settlers were engaged in a battle for land.[4] A key element of the narratives of the struggles in Korogocho was the arrival of the Italian Catholic missionary Father Alex Zanotelli in the early 1990s.

Father Zanotelli was living in the centre of Korogocho, in what is now a well-fortified building which houses visiting foreign missionaries, and preaching at St John's church. He had been working with the Kenyan

Indian lawyer Murtaza Jaffer and a younger lawyer called Jane Weru, who together had established a legal aid office on Luthuli Avenue in Nairobi's city centre. Soon Weru joined the staff of *Kituo cha Sheria*, a legal aid organisation that had been established in the 1970s and which, as already noted, I had observed conducting legal aid and human rights education camps in the Chief's Camp. It was Father Zanotelli who invited *Kituo cha Sheria* to Korogocho. When Weru joined, the organisation was headed by Willy Mutunga, a name that later became famous across Kenya when he became the Chief Justice in 2011. Those still living and working around Korogocho continue to consider him as one of their own, and it was no surprise to them that he returned soon after taking up his position to speak to the congregation at St John's church. But before that, in the 1990s, this group of lawyers worked with the residents of Korogocho to resist the evictions that were taking place. In the early days, *Kituo cha Sheria* offered legal training to community members, the most important for many residents being workshops designed to help them resist the arbitrary power of the Chief. At that time in the 1990s the Chief had the power, in collaboration with various shack owners who claimed that the land belonged to them, to arbitrarily evict tenants, and even charge them fees if they attempted to improve their housing. Various workshops took place, which had to be moved further and further away from Korogocho, especially after the much-feared General Service Unit (GSU) was ordered into one meeting, apparently through the political connections of the owners. Participants at that meeting – which was being held at Mwiki Estate, about an hour's walk from Korogocho – were severely beaten by the GSU.[5]

The 2000s saw the building of an important legal case. Some of the original settlers, as well as others who had come to claim ownership of the land but did not necessarily live on it, formed the Korogocho Owners Welfare Association (KOWA). Key to their argument was a promise made by President Daniel arap Moi on 22 November 2000 when he had addressed a *baraza* (public meeting) in Korogocho, announcing that the residents should be given legal title deeds to the land, a statement they interpreted as directed at them, despite many of them no longer actually residing in Korogocho (Weru 2004), rather than aimed at the tenants living in their shacks. Here was where a new organisation, Pamoja Trust, began working with the actual tenants, who argued that the presidential directive referred to them. Key to Pamoja Trust's work was the process of enumeration, which involved collecting information about residents that could be deployed as part of the process of lobbying (see also Appadurai 2002). Unsurprisingly, this was a politically charged process in the ghettos, where there were many vested interests. In 2001, an enumeration process conducted by Pamoja Trust in Korogocho led to calls by KOWA to arm themselves to resist it, followed by a large protest by the association's members as the enumeration began. Only a heavy police presence allowed the process to continue (Shack/Slum Dwellers International 2001). As this was taking place, KOWA's case reached the High Court in *Paul Kimani (and others) v. Attorney General*. In court they cited the constitutional 'right to live', which under section 71 stated that every citizen had the 'right to live in dignity and protection of one's shelter and means of livelihood'. But KOWA lost the case and returned to Korogocho with assertions that they would sue Moi. Wilson, now the manager of a local government health clinic, laughed as he remembered that day: 'How can you sue the government? It's like suing your father!' he said.

Even though KOWA lost the case, they were in a strong position in Korogocho when an upgrading programme, which I briefly mentioned earlier, brought more changes, as well as hope. Joyce, an elected Women's Representative of Korogocho who first came to the area in 1977, once told me, with her politician's hat firmly on, that she hoped the upgrading would make Korogocho like Switzerland. 'Kocherland!' she added with a chuckle. While her tongue was as firmly in her cheek as her politician's hat was on her head, she sought to give the impression that the ghetto that she was helping to represent had a hopeful future.

The Korogocho Slum Upgrading Programme was a result of an agreement between the Italian and Kenyan governments to convert the Official Development Assistance bilateral debt owed by the latter to the former, into financial resources to fund development programmes. A total of €44 million was generated through this debt cancellation, with the greatest share of this going towards Korogocho's upgrading.

A Residents' Committee was set up at the instruction of organisations involved in the upgrading programme, in order to represent the needs not just of these original settlers and owners of the shacks, if not yet the land, but also the tenants. Each neighbourhood was asked to elect an Elder to sit on the committee. But for many, the elections had no sense of fairness. Intimidation techniques were deployed, and those elected would be the sons and daughters of the landlords, several of whom were part of the group that lost the case in 2008. Furthermore, to the chagrin of many in Korogocho, the Residents' Committee registered itself as a community-based organisation (CBO). Few residents were aware of this change and

Wilson, the manager of the aforementioned government health clinic in Korogocho, expressed surprise to me that a CBO would now have the power and mandate to oversee the upgrading. With claims that too many NGO projects were taking place in Korogocho in different ways and without any regulation, the Residents' Committee had ordered that all future projects must pass through them. A 'fee' of 10 per cent was the generally accepted amount required for a project to be allowed to operate in Korogocho.

The inclusion in the remit of the original settlers' activities of fighting for non-governmental resources is only one example of a wider history of what Jean-François Bayart has called 'strategies of extraversion' common on the African continent (Bayart 2000). That is, attempts by actors within Africa to capture external resources as part of their own political and economic processes. But it is also an example of how attempts were being made not to demolish, but to profit from Korogocho, which was increasingly being absorbed into the wider, charitable economy. I return to this economy in due course.

Mothers in the Ghetto

My description of Korogocho so far has been of the ghetto as it presents itself vociferously and largely publicly. But, interestingly, this description aligns closely with one aspect of the social scientific and journalistic literature, as well as NGO activities, that concerns urban Africa and the lives of its inhabitants. The lens of much of this literature often appears to be trained upon those who are highly visible and often disruptive, often but not exclusively young men: the street children who appear begging on the streets; the bus operators and the conductors who swing from shared taxis as they career around corners (Mutongi 2006); the young men who navigate the street, hustling, stealing and cheating (Mains 2007; Weiss 2009; Thieme 2013; Di Nunzio 2019); or those who protest in the street or in court for land and other rights. Through these studies we often become recipients of a picture that portrays young people in Africa ardently seeking to escape from existing forms of supervision and education, and breaking connections, including generational ones (Diouf 2003).

Particularly influential in this literature has been the work of sociologist AbdouMaliq Simone (2004a), who has argued that in inner-city Johannesburg, a place characterised by poor physical infrastructure and ruined environments, people themselves form temporary and piecemeal collaborations that remake the city and constitute a sort of infrastructure. Yet, what Simone also made explicit, but which has rarely been acknowledged by those inspired by his argument, is that his concept of 'people as infrastructure' did not capture the entirety of urban life for Johannesburg residents. 'Many residents,' he wrote, 'battered by the demands of maintaining the semblance of a safe domestic environment, find few incentives to exceed the bounds of personal survival' (Simone 2004a, 411). This description partly but not fully captures the lives of many of my interlocutors. The women I knew were not simply concerned with the survival of a personal sort, but, as I will seek to show in this book, the survival also both of others, and the relationships that connect them.

One reason, I think, for the emphasis on the roaming of people and goods, and the (re)making of new collaborations and networks in African cities, is that scholars have tended to view young people as childless youth rather than as young parents. Anthropologists, and others, have made significant contributions to understanding the experience of African 'youth',[6] examining the way they socialise and ruminate on the challenges of their lives (Weiss 2002, 2009; Masquelier 2013; Thieme 2013), exploring their pathways through the city (Simone 2004b, 2005; Comaroff and Comaroff 2006), and examining their varied practices of sexuality, leisure and work (Weiss 2002; Mains 2007; Cole and Thomas 2009; Smith 2010). Through these studies we come to learn about the lives of 'the youth', who themselves are struggling to establish a foothold in proper adulthood. Therefore, while we have gained important insights about how youth have experienced the conditions brought about often by neoliberal political economies, it is striking that there is much less discussion about their transitions to parenthood. This attention to the inability of youth to enter into adulthood makes it even more surprising that we do not, as often as we should, hear from the parents who must continue to look after, and out for, these older children of theirs.

Lucy

Humanitarian assistance in countries such as Kenya, as well as social assistance based on a decidedly humanitarian ethos, responds to what is often regarded as an a-historicised and universal suffering. While such endeavours are in themselves, of course, deeply historical and political, their predominant gestures of quantification and generalisation, which undergird the constitution of their objects of intervention, routinely seek to evade such history and politics. As a corrective to this picture, and to show what the grant programmes had to navigate, I introduce Lucy, a cash grant recipient, and explore her life in more detail.

When I met Lucy, in 2011, she was a young, single mother of three children. She was born in the 1980s in Nyanza, the western part of Kenya, two decades after Kenya won its independence, in the midst of the period of structural adjustment and austerity that I wrote about earlier. In the 1990s, Lucy was still living with her parents in Ahero, a town just a few kilometres from Kisumu, the capital of Luoland in Kenya, and around 300 kilometres to the west of Nairobi.[7] Lucy's parents earned a small income as transporters of rice, moving the cash crop from the nearby Kano Plain, a large lowland area near the Winam Gulf part of Lake Victoria, where it was cultivated, to the processing factory in Ahero. This was one of a number of ambitious state-run agriculture schemes, including most notably sugar, instigated by President Kenyatta in the mid-1960s after independence. These schemes and their factories soon became the region's largest employer, as tens of thousands of small-scale farmers produced cash-crops for them, and thousands more worked to trade and transport their fruits (Hornsby 2013, 303).

In 1998, the rice factory that Lucy's parents depended upon for their livelihood closed. Lucy still holds the president at the time, Daniel arap Moi, responsible for its closure. Antagonism between the Luo and the Kalenjin, to whom Moi belonged, runs deep, aggravated by the attempted coup d'état in 1982 for which a number of prominent Luo were held responsible. But the closure of the factory was not simply a tit-for-tat, but part of a larger process of privatisation and liberalisation – an aspect of the infamous structural adjustment policies imposed by the International Monetary Fund – that Moi presided over.

The closure of the scheme meant that Lucy's parents lost their main source of income and were no longer able to pay Lucy's school fees. She was in Form 3 at the time, the penultimate year of secondary school. Here her dreams of finishing this level of education ended. Without schooling she was forced to do what she, and my other interlocutors, referred to as *kukaa nyumbani tu* – just staying at home. However, feeling restless and considering herself, as she once told me, a 'learned person' who could achieve much more, she began searching for new opportunities. Where she was living, and at that point in time, she had little hope for formal employment – even her parents were never formally employed by the now-closed factory – and she had no access to fertile or sufficiently cultivatable land. As a result, Lucy looked to the urban informal economy, an economy that had grown significantly since 1972 when the International Labour Office released its report focusing on Kenya (ILO 1972).

Lucy's stepsister, Angela, thought the best opportunities available to her in this economy could be found in the town of Rongo, located near Homa Bay, around 100 kilometres south-east of Ahero. Angela helped take Lucy there and, upon arriving, Lucy sent word back to her parents requesting a sewing machine with a view to establishing a small business repairing and making clothes that, she reasoned, would offer her the chance to live independently. From the very first time I had met her, Lucy had been keen to stress her business acumen, and this would have been the first step in developing it. But her parents had other ideas. They denied her request, expecting her instead to secure work as a maid in the town. It was at this point that Lucy started to hang out with 'bad girls'. Soon after, in 2000, when she was 19, she met a young man.

Lucy and the man married, and Lucy quickly fell pregnant and gave birth to her daughter, Edda. But it soon transpired that their marriage had gone against Luo patrilineal norms, which require the first-born man of a family to marry before the second-born. Lucy and her new husband were forced to divorce, but any expectations of marrying the first-born son were quickly quashed. The older brother refused, arguing he did not, at that point, have enough income to begin a married life. 'So my life was useless,' Lucy told me, 'like I was an old person.'

One theme of the literature on youth in Africa has concentrated on how those struggling to gain a sufficient income and to marry have interpreted their experience as being suspended in the liminal category of 'youth'. Adeline Masquelier, borrowing from the Middle East Youth Initiative, has referred to this as 'waithood' (Masquelier 2013). Perhaps this was the experience of the older son who was unable and unwilling to marry Lucy, although as Marco Di Nunzio has shown, some people in Africa cannot wait and rely upon others, such as parents, but must exercise their capacity for movement, as well as smartness (Di Nunzio 2019, 19). But as Lucy indicated, on her side the challenge was not being trapped within a single category but instead her too rapid ascent through a series of pre-mapped categories of a life course. In the space of only a few years she had moved from being a young girl in secondary school to a divorcee with a young child and little income.

Lucy stayed for a little while in Rongo. Despite her divorce, her husband's mother, whom Lucy still treated as her mother-in-law, helped to look after Edda, nursing her through the daytime. Lucy was still hustling for money but the economy in Rongo was not as strong as her stepsister had imagined. Thankfully the land was fertile, so fruit and vegetables at the time were plentiful and cheap. But Lucy, again refusing to accept her lot and wanting more from her life, decided to return to Ahero, the small town in which she was brought up, where, at the time, she believed 'there is business and therefore money, but fewer crops'. It was while back in Ahero that she met her second husband, who seemed suitable – or rather was, as she put it to me more straightforwardly, 'very clean and very healthy'. Not only was he interested in marrying her, he also apparently had the capacity to establish their new married life not in Ahero but in Nairobi. Lucy was ecstatic at the prospect of life in the country's capital city. There she would join the hundreds of thousands of other Kenyans escaping small town and village life and harbouring ambitions of becoming *watu wa kisasa* – modern people (Mutongi 2017, 32; see also Ferguson 1999). As a Luo, Lucy would be coming to what was historically a Kikuyu-dominated city, but which, since the Emergency and the restrictions it had put on this ethnic group, had seen successive waves of movement from other parts of the country.

Most of my interlocutors' stories of arrival in Nairobi – more specifically, Korogocho – were filled with recollections of their desire for a better life and an escape from a violent one. Some had recently arrived from another city or village in the country and, in need of somewhere cheap to rent and close to where they might find some work, found Korogocho suitable. Others who were older had had the same idea, arriving years or even decades earlier. It was commonly the older male sibling who was sent ahead to the big city, with requests by his parents to make enough money to support his brothers, sisters and the parents themselves. But girls and young women too, often of school-age, found themselves being sent to Nairobi, often with the promise from kin already settled in the city that they would be provided with education in exchange for their work as a house girl, or *mboch* as they are commonly referred to in Nairobi's Sheng street language. Yet while the girls and young women often kept their side of the bargain, it was rarely reciprocated. They ended up ensnared in domestic work with the promised educational opportunities never materialising.

Worse was to come for Lucy. Her excitement at the possibility of establishing life in Nairobi turned to anguish when she arrived and discovered her husband was, in fact, already married. If this discovery was itself not traumatic enough, the manner in which she made it was brutal: she turned up with her husband at his Nairobi house in the Eastlands' estate of Kariodudu, only to find his first wife already there. Lucy learned from the neighbours that her new husband already had two children with this wife. But the events that transpired would be even worse for his first wife than for Lucy. She was ruthlessly cast out of the house by Lucy's new husband. Lucy was distraught about the whole situation. 'I cried, I wanted to go back home,' she recounted, 'I remember thinking to myself, this is my second husband and he's already got a wife.'

After some time spent adjusting to her troublesome new situation, Lucy fell pregnant again. She travelled back with her husband by bus to Nyanza, in the west of Kenya, to carry her baby to term. When she was with her husband up-country, she began running a little business while also being a member of a *chama*, a merry-go-round savings scheme popular in Kenya. Through her business she was able to buy a few basic things, like cups, to begin making a home. But when her husband saw these, Lucy began to see discomforting changes. Before long he had started drinking and physically abusing her. 'When a man is in alcohol, it is not hard for them to kill you,' she told me once. But it was her unborn son whose life was most endangered. Lucy was only three months pregnant when her husband first lashed out physically, punching her in her stomach. Lucy was later able to flee to her natal home for the remainder of her pregnancy, and then, with her own mother's help, delivered a thankfully healthy boy, whom she named Charles.

Lucy was unwilling to leave her new husband, despite his alcohol problems, and so she departed her natal home and returned to him. Without a husband, social legitimacy would be out of reach for her within the patriarchal norms not only of the Luo, but also of many of the different ethnic groups that she would encounter as a fellow migrant in the towns and cities across Kenya. 'You can't be accepted anywhere with two children but no husband,' she had told me wearily once, when I had been sitting with her in her rented *matope* (mud) shack in Korogocho. Staying together, the young family then returned to Nairobi. Before long, Lucy was pregnant with her third child, went up-country again to give birth to a boy, Bolton, this time without her husband, and returned to Nairobi.

Back in Nairobi, Lucy began experiencing frequent bouts of sickness that began with a fever and diarrhoea. Shortly after, her newborn son Bolton fell ill. With nothing that could resemble a well-functioning public healthcare system available to her in Eastlands, Lucy resorted to private clinics to buy drugs. Soon she found herself afflicted by fits of coughing. Her mind immediately turned to the possibility she had contracted tuberculosis, and she knew what that meant. 'I didn't want to know if it was HIV or if I was alive,' she recollected, vividly associating the disease with death. Even though antiretroviral drugs for the disease had by then become widely available and free to Kenyans, it would take much longer for the association between HIV and an imminent death to dissolve in most people's minds. People like Lucy had seen countless friends and family die from the disease.

Lucy did, however, get tested, and was found to be HIV positive. Yet her husband refused to believe it and declined to be tested himself. This was in spite of the fact that at that point around 7 per cent of Kenya's population had contracted the disease. But, in Lucy's terms, 'he was healthy, I was down'; she was bedridden and looking after her children on her own. It was not long after that he abandoned her, moved back up-country and, she learned later, married for the third time. Lucy was again a single mother, this time of three children – or, as the government and NGOs would designate her, a 'female-headed household', meaning a household that does not have a male-wage earner.

During my fieldwork, it was estimated that over a quarter of the total households in Korogocho in 2010 were female-headed. In this book, however, I do not use this technical term favoured by policy makers and practitioners, including those involved in the grants. Perhaps most obviously, the term is problematic for its subscription to patriarchal, not to mention heteronormative, ideals. But the term is also awkward for two further reasons. First, because it fails to capture what is meant by a household across cultures. In the sociocultural ideology of the Luo, for instance, the man stands as the head of a household, represented spatially in Luoland in the homestead, but it is the wife or wives who are heads of their own houses, which are the minimal units that include a woman and her children (Okeyo Pala 1980). The second issue with the concept of a female-headed household is the assumption concerning its inherent vulnerability. As Margrethe Silberschmidt (1992) observed decades ago, the official status of a household headed by a female ignores that in East Africa there are many households with men where women remain even more overburdened than if they had been alone. As one of Silberschmidt's informants told her, a man was more like an 'extra baby'. In Kenya, while the ideal of a male breadwinner and female dependent has maintained itself since the colonial period, by the 1990s particularly, this ideal was under increasing pressure, largely as a result of economic stagnation. Indeed, such was the extent to which men were struggling to fulfil their new role – not only in the urban environment but also in their rural homelands – that it was even questioned among people in the population whether it was now men, rather than women, who had become the 'weaker sex' (Silberschmidt 1992). To get by, then, both men and women in Korogocho have for decades participated in the informal economy.

Rather than use the concept of female-headed households, I believe it is more helpful to think about these households as exhibiting matrifocality, owing to the fact that men are often marginal to, rather than simply absent from, them (Geller and Stockett 2006, 75). Matrifocality can be understood as a dimension that exists across many different types of kinship systems, where the mother is particularly central in the social structure and the culture, and where people have strong affective connections to her (Tanner 1974, 131). In Korogocho, women as mothers considered themselves and their children as the most enduring, and central, unit, even if kinship did not become unimportant.

In Lucy's case, this matrifocal, relational unit was in danger of falling apart. In order to eat, her children became what Kenyans refer to as *wachokora*. Studying in a Luo neighbourhood in Nairobi in the 1970s, the anthropologist David Parkin (1978) met groups of children referring to themselves as *wakora* (a variation on the word *chokora*), which he translated as 'rogue'. This idea of a rogue child has travelled more widely, and now is used across the city to refer to the, mostly male, children who congregate with others in gangs and together sleep at night on the streets. The English translation of *chokora* as 'rogue' adequately captures this particularly tragic phenomenon, pointing as it does to behaviours exceeding the bounds of normality. For many people, the behaviour of *chokora* emerges from their lack of attachment to wider society, but also to their lack of any proper relationships of socialisation, care and discipline of the family, and particularly with the mother.

One day, Lucy borrowed her neighbour's mobile phone to call her mother. She told her mother she was dying and begged for her and her father to come to Nairobi to collect their grandchildren. The parents sent their other daughter's husband to Nairobi to pick them all up. It was now 2007. When she had been in Nairobi, Lucy had been unable to buy enough food to allow her to begin the course of the drugs she had been given to treat the tuberculosis she had contracted (see also Prince 2012). But back up-country, her parents were able to feed her properly, allowing her to take the drugs for six months before she could begin the next course of the antibiotic Septrin (*cotrimoxazole*). With her viral load by then dangerously high, Lucy had to take these antibiotics to prevent any opportunistic infections.

By 2008, three years before I first met her, Lucy had begun taking antiretroviral drugs, which reduced her viral load. She was now feeling a lot stronger. At that point, her mother had persuaded her to go and find her second husband, whom she believed she had contracted HIV from. Lucy arrived in Nairobi and set out on what would be a fruitless and time-consuming endeavour. She stayed with a friend for a while before being chased away, at one point finding herself sleeping in an outside *choo* (toilet). She sought out other friends who might offer her a place to stay, but with her HIV-positive status it was difficult. 'If you'd stayed there for a few days, they would give you a bit of food but then tell you to leave so that the house could "freshen",' she told me. A pastor at a church gave her KSh400 (£2.72) and recommended Korogocho as a good place to find refuge. This period was bleak for Lucy, or, as she called it, 'black'. She was sick, depressed, without a husband and skipping between short stays at friends' homes. Even when she eventually found a place with a barely affordable rent to move into, her problems did not end. When the landlord learned of her HIV-positive status, he threw her out, claiming that if Lucy died in the house, he would find it hard to secure tenants in the future.

During this time, Lucy was not able to rely much on her kinfolk. She joined others in Korogocho who had found themselves excluded from kinship networks and their redistributive mechanisms. One male widower I knew, struggling to put his three children through school, once complained to me that the days of kin selling cattle to assist with school fees was now past. For both men and women in Korogocho, the rights and obligations around assistance associated with their own ethnic and kinship groups no longer seemed to be as firm or generous as they had imagined them to be in the past, even if other sorts of norms, as we saw with Lucy's first marriage, often remained rigid. To be excluded from kin-based forms of solidarity was not, then, a situation exclusive to women – but it was certainly worse for them.

In fact, the reason why many men and women migrated, often from rural but also from other urban areas, was because kin relationships were under such strain. Lucy was a young woman, but others in Korogocho had moved at much younger ages, partly owing to the lack of opportunities in their rural areas. As I have mentioned, some had received promises from urban-based kin of receiving education, only to find themselves in what might be described as domestic servitude. Others, like Lucy, migrated later, when called on by their husbands to join them. Some women I knew had lost their husbands through AIDS. Several of them vowed never to get married again, and I often heard those who had become Born Again claim that they were now married to God. But others responded to a need and desire to forge new relationships with men for companionship, survival and security, and social legitimacy.

After the deaths of their husbands, many widows also found that they no longer had the support of kin either in their late husband's or their own natal family. Nor, crucially, did they have access to land. While I knew people from several different ethnic groups, a number of the women belonged, like Lucy, to the patrilineal Luo, who practise exogamous marriage and virilocal residency. Because of the stigma associated with HIV/AIDS, Luo widows had been forced from their marital homes and found they were also no longer welcome in their natal homes. Nor were the women considered eligible for levirate marriage, *tero* – that is, where a woman is eligible to marry her late husband's brother – leading to a general decline of this custom among the Luo (Geissler and Prince 2010, 263).

Korogocho therefore became a place of refuge for those people, and for those who might have been affected by domestic, political and other forms of violence back home. Some women had plans to purchase their own plot of land up-country in readiness for their retirement, and to re-establish themselves in the cultural and social life there. Yet most of these plans remained just that. Their lack of land meant that they would struggle not only to carry out either subsistence or market-based agriculture, but also to fulfil other associated rites of passage. For example, among the Luo, but also other ethnic groups, without land one cannot build a house, and without a house one cannot establish oneself fully as an adult woman.

In Korogocho, the Chief was able to give Lucy another KSh400 (£2.72) and a small amount of maize to get by. But Lucy was uneasy about relying upon handouts. 'I want my children to eat', she once told me, 'but I don't want that support.' Handouts for food and other basic commodities in Kenya had become something associated with the poorest and most needy, particularly during the 1990s and into the 2000s. Before then, in the decades after the country gained independence, Kenya's predominant mode of ensuring its citizens were fed was through the implementation of state price controls. Beginning in the early 1970s, the government introduced these controls for basic commodities, including the staple maize. The controls for the prices paid by consumers grappled with classic tension between the interests of farmers and the interest of workers, including in the newly and increasingly recognised informal economy. The government's position, supporting the urban worker, held out; the Maize and Produce Board was established, becoming the sole buyer of maize. But price controls were introduced not only for the consumer but also for the producer. The result over time would be ongoing political negotiation between the interests of the consumer and those of the producer, with the Treasury sometimes taking up the shortfall when the competing interests could not be reconciled. After a brief resistance in the early 1980s to the International Monetary Fund's demands to put an end to the state's control over agriculture and food supply, the government was forced to accept defeat and began to liberalise the sector. Although there was never total acquiescence to these demands (Hornsby 2013, 434), and although it did not happen immediately, the liberalisation of agriculture was far reaching. By 1994, all price controls had been eliminated.

With no price controls over food, or other important expenses such as rent or water, Lucy and her fellow urban slum dwellers in Nairobi were increasingly battered by the forces of the free market. They laboured across the city barely able to, or often not even able to, cover their daily expenses. Men worked in the growing construction industry, in *jua kali*, in the factories in the Industrial Zone, and in the markets trading and transporting goods. Others turned to petty or more organised crime. Young men also looked around the ghetto itself, for casual work, and listened out for opportunities for something more substantial. Key to their livelihoods is a certain openness to being mobile, willing to go up-country or at least around the city (Simone 2004a). Young men in particular must be flexible in work, ready, at only a moment's notice, to be picked up by trucks and taken for work, even if this is outside Nairobi, where they might stay for weeks.

There were two common ways for women in Korogocho to earn income. First, continuing a livelihood tradition that stretches back to the establishment of Nairobi in the early twentieth century that I have already detailed, many women hawked vegetables or other foodstuffs. Second, in a more recent development – after the 1980s at least – women had begun to turn to domestic work, either within Korogocho for 'wealthier' homes, or, more commonly, outside the ghetto in neighbouring housing estates (Robertson 1997, 155). In Korogocho today, many women wash clothes for those people referred to in street language as the *warya* – the eastern-Cushitic population – in Korogocho, or in Eastleigh, a Somali-dominated estate a few miles away. Because providing domestic services for another family is considered shameful, some married women learned to keep it secret from their husbands. Mothers also struggled to balance childcare with securing an income. Children could usually be incorporated into hawking, but often not into domestic work, forcing some mothers to leave them home alone or to pay for childcare.

Women sometimes juggled both forms of livelihood, especially because the income from each was extremely precarious. The difficulties in hawking and generating income were already being exposed in the 1960s (Robertson 1997, 150), and things had not become any easier. While a newly forming elite class of Kenyans was still enjoying the benefits of economic growth, often through the state bureaucratic structure, these benefits did not reach the migrants of either gender in Nairobi's ghettos. A post-independence plan to establish an export processing zone in Nairobi that would have constituted a major source of employment for women was never realised, and few women were able to find factory work. Moreover, many of the women were landless, and thereby had little incentive to return to their rural areas for the harvest period, which would otherwise have been able to provide them with at least some food for part of the year.

When I first met Lucy, she was running her own small roadside food stall – in reality simply a stool to sit on and a piece of wood to display the food – on the side of the main road that ran through Korogocho. Like many others in Korogocho, while she had little actual contact with Kenya's middle or upper classes, her own livelihood relied upon the by-products of their lifestyle. Most significant was that which came from the city's growing fast-food sector.

Korogocho's entrepreneurial traders had learned to tap into the flows of waste that came from the factories supplying the fast-food outlets. Bringing it back to Korogocho, the traders would sell it on the side of the road to the hungry workers who trudged back from the Industrial Area each day, or to the children coming home from school. One of the most prominent waste foods during my fieldwork was *anyona*, the cut-offs and scraps of bread from Nairobi's bakeries. *Anyona* is a Dhuluo (language of the Luos) word meaning 'stepped on', which describes its crumbled condition. Originally the bakery would sell the waste offcuts of bread, which had been rejected for human consumption, to pig farms. But local rumour has it that one female resident of Korogocho started to buy up the bread to sell it to residents, and since then numerous *anyona* sellers have appeared in the ghetto. Another less widespread but popular food source was the airline industry. With Korogocho being situated near both the dumping site and the country's main airport, Jomo Kenyatta International, some traders had managed to intercept the leftover in-flight meals of transnational airlines before they were thrown away.

Lucy sold chicken offal (the heads and feet) that would otherwise be thrown away by the factories that fed the ubiquitous fried chicken shops across the city frequented by the lower-middle and middle classes. During the day she would collect and prepare the heads and the feet, and as the night fell, she would move to the roadside, which lay a hundred metres or so from her shack, to fry and sell the food to the workers. Her returns averaged KSh250 (£1.70) per day. This meant she and her three children were each living on £0.43 day – over two and half times below the World Bank's extreme poverty line at the time.

As I hope I have conveyed thus far, Lucy was exceptionally hard-working and was unenthusiastic about relying on others' support. Nevertheless, her circumstances forced her, reluctantly, to accept her inclusion on the urban grant programme. She had no desire to identify as a recipient of charitable aid, but it was the only way in which her poverty and suffering could be temporarily and only minimally mollified through what was growing into an increasingly significant, but never sufficient, charitable economy. It is to this charitable economy that I now turn, in order to situate the cash grants that arrived in Korogocho.

The Emergence of a Charitable Economy

There had been efforts, ongoing since as early as the 1900s, to transform Kenyans into particular kinds of gendered, modern subjects through programmes of welfare and development (Seeley 1987). During the colonial period, the authorities aspired to create a particular sort of gender equality along with a template of a stable, modern, urban family life. Yet this model of family life nevertheless maintained the ideal of a male breadwinner and a female dependent (Francis 2002). This 'modern' idea of the household was taking hold amidst urban migration, changing ideologies brought by Christian missionaries, as well as demographic changes. A woman's responsibility to feed the household through her own control of land was being reduced, but with this came a greater capacity to make claims on male incomes, which began to rise as wages increased in the cities of Kenya in the 1950s (Francis 2002).

Efforts around welfare and transformation intensified after the Second World War, which was, according to Joanna Lewis, 'the midwife to a moral rearmament' for an imperialism that began increasingly to emphasise the importance of state 'welfare' in its colonies (Lewis 2000, 17). After the war, with the Labour Party in power in Whitehall, the British colonial government led the way, its efforts extending to Kenya – although as I have already mentioned, its promises of financial resources were never matched by what was actually delivered.

By the 1950s, Britain's welfare efforts in Kenya, together now with the US, began a process in which they sought to construct an African class-based, gendered economic system in the country. Certain men in Kenya, for example, were singled out and offered business loans and financial training, as well as instruction on a range of topics including agriculture, community development, citizenship. Women, despite their already significant role in trading networks that crossed the country, were offered courses on needlework, cookery, laundry and child welfare. As Robertson writes: 'If a few African men were to be taught trading skills in order to raise their status to that of petty bourgeois, then it was considered suitable that they marry Western-style housewives' (Robertson 1997, 127). Of course, gendered and class civility were not simply foreign impositions but also concerns of the African population in Kenya during this period. Many male and elder Kikuyu expressed, for example, their worries that female traders coming into Nairobi had become 'immoral' as a result of their ability to evade the sorts of structures of authority and surveillance present in their rural areas.

Despite increasing welfare spending in Kenya, the colonial authorities had little appetite to create anything that might resemble the sort of welfare state that was being built in Britain under Nye Bevan in the post-Second World War period (Thomas 2003, 141). The reasoning behind this reluctance was drawn not only from an economic rationale, but from the colonial authority's perception that Kenya's own social and cultural make-up made the country an unsuitable object for state, bureaucratic forms of welfare. This thinking was first conveyed when the British government's Colonial Office issued a circular just before the end of the war. This notice justified their decision not to pursue a project of state welfare building in the colonies on the differences between 'traditional agricultural societies with their own basis of social security provision' and 'more sophisticated and industrialized societies' like Britain, in which national systems of income redistribution and social security measures have 'developed gradually' (cited in Thomas 2003, 142). To some extent, there were existing forms of social security – and not only in the rural areas. In the cities, for instance, 'tribal associations' had formed which often aspired to protect the welfare of their members (Seeley 1987, 544).[8] But it would be difficult to argue that these were part of a 'traditional' agricultural society or that they were sufficient to protect the many landless people now coming to the cities.

The hard and tragic fight for independence in Kenya led to expectations among the populace for free education, healthcare and social services (Hornsby 2013, 128). Kenyan citizens, however, were to be disappointed. First President Kenyatta prioritised economic over social development, the latter seen as naturally following a predefined teleological path of progress. The new government reneged on its earlier promises, arguing that fulfilling them would bankrupt the state (Hornsby 2013, 138). But this should not have been a surprise. As early as the 1920s, Kenyatta was proclaiming the importance of production, especially larger scale farming and foreign exports, rather than social redistribution as essential to the development of the country. Then, in the 1965 governmental sessional paper *African Socialism and its Application to Planning in Kenya*, this priority was made even clearer, maintaining that issues such as unemployment and welfare services 'must be handled in ways that will not jeopardise growth' (cited in Seeley 1987, 553).

Kenyatta emphasised that the state would not be able to provide welfare and other forms of assistance on its own and that the voluntary organisations, such as missions and charities, that had played a prominent role in welfare for the African population during the colonial period would continue to be required. Despite a greater recognition of the need for more comprehensive state welfare in Kenya, the government's approach forked into two broad routes. One route was for the wage-labourers in the formal economy who, from 1965, received state-provided social security, through the National Social Security Fund, a compulsory saving scheme. The other was for everyone else, in which welfare would metamorphose into 'community development'. This took the form of the aforementioned *harambee*, a concept that was unique to Kenya. On 1 June 1963, Madaraka Day (Self-Governance Day), Jomo Kenyatta, in a public address broadcast on the radio, argued that the national slogan should no longer be *uhuru*, meaning freedom, but *harambee*, meaning 'let's pull together'.[9] This, he proposed, would constitute a system of welfare and development in which communities of citizens would play a central role in the building of schools, health clinics and other physical infrastructures. Villagers would raise money, solicit in-kind donations and provide voluntary labour. Even though it resonated with existing ideas of community self-help, such as communal labour and work parties, as well as colonial ideas of community development, *harambee* was a new word for Kenyans and, more importantly, a new experience of government (Mbithi and Rasmusson 1977, 147–8). Into the 1970s, as a result of various economic and political constraints, the government remained wary of taking responsibility for issues of health, education or housing – and therefore continued to stress the importance of *harambee* (Seeley 1987, 557–8).

During this period, there also continued to be a growing attention among members of the international aid and development community, to the 'basic needs' and the 'poorest' in the global South. In Kenya, this attention also began to be matched by an increasing number of foreign aid donor-funded programmes and projects. These often worked through NGOs and non-state actors including UNICEF, CARE and Oxfam, in partnership with the Kenyan government's Community Development Office. Many of these continued the focus on 'self-help', by helping develop and work through different sorts of groups, for example, women's groups. As Seeley writes: 'governmental social services in Kenya continue, then, to rely very heavily upon the voluntary efforts of individuals and groups' (Seeley 1987, 559).

The role of central government remained minimal, its responsibilities generally confined to training and some specialised social services. Local government was responsible for the provision of social services in its urban centres, including the delivery of primary education, healthcare, road maintenance and water supplies. But not only did this leave out rural dwellers in principle, but in practice did not necessarily result in anything comprehensive, even in the urban locale. City councils were not provided with enough governmental resources and, even as early as the 1960s, some were looking to foreign donors, such as USAID, to fund their public social services plans. Churches and mosques, along with politicians and businessmen, also continued to provide some social services to their members and others in the community. The infamous and devastating policies of structural adjustment, when they were forced upon Kenya in the 1980s, imposed further cuts on government spending and introduced cost-efficiency measures, such as requiring patients in the public healthcare system to pay some fees.

The ending of the food price controls in the late 1990s had meant that people like Lucy now turned, where they could, to the support that was being offered in the way of food aid, whether from the government or from foreign institutions. The 1990s had seen in Kenya the beginning of a series of droughts and incidents of political violence which would combine to produce episodes of mass hunger and starvation, to which international organisations responded. In 2000, 4 million Kenyans were relying upon US-donated food aid, delivered through the World Food Programme, and in 2004–6, the government and donors spent US$230 million in Kenya on food aid (Hornsby 2013, 736). The post-election period in 2008 brought even more violence to the country, including Korogocho, and another increase in food aid. Also, in the late 1990s and into the 2000s, large amounts of aid money flowed into Kenya in an attempt to tackle the HIV/AIDS crisis, for instance from the US's PEPFAR programme (President's Emergency Plan for AIDS Relief). Much of this went on the supply of antiretrovirals for HIV but, with the realisation that the drugs could not be taken by people when they were hungry, modest amounts of money went into food aid and poverty alleviation programmes (Prince 2012).

It would be a mistake to assume that structural adjustment dismantled any sort of substantial welfare state already in existence in Kenya. However, the end of the Moi era was, for many of my interlocutors, associated with if not a sea change, then at least an increase in what flowed into their communities in the way of service delivery and assistance. Ann, a Korogocho resident in her forties, put it like this:

You know, under Kenyatta and Moi, there was nothing, no help, but now with Kibaki there is lots of help, CDF [Community Development Fund], LATF [Local Authority Transfer Fund], all of these things. NGOs are here too now, but they mostly come with packets of *unga* [flour] for a bit and then they disappear.

Ann succinctly summarised the views of many Kenyans who had a long experience of outsiders, often from abroad, seeking to assist their communities. These efforts have never translated into anything that could be described as a universal, as in national, system of welfare. Rather, they have remained piecemeal and fragmented, shaped by a diverse and often competing array of values, norms and often shifting strategic priorities. For

Ann, foreign aid and NGOs seemed to be helping to support the lives of some, but certainly not all, people. But their presence, often made visible through promotional materials, with logos emblazoned onto signs and leaflets as well as t-shirts often given away, was not necessarily matched by what they provided. Moreover, they had the tendency to 'disappear' after a while, as Ann stated. Many Kenyans, and not only in Korogocho, had experiences of NGO projects that came and went, as donor funding priorities shifted rapidly. In contrast, while government schemes like the Community Development Fund and the Local Authority Transfer Fund were often difficult to access, and were linked deeply with patronage, they remained a more long-term and stable feature across the country. But differentiating between government and non-governmental assistance was not always so clear-cut. As we will see in the next two chapters, both the government and NGOs had worked, sometimes together and sometimes in competition, to produce through their varied programmes of care and assistance, a charitable economy within Korogocho; an economy that was surrounded and maintained by a collection of what I call ghetto-level bureaucrats.

It is from this economy that the grants that reached Korogocho, and people like Lucy and Beatrice, who I mentioned in the introduction, emerged. Together, the government and NGOs, along with major aid donors, such as the World Bank, worked to create a national system of social assistance that would concentrate not on the self-help of the independence-era *harambee* movement but more on help for different individual selves.

Conclusion

Lucy's life, and those of others like her in Korogocho, was shaped by a long process of differentiation and stratification along lines of class, gender, race, and ethnicity. This process has forced these people to navigate the margins of both Nairobi's informal economy and networks of care and solidarity that stretch beyond the city, incorporating kith and kin, and state and non-state institutions. Such navigation does not translate into a highly mobile and expansive form of city-wide economic collaboration (Simone 2004a), but nor does it equate to a form of waiting (Mains 2007). Instead, navigating life on the absolute margins for women in Korogocho, situated at the lowest rung of Nairobi society, is more concerned with attempting to maintain some form of safety and security for the domestic environment. This is a life already full of risk, in which further risk-taking must be carefully considered. Moreover, it requires regularly responding to both the emergencies and the opportunities that appear in the exigencies of everyday life, often only for the briefest of moments, to sustain the life of oneself and one's children. But this can never be reduced to sheer survival, as if such attempts to survive are somehow divorced from social norms, moral values, dreams and aspirations that women in Korogocho in fact held onto in often desperate circumstances.

It is these lives on the margins of Nairobi society that the cash grants had to contend with. But the grants did not grapple with them in the same way as traditional forms of assistance, still present in Korogocho, that sought to cajole and prod people in their attempts to create particular sorts of healthy, educated and economic subjects. Instead, as I will show in later chapters, the grants, while providing minimal assistance, created circum-scribed spaces of freedom for recipients. In these spaces, recipients were able to utilise the financial resources afforded to them, inserting them into their lives navigated on the margins of redistribution and exchange in the city. However, in order to create these circumscribed spaces of freedom, the recipients first had to be identified.

The next chapter turns to the identification of those who would come to be enrolled onto the urban grant. It shows how this process, while premised on a recognition of the importance of the social body, had to nonetheless cut through this body to find the poorest and most vulner-able. I chart how this contested process revealed the importance of a range of social relationships not fully appreciated by the designers of the grant programme.

2

Scoring the Poor

Money has been an integral part of Korogocho life since the slum emerged in the first half of the twentieth century. Money has circulated in the market economy, and has flowed, hopped between, and suffered blockages within kinship and other forms of networks of support. It has also left the slum when its residents are forced to 'purchase' services, many of them from the state itself: education and health, police reports and mortuary certificates. Money's incursion into Korogocho has largely been through the ingenuity of its inhabitants as they hustle in the informal economy. But it has also been injected through the apparatus of individual development-oriented debt, known popularly as microloans, that has today morphed into a behemoth of mobile, digital debt that has extended to Kenya those infrastructures and experiences of debt seen in other parts of the world (Han 2012; James 2014; Donovan and Park 2019). Therefore, for Korogocho's residents, receiving 'free money', a grant payment, was a novel and often unsettling experience. Discussions with residents and others I knew in Korogocho about the arrival of these grants sometimes turned to questions about why people were selected, where the money was coming from, and what might be expected in return.

I was told that when the first cash grant programmes appeared, before the period of my own fieldwork, some residents staunchly refused to be included, reasoning that doing so would constitute entering into a perilous pact with the devil. Their concerns about the grants connected not only with wider discourses in Kenya around devil worshipping but also more particular to Korogocho concerning the abduction of children. It was not unusual to see in the ghetto missing-children posters pasted onto the outer walls of shacks or on electricity poles along the main road, and I frequently encountered stories of children who were said to have vanished. Some children would, as one friend put it, 'wander off as children do' and become lost in the maze of alleyways but most would often soon be found again. As we saw with Lucy, and I will show further in chapter 5, children also become *wachakora*, and end up joining gangs of other children roaming

Nairobi's streets. But sometimes the explanations appeared to residents as more nefarious. What was known locally as the 'Chinese' church, situated in a nearby estate in Eastlands, and which picked up some of its congregation in Korogocho each Sunday by bus, had been implicated by residents in the case of one missing child a few years before my fieldwork. 'They give you 500 bob [KSh500 – equivalent to about 30 pence] and even lunch, but one boy', Jude, once told me, 'did not return after going to that church, and nobody knows what has happened to him.'[1] The story was tragic but not uncommon. I often heard people's own painful and intimate experiences of their own or their neighbour's children going missing. Nobody knew for sure why children were lost but most were aware, long before investigative journalists revealed child-trafficking networks in Nairobi, that they were being stolen (Murimi et al. 2020).

In this context some people worried about whether the cash grant programmes were a ruse, perhaps associated with the pact with the devil – in the same way as they perceived the 'Chinese' church – to rid people of their children. Neighbours similarly sometimes wondered if those who suffered misfortune after agreeing to receive a grant had somehow been brought into the world of the occult. Jude had once speculated if its workings were at play around a couple we knew who had fought after the husband had accused his wife of not disclosing to him her status as a grant recipient.

One day, soon after the conclusion of the urban grant selection process that I will explore in this chapter, I was with Caroline, a community worker well known in Korogocho, in the corrugated metal shack she called her office on the ghetto's main artery road. Sitting down on one of the hard wooden benches, I had asked her what she thought people in Korogocho understood about the grants. She chuckled, explaining that some had refused the grants when they first arrived lest they become contractually beholden to the devil. But, she said, these days, since the first grant programme had finished and people who had accepted the grants had experienced no misfortune, others were now more willing to accept them too. '*Ni pesa ya wazungu tu*', it is just foreign (white person's) money, she said, and added that she also reminded others who would listen. For her, *pesa ya wazungu* meant charitable aid, a particularly technical type of assistance within a specific political economy, intended to flow to the poorest.

In seeking to situate the grants in specific charitable social relationships, Caroline had occluded their presence in potential others, also still involving foreigners. But, as she knew from her long experience of working within such specific relationships, charitable aid raises not simply technical questions but also deeply moral ones about needs and responsibilities. Charity, such as the cash grants, she explained to me on another occasion, needed to locate, using a common phrase, the 'needy', differentiating this group from another, also characterised by a particularly Kenyan-English term, the 'wanting'. To do so the grants, as part of relationships of the political economy of charity, depended upon technical expertise and artifacts, from surveys to algorithms.

Following the anthropologists Penny Harvey and Hannah Knox (2015), I am interested in the ways in which technical forms of knowledge are a means of understanding and working upon relations, and should be considered not in opposition to, but as equivalent to, those forms of knowledge circulating around the occult or the spiritual domain. In other words, ghetto-level bureaucrats, like Caroline, and residents deployed particular epistemological resources as they sought to make sense of the often intractable relations that shaped the flows of *pesa ya wazungu*. One form of explanation is not necessarily more rational than the other. As Didier Fassin (2007) has also shown in his discussion of suspicion and denial around the connection between HIV and AIDS in South Africa in the early 2000s, we must understand how people encounter and comprehend the world through their own histories situated in particular political economies. Of course, as Jude showed, different forms of knowledge were hardly circumscribed by occupation or role, but also existed as a resource to be considered, in an almost quasi-Bayesian manner, as events unfolded.

While Harvey and Knox's particular interest concerns how technical infrastructures and epistemologies are a way of both understanding and engaging with the relations between material substances, my own interest is how they work on and through social worlds. Moreover, I am interested in how this unruly social world came to bear on this technocratic infrastructure.

I begin this chapter by introducing the grants themselves, showing how they emerged out of a policy world shaped heavily by global health and humanitarian interventions that concentrated on the biological body, but which had begun, in a more concerted fashion, to recognise the importance of the social body in Kenya. However, as I show, a more abstract recognition of 'the social' by a charitable, technocratic apparatus became unstuck, and sought to unstick itself, as it encountered the messy realities of a tension-ridden social fabric of the ghetto.

This chapter focuses ethnographically on the selection process for the urban grant and a three-week bureaucratic operation involving often precariously employed personnel both from outside and local to the slum.[2] What would turn out to be a tense and disputed operation had as its aim to cut through Korogocho's social cloth in order to extract from it particular individuals – largely, vulnerable women and their children – who would thereafter receive a grant.

This contested process of extracting, which constituted one of the early technocratic building blocks seen as necessary in efforts to construct a national social assistance system, revealed, through the texture of people's contestations, the relational entanglements and disentanglements of differently situated actors in and around Korogocho. Moreover, this process showed the ways in which an effort to carve out the individual, largely female poor was interpreted as a way through which the humanitarian NGO sought to extract itself from the ghetto's relational matrix. By drawing attention to ways in which practices of technocratic knowledge aimed to navigate through, alongside and outside of this social fabric, this chapter lays the foundation for the remaining chapters that explore how different actors within and around the ghetto aspired, through their particular acts of care, to repair the fine and fragile threads of that very fabric. I now turn to the grants themselves.

The Grants

Acts passed in parliament in Britain in 1945 and 1946 established a system of social security payments made to those within the country, or British citizens outside it, including families with children, the unemployed or sick, and the elderly. These benefits were not extended to the indigenous, African population in Kenya nor in any of Britain's other colonies. Upon Kenya's independence, Jomo Kenyatta publicly declared his desire to put an end to poverty, ignorance and disease. But as I detailed in chapter 1, his subsequent attention to increasing the country's production rather than sufficiently considering how resources would be redistributed within it, meant that under his rule he paid little attention to building anything that might resemble a national welfare state.

It would not be until the twenty-first century, almost fifty years after independence, and after a hard struggle to win a multi-party democracy, that the Kenyan government began to take tentative steps towards the design of a social security system capable of benefiting people who occupied the lower rungs of society. The story begins in the campaign for the presidential elections of 2002, when Mwai Kibaki put an end to Daniel arap Moi's over two decades in power. Kibaki's subsequent rule until 2013 will likely be remembered as much for his inability to curb rampant corruption in the country as his role in the election violence following the 2007 presidential election that resulted in more than a thousand deaths and the displacement of over half a million people. However, for some Kenyans his legacy includes the introduction of ostensibly free primary and secondary education earlier in his tenure, even if the outcome of this, partly due to the insufficient allocation of funds, was not generally considered particularly impressive. Less publicly discussed, however, has been Kibaki's role in the introduction of government cash grants as a form of social assistance to the poor in Kenya. While this social assistance, as we shall see, remains both minimal and essentially understood as charitable, the policy to give cash grants to the poorest and most vulnerable was at that time unprecedented in Kenya, and represented a new sense of social responsibility of the state towards its citizens – shaped and influenced, of course, by foreign actors.

A key milestone was 2013, after the period of my fieldwork, when the government launched its *Inua Jamii*, or National Safety Net Programme, funded predominantly by a World Bank loan of US $250 million. This launch was the culmination of work that began more than a decade earlier as largely donor-funded non-governmental advocates and designers of grants sought to persuade the government, with varying degrees of success, that the grants should be moved from short-term humanitarian and charitable relief into forms of social assistance for which the state should take responsibility. At its inception *Inua Jamii*, included five individual grant programmes, two of which, the urban and child grant, had reached Korogocho during my fieldwork.[3]

The child grant was for a long time the Kenyan government's flagship social assistance programme. While its official policy was to target households with children who fell into the category of 'Orphans and Vulnerable Children', the emphasis was largely on vulnerability. As one staff member at the secretariat for the grant told me, referring to the son of Kenya's first president, and who would later become its fourth: 'You see, not all orphans are vulnerable. Uhuru Kenyatta is an orphan, but he's not vulnerable.' At the time of writing, just under 25,000 households receive KSh4,000 (£27.08) every two months. During my fieldwork, 400 Korogocho households were enrolled on the programme, with the payment deposited into the caregivers' account in the post office, Posta.[4] While it reached a relatively small number of households in Korogocho, the child grant was also a more long-term grant, with caregivers receiving it until the youngest child in the household reached 18 years of age.

The urban grant, in contrast, was spearheaded by a consortium of transnational development and humanitarian NGOs with the ultimately unfulfilled hope that the government would adopt it as part of the emerging national social assistance programme. While this grant was a direct response to the specific hunger crisis that affected the Horn of Africa in 2011, it was also linked to the cycles of hunger and drought that had been affecting Kenya since the 1990s. The specific urban grant that came into Korogocho was the responsibility of one transnational humanitarian NGO, which I call Global Relief. But also involved in the implementation of the grant, was a local faith-based NGO that I refer to as Living Faith. The urban grant had a far greater reach in Korogocho than the child grant: around 3,000 households (compared to 400) received KSh2,000 (£13.54), which was deposited in the nominated caregiver's *Mpesa* mobile money account each month. Due to the insistence of the government, because they wanted it to align with the other government grants, this was exactly the same monthly amount as the child grant. Yet, while the urban grant was wider in reach than the child one, it was much narrower in regard to its temporality, lasting only eight months.

The move towards social assistance, as the name suggests, hinges on theorisations of the social, that nineteenth-century European invention (for a discussion see Ferguson 2015). From Durkheim onwards, issues such as suicide or crime that were once viewed as the outcome of moral character failings of an individual were increasingly seen as 'social facts', understandable through their relationship to other measurable ones, such as unemployment, gender, and age. This also means, as James Ferguson (2015) has argued, that framing problems as social ones meant asking questions about probability and risk, which in turn led to social solutions that were particularly technical in nature. However, the social aspect of these technical solutions was not simply about connecting 'social facts' but recognising that these facts were part of wider social relationships that constituted a society that was deemed responsible for delivering them. Social assistance, then, can be understood as an outcome of the solidarity through which a society protects its constituent members.

In Kenya, this solidarity that manifested itself in new and developing forms of social assistance was one that was not in any way confined to the nation-state, but was instead heavily built out of relationships, values and ideas that incorporated a range of different national and international actors, including the government, donors, and local and foreign NGOs. This collection of actors continues to emphasise economic development, particularly in agriculture but increasingly in other sectors, such as in the informal economy, and more recently in the service and IT sectors. But for decades, as we have seen, many of them have pursued a form of global health and medical humanitarianism that 'emphasizes the physical (and increasingly the psychological) condition of suffering people above all else' (Bornstein and Redfield 2011b, 6). The two grants that reached Korogocho as an attempt to create a form of social assistance emerged out of these transnational global health and humanitarian policy worlds, and therefore exhibited a particular intertwining of the social and biological.

The connection between the biological and the social has been theorised particularly influentially in Foucault's (2009) novel expositions concerning biopower. His arguments broadly spoke to the way in which the biological dimensions of a population had, in Europe, increasingly come under the jurisdiction of the political domain since the eighteenth century. Social scientists have drawn on these ideas, including in the field of humanitarianism and global health, to explore new constellations of the biological and the social, for example the ways in which access to state- and non-state-provided social assistance in certain contexts has become dependent upon one's biological condition (Petryna 2002; Nguyen 2010; Ticktin 2011), even though the distribution of this assistance often remains strikingly unequal (Marsland and Prince 2012). In these situations, a biological condition is viewed in itself, often as a result of hard-won victories, as a vulnerability and therefore a basis for an inclusion in society and its protective mechanisms. As others have shown, political movements, sometimes involving humanitarian actors, have established themselves firmly in Africa, particularly around HIV/AIDS (Robins 2009; Nguyen 2010). Hence, in contrast to either an explicit self-identification with political neutrality or under the guise of technical assistance, the fields of humanitarianism and global health have always needed to make uncertain and unstable attempts not only to enact but to draw upon power in the places in which they operate.

The Child Grant and the Urban Grant

In 1999, President Moi declared HIV/AIDS a national disaster. In converting this biological illness into an official political declaration, he recognised, as did many other leaders at the time, not only the disease's effect on individual bodies but also how it was having, and would continue to have, important ramifications for society. A few years later, when his two decades of rule ended, these consequences were becoming increasingly acute, as the extent to which the disease had created new forms of vulnerability for children, many of whom had been orphaned, became ever more apparent. In this sense, rather than a biological status viewed exclusively as a vulnerability, it was instead considered as a contributing factor and an aspect of a wider assemblage of vulnerabilities that were at the same time social and biological.

It was, however, the election campaign preceding Mwai Kibaki's victory in 2002 that sowed the seeds of the cash grants. The United Nations agency UNICEF, headquartered in New York, took these elections as an opportunity to advocate for Kenya to be one of the first countries in Africa, besides South Africa, to experiment with a social and humanitarian policy idea that was being increasingly talked about across the world. In Kenya, the interest in the grants was never simply a recognition of the social determination of vulnerability tacked onto an understanding of biological needs. Instead, it went to the heart of issues of state sovereignty, control, and order. The control of women and children has often been central to statecraft (Thomas 2003; Das 2006), including in Kenya, but HIV/AIDS had begun to threaten the state's capacity to assert its authority over these groups. When I spoke with key staff involved in the child grant programme, they revealed their fears of a new generation of Kenyans becoming unmoored from their familial relations, gesturing towards the loosening of the societal knot. To substantiate their fears, they pointed to the ways in which they saw Kenya's cities overrun by street children while witnessing the proliferation of children's homes, many of them run or funded by foreigners.

Therefore, while members of the government understood grants as having the potential to tackle issues of extreme poverty and poor health outcomes in the country, they also recognised their other social potentials, offering the country one possible solution to the restoration of proper and traditional kinship forms of social security that had been further damaged by HIV/AIDS. As a way to illustrate the social restorative potential of cash grants, high-level and middle-class Kenyan civil servants involved in the programme often felt compelled to provide me with examples of what such a restoration should look like. To do so, they regularly turned to the Maasai. One official in the child grant programme once told me that a Maasai mother would respond with incredulity if an outsider visited her homestead and asked her to identify her child. 'They won't understand, they'll tell you all of them are her children,' she said to me, 'they don't differentiate between their children.' For the Kenyans who mentioned it to me, the idea of the Maasai as an ethnic group that had retained its 'traditional' cultural practices, in which kinship was an expansive and undifferentiated network beyond the nuclear family, was a symbol of a virtuous form of solidarity that had collapsed among Kenya's other ethnic groups. Therefore, it evoked not the Maasai's perceived failure to 'modernise' but their retention of positive kin-centred aspects of life which could be rejuvenated in other groups through social assistance. Through this synecdoche that was, at least to my mind, at the same time both romantic and hackneyed, the civil servants I spoke to saw Maasai 'adoption' practices as standing for the rehabilitation of kinship for the whole country. While the World Bank, as we saw earlier, saw social assistance as a replacement of failed kinship-based forms of social security, Kenyan civil servants saw it as holding promise for their rejuvenation.

But the Kenyan government was not the only institution interested in rejuvenated social relationships. In 2004, with Kibaki in power, Vice President Moody Awori entered discussions with UNICEF and the new parliamentary Orphans and Vulnerable Children Committee, as well as with other NGOs, the outcome of which was the decision to go ahead with a pilot cash transfer programme, with Korogocho being one of three locations across the country chosen for this experiment.[5]

The early 2000s saw a widescale attempt by foreign donors to experiment with cash transfer programmes, and soon they began to publicise their evaluations. One of the most famous of these was the Kalomo Cash Transfer Scheme in Zambia, which began in 2003, the same year the child grant in Kenya was piloted by UNICEF. UNICEF had particular ideas around the aims of this pilot. It was partly to provide technical advice concerning how a grant might operate in a variety of different contexts and modes of production, from the urban informal economy to rural pastoral and agricultural forms. But another of the aims envisaged how the pilot might serve to revitalise the state social contract. Two UNICEF staff members who were involved in the process described it in a report like this (Alviar and Pearson 2009, 15):

Having a programme on the ground became a major boost to encouraging political discussion and policy debate on its merits and worth. Politicians and policymakers could now travel to very diverse parts of the country to see a programme in action and decide for themselves whether it was capable of reaching the very poorest and whether the money was being well-spent.

This sort of thinking became integral to efforts by many transnational NGOs in the 2000s as they attempted to re-establish their legitimacy. Activists, journalists and academics had for some time been pointing out, and usually criticising, the manner in which NGOs had often served to fill the gaps in the government's social and welfare services (Schuller 2009). Critics saw this as a politically illegitimate transfer of responsibility for social policy and welfare from the government to NGOs. Responding to such criticism, NGOs increasingly began to launch pilots and experiments, and then insert the resultant evidence into political processes both nationally and globally, in a process that Arjun Appadurai (2002) has called 'precedent-setting' and which involves a 'border zone of trial and error' (2002, 33–4) . Instead of displacing the state's responsibility for its citizens, these NGOs envisaged their role as strengthening it, thus playing an increasingly political rather than merely technical role in Kenya. Of course, in doing so they carried with them their own norms, values and expectations around the political process: in the case of UNICEF, assuming that Kenya's citizenry thought it a priority, and trusted the government, to ensure flows of money would reach the very poorest.

In 2009, five years after the government's child grant was first piloted in Korogocho and a year before I arrived in Kenya, the first urban grant arrived, backed by similar political motivations. In the middle of the first decade of the twenty-first century, there had been growing international concern over the urban slums, an interest fed by the publication in the same year of *Planet of the Slums* (2006) by Mike Davis and *Shadow Cities* (2006) by Robert Neuwirth. In 2007, the Oxfam country office conducted a National Strategy Review. 'We realised', Patricia, a senior manager there recounted to me later, 'we were making zero impact!' Their strategic focus settled on two types of area: Arid and Semi-Arid Lands (ASAL), and urban informal settlements, their technical term for Nairobi's slums.

For Oxfam, attempts to put urban vulnerability onto the humanitarian map were proving difficult. Their work started in 2008, when they carried out, in collaboration with other humanitarian NGOs in the previously mentioned consortium, a contextual analysis of the informal settlements. As a result of this analysis, they were willing to implement a cash grant programme themselves, with one of their main aims being to convince the government that the urban poor specifically needed protecting as much as other more specifically targeted populations, such as orphans and vulnerable children or the elderly. But NGOs, constrained by resource availability, usually have an eye not only towards the national governments in the countries where they operate, but also towards the globally oriented networks that shape the movements of ideas and money.

The transnational humanitarian apparatus is a case in point. Cities, unless they have been affected by severe shocks such as earthquakes or disease epidemics, have rarely been considered as sites of disaster that require the response of this apparatus. This has begun to change as different actors in this apparatus have begun to recognise what they have called a 'silent crisis' in the city; a crisis which includes hunger and malnutrition (Lucchi 2012). For these institutions, the feeding of African cities had deteriorated into a distinctly partial and patchy affair (Guyer 1987). The consortium of NGOs in Kenya also endeavoured to play their own role, generating and deploying statistics into the humanitarian biopolitical terrain in order to shift perspectives around urban suffering within it.

As I was told by workers at Global Relief, humanitarian organisations have largely depended upon indicators drawn from interventions and experience in rural settings. This meant that what constituted a food emergency for the humanitarian apparatus was triggered by high rates of malnutrition – in other words, a high proportion of malnutrition in the population. The NGOs now becoming involved in urban food insecurity argued that in the sparsely populated areas characteristic of ASALs, high rates of malnutrition in particular districts could, and often did, equate to fewer *absolute* numbers of those malnourished in comparison to the densely populated areas of the cities. As a way of an example, they argued that a Global Acute Malnutrition rate of only 2.3 per cent in a Nairobi informal settlement would lead to 8,000 cases of malnutrition in children, whereas in a typical sparsely populated rural area, a higher rate of around 15 per cent, which would trigger an emergency response, might produce 'only' 3,000 absolute cases. The consortium was well aware that its efforts to turn the urban informal settlements into sites of humanitarian crises would be difficult, largely due to the limitations in available global humanitarian funds. Moreover, staff knew that the funders of humanitarian action were wary of entering into the informal settlements, not because they were unaware of or indifferent to the suffering often experienced in them, but because they struggled to see how their intervention would make a discernible and significant difference, provoking anxieties that they would be caught up in the settlements forever. It was not, then, that humanitarians did not want to enter the ghettos of Nairobi because they failed to recognise a need, but because they did not know how to meet those needs within the temporalities that define traditional humanitarian action.

Although the Kenyan government had its own reasons to be wary of bringing cash grants into the country's slums, it did, at one point, look as if it would make a financial contribution – about KSh1 billion (around £710,000) – to create the Urban Food Subsidy Cash Transfer. The name, interestingly, represented the legacy that I have spoken about earlier of previous, since abolished, price controls in Kenya. Political wrangling saw the government withdraw its support for the programme, leaving the consortium of NGOs with only KSh40 million (around £28,000) from the Swedish International Development Cooperation Agency SIDA. This meant that only two informal settlements, one of which was Korogocho, would be reached. While the programme was never realised in the form that was originally intended, the consortium of NGOs considered their work a partial success. This sense of accomplishment related to their other goal, similar to that pursued by UNICEF in the child grant, of persuading the state to fulfil its own social responsibilities towards its citizens. To this end, the NGO consortium managed to establish an Urban Food Subsidy Taskforce within the Prime Minister's Office, which, considering that humanitarian aid has historically always been directed towards ASALs, was viewed as a significant step towards better state recognition of the needs of slum dwellers.

In 2011, the NGO originally responsible for the early urban cash grant, arrived again in Korogocho to implement a second cash grant programme that would last eight months. This programme was a direct response to the hunger crisis that was affecting the whole region of the Horn of Africa. What also became apparent was how this urban grant was premised upon a further consideration of the social. While the actors involved in the child grant often talked about it responding to the societal *outcome* of a biological disease (in this case, HIV/AIDS), the actors behind the urban grant often referred to social factors as a way to *prevent* a disease (malnutrition). They were, as an American NGO worker involved in the programme put it to me, trying to 'catch malnutrition upstream'. Some scholars might refer to these attempts of offering cash grants, often as part of national social policies, as embodying a particular recognition of the social determinants of ill health. Of course, however, the grants remained minimal, constrained both by their scope and temporality, and therefore represented a limited attempt at preventing ill health through a social intervention.

A Ghetto-level Bureaucracy

As I have attempted to show both in the introduction and so far in this chapter, a sense of the failure of the state and other kinship-based forms of solidarity lay behind the conceptualisation and implementation of the grants, seeking, as they did, to incorporate a recognition of the social body into an understanding of the biological one. But while these tended to be based on a more abstract, and sometimes idealised, sense of the social, more concrete situated relationships of sociality had to be encountered as the cash grants programmes entered Korogocho. To consider these, it is helpful to think about the 'unconditionality' of both grants and how this entailed a particular attitude to expert knowledge.

The community of experts behind the grants, a collection of policy makers and practitioners for both governmental and non-governmental institutions, simultaneously assert their own expert and technocratic knowledge, by designing, funding and implementing a programme they deem most appropriate, and deny it, by the very nature of a programme that aims to prioritise and value what might be called the epistemological sovereignty of the poor. Yet, what also transpires is a particular orientation that results in the devaluation of the relational, embodied knowledge and practices of what I am calling ghetto-level bureaucrats: those actors who stand between the designers, funders and implementers in their air-conditioned governmental and non-governmental offices and cars, and the recipients in the hot and dusty ghetto.

What I am referring to as a ghetto-level bureaucracy comprises a group of Village Elders, social workers, community workers, and community health workers, who worked, and often lived, in Korogocho. Village Elders, or *Wazee wa Kijiji* in Kiswahili, were non-salaried but elected members of the Provincial Administration. Social workers were often employed by institutions located outside but serving the local area, such as Living Faith for the urban grant, while community workers and community health workers, although sometimes living outside the strict cartological boundaries of Korogocho, were to a greater extent embedded in the dynamics of its social life. Most of these workers, however, emerged out of a decades-long growth and layering of donor-funded global health and humanitarian programmes, on issues from HIV/AIDS to water and sanitation to hunger, as well as development and human rights ones, many of them implemented by NGOs, or partnerships between NGOs and the government. Within this complex, multifaceted and diverse assemblage of care, these workers were often precariously employed, as well as poorly remunerated, on a series of short-term projects. I would regularly encounter these workers, over the course of a week or month during my fieldwork, engaged in a hotchpotch of activities. One day a community health worker or community worker might be weighing babies on an NGO nutrition project and the next day organising a government 'youth empowerment' workshop. I have given names to many of them that feature in this book: Congestina, Lynn, Ana, Achieng, Caro, and Caroline and my research assistant Jude, both of whom we have met already.

What I call a ghetto-level bureaucracy is therefore dissimilar to either the formal bureaucracies, whether governmental or quasi-governmental, that have been extensively documented by anthropologists (Herzfeld 1993; Feldman 2008; Gupta 2012; Mathur 2015). It is, however, inspired by and a little closer to the street-level bureaucracies influentially described by political scientist Michael Lipsky (1980), comprising schools, police and welfare departments that are responsible for implementing policy.[6] The ghetto-level bureaucracy in Korogocho operated in bureaucratised spaces of rule-making and regulation, however, it was not simply involved in the implementation of policy but formed, as I will show in much more detail in the next chapter, a part of the fragile networks of care and solidarity in the slum.

The Selection Process

In late 2011, a bureaucratic apparatus suddenly appeared in Korogocho, or in some cases was reactivated. Its materiality appeared on the ground and its conflicts appeared in people's discussions: pens and paper, social workers, community workers and community health workers, algorithms and computers, queues and crowds, confusions and clarifications. I was in Korogocho from the beginning of the process of the urban grant and through its entirety as it culminated not only in the selection of recipients, but in their insertion into a telecommunication-mediated financial infrastructure that was being rapidly built across the country at the time. The port of entry into this infrastructure for these recipients was the fingernail-sized green and white Safaricom Subscriber Identification Module (SIM) card. Once recipients received this SIM card, they had not only a phone number but also an *Mpesa* mobile money account; for some but certainly not for all, this was the first time they had had such an account.[7]

'We're going to have to go line by line now,' Mutuku told me when I arrived one morning at the field office of Living Faith, the local implementing NGO for the urban grant. The organisation's office was on the edge of the ghetto, and their social workers, who were on longer-term contracts, would sometimes travel into it, squeezed into the *matatus* which were themselves packed within the city's notorious traffic jams. But the local NGO also relied upon community workers and community health workers who lived in, or at least had a much closer and often longer engagement in, the ghetto. I had been invited by Living Faith to observe the selection process for the grant. As it turned out, this would involve accompanying the salaried social workers, like Mutuku, but also the community workers and community health workers, who were compensated for their time with a small payment. Over the course of three weeks, I accompanied these ghetto-level bureaucrats as they made their way across Korogocho with their rucksacks and stacks of paper questionnaires. I also spoke to as many other people as I could, from local administrative staff to Village Elders to residents.

With his breakfast of a tin cup of hot chai and a fresh *mandazi* (deep fried doughnut), bought from the roadside stall nearby, in his hand, Mutuku leaned back in his chair and elaborated. Referring to the transnational NGO in charge of the urban grant programme, Global Relief, he said that they 'have told us they now want us to fill a form for everybody'. This, it would transpire, would mean visiting and interviewing 12,000 households. Initially, Global Relief had asked for social workers from Living Faith to work with community health workers and Village Elders to identify potential households who could then subsequently be interviewed. But they had been forced to change their strategy. Complaints were filtering through to them that some of the community health workers, whom the social workers from Living Faith relied upon, were selecting friends, family and those from their own ethnic groups.

Later that day, I was at Provide Health Centre, a small medical facility in Grogan neighbourhood, out of which operated several global health and humanitarian programmes. There I bumped into two NGO workers from Global Relief headquarters – from the team running the urban grant programme – waiting for their driver to pick them up. After introducing myself and my research, we began discussing the grant, and particularly the process used to identify and register recipients. Sally, an American

woman, brought up a previous occasion when the organisation registered people for grants in Korogocho, telling me that then: 'the selection
process was too subjective. This time we are going to be more objective.'
She explained how the local volunteers they had used, including some of
the community health workers, who were working at that moment at the
health centre, were not making 'objective' decisions about who was the
most vulnerable, requiring, she explained, Global Relief to step in.

She made clear her worries that each of these volunteers had their
own ideas about vulnerability that rendered the process unfair. However,
in later discussions with staff from the NGO, it was also apparent that
they were equally concerned about the way in which existing relationships, particularly those networks of kinship and ethnicity, would shape
the selection process. The knowledge of residents and those working in
Korogocho and research from other slums had originally helped to define
some of the indicators. But the actual process of finding particular people
who matched these criteria needed health and social workers and volunteers to be detached enumerators rather than engaged, knowledgeable
and relational persons. This would entail what Donna Haraway (1988)
has famously called a 'god trick'. That is, the illusion that one can, within
spaces of science and technology, ascertain objectivity without 'situated
knowledge'. To see, she wrote, 'everything from nowhere'.

Fleeing the Subjective

Global Relief, and their implementing partner Living Faith, seemed to
want to steer clear of the formal political system in Korogocho, and there
was therefore very little attempt to actively involve in the process the
Chief, his Provincial Administration, or the elected Village Elders. The
NGO deemed the Provincial Administration incapable of 'objectively' representing the multi-ethnic citizenry of Korogocho. If the state is sometimes
seen, in its idealised form, as a formal form of solidarity, defined through
the social contract between it and its citizens, for the NGO encountering
the sociality of the slum it appeared as something failing the very poor.

It was not only the NGO that had concerns about the state, however.
Recent survey data has suggested that the Chief is the most popular
institutional form of dispute resolution in the country, albeit far less so
in urban areas than in rural ones (HiiL 2018). Those I knew in Korogocho, however, were largely disillusioned with the Chief and her or his
Provincial Administration, even if they knew that their authority was ines-

capable. Disputes in Korogocho, I was told, were resolved neither through a bureaucratic detached rationality nor a rationality based upon patronage, but through one that turned on a temporal and economic calculus. I heard many stories throughout my fieldwork of complainants arriving at the Chief's office too late, after the other party had already reached it with a payment deemed sufficient.

If the avoidance of this local governmental authority was understandable, albeit problematic in its own way, the attempt by Global Relief to avoid the knowledge and relationships of another subset of Korogocho's ghetto-level bureaucracy, community health workers and community workers, was more puzzling.

As others have shown, community health workers have occupied a crucial role in both global health practices and imaginaries (Prince and Brown 2016). Across Kenya and the wider African continent, community health workers in Korogocho are expected to perform a wide range of tasks: they visit patients, screen residents for disease, administer vaccinations such as polio drops, and conduct health campaigns. At Provide Health Centre, where I spent some time during my fieldwork, through the malnutrition programme they facilitated sessions educating mothers about nutrition, measured children, and helped to provide 'food baskets' and ready-to-use therapeutic food. This is where I first met Mama Joseph and her sick child, Faith, to whom I turn in the final chapter.

During my fieldwork, community health worker positions were voluntary, and while some considered them a 'call' and expressed to me their interest in helping others, they would often justifiably complain about lack of remuneration for their work. A few were able to access *per diems* for attending workshops, while others managed to find NGOs that paid them a small, and time-limited contractual salary. But the level of remuneration was a topic fiercely debated, not only in Korogocho but across the country. This issue became especially acute when the health workers visited patients and, for example, found them without food or bedridden. They complained that they would have to dig into their own pockets to help them, meaning that they were often not only volunteering but paying for the apparent privilege.

In 2010, the government, in partnership with USAID, had been rolling out its Community Strategy across the country as part of its Vision 2030 policy. AMREF, a large and increasingly influential global health NGO with its head office in Nairobi, was instrumental in this process. Not only was it providing health worker training but it was also the first to test whether the Community Strategy was implementable in the urban slums. While AMREF have claimed that the strategy was effective, conversations with community health workers in Korogocho revealed something different. Most community health workers, Congestina, who also happened to be one, told me, were 'just dormant. They all have the bags and materials in their house, but they don't ever use them.'

Others explained to me that in many of the neighbourhoods, the Village Elders had managed to bring in their own friends and family, who lived away from Korogocho and who would never come and work there. Because community health workers had the potential to access foreign resources within a global health and humanitarian space which had been expanding in Kenya since the early 2000s, they have become politically important. This was made clear to me when I paid a visit to Caro, a community health worker whom I would often bump into during fieldwork. When I arrived at her modest two-roomed home, Caro was already entertaining another visitor, and she asked me to wait a little while. I sat with them in her living room as they finished their conversation, the evidence of her occupation visible around me: a community health worker bag on a table, a World Food Programme sack of food in the corner. The guest, as it transpired, was a councillor from the local area. After a short time he left and Caro explained to me that he had asked her to consider standing for the Women's Representative position in the up-coming local elections. She had little interest in standing, she told me. Many others in Korogocho had had these sorts of invitation. Another community health worker, Achieng, had followed this same path, and I would often hear complaints that she was no longer with the 'people', because she was using her new position for her own ends, for instance requesting payments in exchange for assistance. During my fieldwork I would encounter not only these sorts of complaints but also more active efforts by people to force out those community health workers who were perceived as not working fairly for the poor.

A desire to serve the public good was considered by those providing community health training to be a prerequisite for the health workers. Congestina further explained the training she received.

They told us community health workers must be selfless, that it's a voluntary job and you need to have the right attitude. You can't be tribal. It is also like a church thing. If you give with your left, you will receive with your right hand. They told us it's good to help others. But you know, it's difficult. I have my own daughter to look after too.

As she explains, the training sought to instil in the community health workers a Christian ethic of selflessness rewarded through a divinely inspired reciprocity that would shift them away from their ethnic affiliations. Glossing these loyalties as 'tribal', she paints them in a negative light. As many Kenyans told me, the sorts of obligations or reciprocities that might exist in what Lonsdale (1994) has called 'moral ethnicity' seemed today to be less visible than what he calls 'political tribalism'. Yet, as she also made clear, this ethic of selflessness towards an abstract citizenry also ignored the competing and crucial obligations between herself and her child. The apparent inability of these community health workers, despite their instruction, to exercise a sort of Weberian bureaucratic rationality meant turning to a new 'objective' approach. This was something called the 'scorecard', a device designed to aid the decision-making process within humanitarian and development modes of assistance.

The Scorecard

Decisions around selection, concerning to whom to give – and not give – the grant, are regarded by academics and policy makers to be one of the most controversial issues around cash grant programmes (Hanlon et al. 2010, 97). Policy makers have identified several methods through which such decisions are made, including establishing and populating fixed categories of persons or geographical areas, handing the process over to a 'community' to select people, and allowing recipients to self-select. As we have seen, Global Relief displayed little confidence in the 'community' selecting who the organisation considered the 'right' people. Nor did they think, in a context of widespread suffering, that allowing individuals to self-select would constitute what they would consider an effective strategy. Instead, they chose to survey the whole of the slum's population and select those households, around a quarter of the total number of households in the slum, that they calculated to be the most vulnerable to malnutrition. Of course, they could not ignore those *already* malnourished. Those people, particularly children, with malnutrition, who were identified when community health workers measured the circumference of their upper arms, using a specially designed tape, were also referred to a clinic nutrition programme.

To look at the social and biological dimensions of vulnerability to malnutrition, Global Relief turned to the concept of scorecards that first emerged in the 2000s, pioneered by Mark Schreiner, an American development economist and microfinance specialist. As Schreiner (2015) himself has argued, the idea for a scorecard emerged out of a donor and NGO climate that demanded accountability and sustainability in microfinance but where alternatives to traditional financial metrics were deemed necessary. This development also draws attention to how the rise in governing-by-indicators borrows less from earlier statistical techniques associated with the emergence of the nation-state, and has more to do with how neoliberal techniques bring businesses and the market into new domains (Merry 2011). While giving rather than lending money, Global Relief considered the scorecard a helpful way of ensuring accountability, particularly so as to stay close to their humanitarian aim of focusing on those suffering most, or, crucially, those most vulnerable to suffering. Like the child grant, the concept of vulnerability was important in the urban grant. Unlike the concept of 'poverty', which is largely an ordinal and static ordering of a phenomenon, vulnerability points to a diachronic understanding of suffering, as something that may happen in the future.[8] If the etymological roots of 'vulnerability', from the Latin, *vulnerablis*, refers to a wounded soldier on the battlefield, Global Relief was interested in how both social and biological woundedness intertwined.[9]

To develop the scorecard, Global Relief depended upon both social, for instance demographic, and biological indicators that were collected by the African Population Health and Research Center's Demographic Surveillance Survey, as well as a more recent research programme on urban emergencies. The form, that would produce the data to be subsequently analysed by the algorithm, was divided into seven parts: (1) household composition as well as school enrolment and malnutrition status, (2) food (sources, cost and consumption), (3) housing and tenure domain, (4) household assets, (5) household income, (6) coping strategies, and (7) other questions regarding other sources of support, disability in the household, and whether there were women in the household who were pregnant or breastfeeding. Global Relief also made a decision to divide these parts into measurements that are chronic and acute; in other words, long-term conditions that underlie people's vulnerabilities and signs that indicate an immediate crisis. However, when it came to malnutrition, the issue that brought the urban grant to Korogocho, the overwhelming interest was in the acute type. There was a notable absence of any discussions around stunting, the principal symptom of chronic hunger that manifests itself quietly but devastatingly over many years of a child's life. Instead, Global Relief staff referred regularly to *kwashiorkor* and *marasmus*, signs of acute deficiency in protein and calories, respectively.[10] The NGO's mandate with the grant was to tackle the acute food crisis, not to address the undoubtedly more difficult task of long-term hunger. They worked within the human-itarian temporal register, one in which emergencies must be identified and responded to rapidly. It is little surprise, then, that a final decision was made to weight criteria that suggested an 'acute crisis' double those of 'chronic vulnerabilities'.

Also important was the gendering of need. During a meeting I attended at Global Relief's country office, two consultants fed back their findings from their short research into the targeting process and were at pains to praise the NGO for the high proportion of female recipients they had selected for the grant. This emphasis on women seemed to rest on two assumptions. On the one hand, of women's vulnerabilities: many of those women belonged to 'female-headed households', as described in chapter 1. These households, as mentioned earlier, are often assumed to be highly vulnerable, an assumption that is also part of a wider feminisation of policy across the globe, and which has already been critiqued (Roy 2010, 70). Sylvia Chant, for example, has argued for Latin America that there is often insufficient evidence to say that such households are necessarily poorer than their male-headed counterparts (Chant 2006, 202). On the other hand, the emphasis on women rested on an assumption not of women's vulnerabilities but their strengths. While women's inclusion in poverty alleviation programmes, especially microfinance, stems from the percep-tion of their 'inherent talents and abilities as entrepreneurs' (Rankin, in Roy 2010, 71), in both grants their inclusion was premised more often on their role as caregivers. In short, then, the aim was to identify women as caregivers, who were considered not only vulnerable but urgently so.

The Fabric of Ethnicity

With questionnaires based upon the scorecard in hand, the group of enu-merators set to work. Teams were assembled by Living Faith, each one made responsible for the surveying of one of the seven neighbourhoods that comprised the slum. These teams were headed by a social worker from Living Faith but included those community health workers and com-munity workers who were better known to the residents. Almost 12,000 households had to be surveyed over the period of three weeks, with team members often visiting households on their own to complete the task in time. The teams aimed to move systematically throughout the ghetto, trying to enter each shack to speak with the occupant. I would usually accompany Martin, a Kikuyu social worker in his fifties, also living in Eastlands but not in Korogocho. Now a social worker, before this he had worked at a microfinance institution in Nairobi. When this institution became a regulated banking institution Martin was made redundant, as he lacked the requisite formal accountancy qualifications. Microfinance, however, was still in his blood, and he would often talk to me about another microlending programme Living Faith were running, outlining the different business ideas that people had come up with. Like many other NGO workers, Martin was himself a little suspicious of the unconditional cash grants, which he viewed as mere handouts that would neither have sufficient longevity nor, crucially, would create the sorts of economic subjects capable of escaping from their own impoverishment.

Most mornings over the three-week period of surveying, I would meet Martin at the Living Faith office. He was always dressed in smart, pressed trousers and shirt, which, together with my own presence as a white man, made us both stand out to the residents of the ghetto, particularly as we also both often carried a rucksack and a stack of paper. As I mentioned earlier, carrying paper in Korogocho was to residents an indubitable sign of the arrival of a government or NGO intervention. But the significance of the intervention was made even more apparent by the numerous enumerators who moved systematically through Korogocho seemingly visiting all the households.

One problem was that Global Relief, in wanting to select the 'most vulnerable' to malnutrition, assumed that these individuals and their households could somehow be cut out easily from Korogocho's social cloth. This ambition accorded with how the leaders sought to then assist, by offering cash grants without conditions, in a way that aspired to further evade this wider fabric. More will be said about this in the next chapter. The first indication that to avoid the interweaving of relations in the ghetto would not be straightforward was when the Village Elders appeared. I experienced it first-hand myself as I accompanied Martin, but I also learned that other enumerators had shared a similar experience.

During the process, Villager Elders would often direct me and Martin to particular households. 'Come to this one,' one said to us, as he took us to a young woman whom he declared to be particularly 'needy'; again, that Kenyan-English categorisation, which was used more commonly in Korogocho than the grant's preferred concept of 'vulnerability'. But this was not the only way in which the Village Elders sought to take control over a process they considered to be rightfully part of their own political mandate. 'They are telling their people to hide their TVs,' Caroline, the community worker we met earlier, told me as Martin and I passed her one day. Residents would also gather in groups and follow enumerators, asking, when they came out of a particular house, why they had not come to theirs yet.

This new strategy to interview the representatives of each household did not, then, ease tensions. One reason for this was that not everyone was confident that all the households would be interviewed. Leaving a house after an interview, we would be greeted by curious onlookers and invited into their own homes, only for Martin to reply that he would get to them eventually. 'We just wait then?' asked one lady, with a tone and expression that suggested she thought nobody would return to interview her. Part of the reason for the lack of trust that everyone would be interviewed, it soon became apparent, revolved around the issue of ethnicity, particularly as the grant appeared only a few years after the devastating post-election violence. The spatial orientation of Nairobi has long been shaped by ethnicity, since as far back as the colonial period as I detailed in chapter 1, with certain neighbourhoods and slums becoming associated with particular ethnic groups (see also Parkin 1969). While Korogocho is a multi-ethnic slum, its constitutive neighbourhoods are associated strongly with ethnic groups, reflected in the names of the areas; for instance, Kisumu Ndogo, meaning a smaller version of the Luo capital, Kisumu, in Western Kenya. While such associations were often belied by the areas' actual ethnic make-up, they nevertheless have proven to be not only enduring but powerful categorisations, particularly during the post-election violence.[11] The land grabbing and counter-violence hardened particular ethnic groups' attachment and sense of belonging to land (Lonsdale 2008). Residents in Korogocho told me that skirmishes, murders and mob justice had frequently taken place on an ethnic dimension before the post-election violence, but that they had become more intense during and afterwards. The violence aggravated existing fault lines, including tensions, also mentioned in the preceding chapter, that existed between landlords and residents. Many of the Kikuyu landlords who no longer lived in the ghetto, were dispossessed of their shacks. And during my fieldwork, three years after the violence, these shacks housed residents who, I was told, continued to refuse to pay rent for them.

As I accompanied Martin, I would see glimpses of the tension between ethnic groups. One mid-morning during this process, we passed several compounds in order to reach the start of a row. As we did, a lady called out from inside one of those that we passed, inviting us both in. Then, addressing Martin directly in Kikuyu, which he later translated for me, she added, 'You are one of ours, come in and talk to me,' drawing attention to the obligations that apparently pertained between them as fellow Kikuyu.

But the legacy of the violence and the dispossessions also affected the surveying process in other ways. Rumours abounded that the forms were being manipulated by some of the Kikuyu enumerators because, according to one, 'of the evil the Luo have done'. Despite attempts by Global Relief to pursue an 'objective' identification of vulnerability, many residents experienced the whole process as mired in favouritism. A pastor and Village Elder of one neighbourhood told me he that he feared there would be *muaji*, a massacre, in Korogocho. He had tried to follow the enumerators one day in an attempt to understand the process, but, he said, 'some thugs started following me and threatening me, so I stopped. If Global Relief doesn't do anything, there are going to be wars and even killings in the community.' Despite the significant amounts of money that would be flowing into Korogocho, he said he was no longer interested in being any part of it.

Global Relief tried to cut the poor from the social fabric of the ghetto by essentially also cutting out other modes of relating, for instance around ethnicity. But this was seen as only exacerbating tensions around these relationships. Another way that was suggested to me was for Global Relief to more meaningfully engage in this very fabric.

Filling in the Forms

As we moved through Korogocho, Martin and I listened to the sorts of complaints being made, with Martin sometimes responding in a way that he thought might reduce the tension. But Martin told me he had a specific job to do and did not have time to spend longer than necessary on the street. As a result, he tried to get us into and out of the compounds as quickly as possible. Ducking through one of the ubiquitous, rusting makeshift corrugated-iron doors, always open during the day, that separated a compound from the ghetto's streets, we would be met by a tenant, invariably a woman, as the men were often working or hustling for work elsewhere in the city. We would usually be invited into one of the shacks, generally a small one-room affair, with a curtain separating the bed from the living and cooking area. A child would be called to scramble for something that could serve as a seat – perhaps an upturned plastic bucket – while the respondent sat on the bed. Once we all sat down, Martin would go through the form methodically. His eyesight had begun to fail him, and the windowless rooms meant that light only filtered through the door, or sometimes from a dimly glowing bulb. Martin would therefore often ask me to read aloud the words that he could not quite make out. As the respondent gave their answers, I would often notice their eyes darting towards me nervously, giving the impression that they were unsure as to whether they had answered 'correctly'. Martin never told them why we were interviewing them because he feared this would shape how they answered. As an outsider, he had no intimate knowledge of the respondents and therefore was unable to otherwise ascertain the veracity of the responses.

Inevitably, the closed questions were never enough to capture the complexity of a particular respondent's situation, and often they would try to give a longer explanatory narrative. Martin was patient and listened, but the only space to record this information was at the end in the 'comments section'. Here Martin, and the other social workers, would convert some of the information they gleamed from these narratives, spoken in Kiswahili or Sheng, into English terms, for instance, 'child-headed household' or 'single mother'. They would invariably write down that the respondent required assistance and was 'needy', which they would contrast, but not write down, with 'wanting' – that word again, meaning desiring, but not deserving, of support. It was one of the few moments in which a sense of 'subjectivity' was explicitly and formally allowed into the process, although it had little influence on the selection process, as it never reached the techno-rational workings of the algorithm.

Lucky Recipients: The Work of the Computer and Its Algorithm

After three weeks, the intensive ghetto-level bureaucratic surveying work that I witnessed came to an end. The now dog-eared questionnaire sheets that had been filled in by hand by the various enumerators in Korogocho were handed in at the Living Faith field office. There the staff went about collating them before sending them across Nairobi to the Global Relief country office. In the office, the hand-written answers were digitalised into the STATA *dta* format. Then, a composite index was designed to determine the level of need, before being subdivided into a 'chronic index' and an 'acute index'. As mentioned earlier, the programme was a humanitarian emergency-oriented one, and therefore a decision was made to weight the acute index as double that of the chronic index. The overall composite index was then standardised on a scale from 0 to 100, where 0 indicated they met all the criteria for targeting. Based on a sample of previous beneficiaries, a cut-off was set at 59. Those falling below the cut-off were considered households with members most vulnerable to food insecurity and malnutrition and would be included on the programme.

Back in Korogocho, while residents waited, some of them also began to ask the enumerators, as well as community health workers and community workers, what would happen now that these forms had been filled. Some were battle-weary from their many years of involvement in the African Population and Health Research Center's Demographic Surveillance Survey that had produced, from their perspective, few direct tangible benefits. The institution had tried to persuade many of them to continue participating by arguing that respondents should not expect a direct exchange of information for material support. Demographic Surveillance Survey enumerators were told to convince reluctant respondents that participation in the survey was a way of serving the public good; that through the research, more would become known about the struggles among Korogocho's residents, which would in turn, it was argued, inform policies and programmes that would address these struggles. But after years of participating, respondents wondered when these policies and programmes would actually materialise. Informally, the other enumerators of this Demographic Surveillance Survey also started to tell residents that the urban grant was their recompense for years of their participation. There was a partial truth to this as the African Population and Health Research Center's survey and its data were integral to the arrival of the grant. But residents, all of whom had participated in the Demographic Surveillance Survey previously, knew that not everybody would receive the urban grant.

When residents, as well as community health workers and community workers, asked who would receive the grant, Living Faith members of staff often replied, *kompyuta itaamua* (the computer will decide). This response became an almost ubiquitous refrain as people across Korogocho discussed the grant among themselves. One day, as I sat with a group of young men I knew in Caroline's shack-cum-office, one of them told me:

> The government, they are always covering things up. You see on the TV there is this [cash grant] programme for elderly, but when you ask here, they say there is nothing like that. But everyone knows about Global Relief, even the little kids know. They give the form to everyone and then there is no cover-up, and then the computer will decide.

In contrast to the government, Global Relief, as an NGO, was understood by this man as capable not only of delivering vital resources to Korogocho, but in doing it in a way that was deemed, as a result of the work of the algorithm, as transparent. The NGO had supplanted the government not only in being capable of delivering a social service to the residents of Korogocho, but in doing so in a way that fulfilled the bureaucratic rationality that was integral to dominant conceptualisations of the public good.

But the algorithmic rationality was far from universally praised. Grace, the manager of the Living Faith Korogocho office, told me:

> I am telling everybody it is the 'index' that is sorting things out, but it's left so many needy people. I don't want to talk bad about them, but Global Relief should be explaining the process and why certain people have been selected. They need to be talking to the people who have not been selected.

It was only after my fieldwork that I noticed how Grace's understanding of the index as 'sorting things out' accorded so closely in meaning to Bowker and Star's (1999) influential book, *Sorting Things Out*. There the authors showed the ways in which classification systems come into being and influence our lives. As they also showed, such systems are never uncontested. Grace made the same point, showing how the algorithm was failing to properly populate the classification of 'neediness'. But not only did the algorithm fail to select many 'needy' people, it was also a black box that provided no explanation to those same people. After the furore of activity from the targeting process had subsided, I could feel this sense of confusion in Korogocho. 'Why did I get selected, but not my neighbour?' one lady once asked me at the end of an interview.

Critics of algorithms frequently point to the lack of 'explainability' around their more complex forms, such as deep neural networks, arguing that algorithmically mediated life becomes potentially dangerous if we do not know how decisions are being made. But the issue with Global Relief's more rudimentary algorithm or 'index' was not that the institution could not explain how it worked, but that its functionality to select the most vulnerable required a particular sort of opacity vis-à-vis Korogocho residents. While most residents would object to being categorised by others as *maskini wa mwisho*, a Kiswahili term used to denote the very poorest, most I knew would argue that they were nevertheless in need of assistance, even if that were not necessarily to take the form of a 'handout' like a cash grant. The necessity for an algorithmic opacity was made clear by a consultant to the programme, who put it like this to me: 'All these people who are advocating a rights-based approach, saying that we need transparency, what would they do in this situation? How do you select people if they have learned the criteria?' The same point was made when authors of the influential book *Just Give Money to the Poor* argued: 'Transparency can undermine a proxy means test because if households know the indicators, they can manipulate the results – for example, by hiding a radio or bicycle, thus the criteria for proxy means tests are sometimes kept secret' (Hanlon et al. 2010, 110). In short, impoverished people exercising their capacity for opacity, as we saw earlier concerning the Elders instructing people to hide their TVs, is met with a tit-for-tat as institutions offering assistance strategically do the same. Nevertheless, it does seem unlikely that institutions can effectively win the battle by keeping the criteria secret. For those in Korogocho, it would hardly be difficult to guess what sorts of indicators an institution like Global Health might use to signify vulnerability.

It is conceivable that residents were able to game the system, leading to Grace and others lamenting that the process did not select many of those that needed assistance. But it might also be the case that in Korogocho the population that needed assistance was far greater than the numbers that could be taken onto the programme.

Because the algorithm did not seem to many people in Korogocho to actually be finding the 'neediest', or at least selecting some that were not 'needy', it began to be interpreted as a lottery, or sometimes as a result of the divine. *Ni bahati tu* (it is just luck) I would often hear, or if they had not been selected, *Jirani yangu ako na bahati* (my neighbour has luck), and sometimes *Mungu alinibariki* (God blessed me). Related sorts of interpretations of cash grants in Kenya have also been found by the anthropologist Vickie Muinde (2018) in Kwale, one of the other three pilot sites of the child grant, where female recipients would talk about their grants as *riziki*, which Muinde translates as simultaneously sustenance and a blessing.

Preserving a Reputation

One evening, back at the Living Faith office, I was sitting talking to Mutuku. 'Yes, we are interviewing people who we know are not needy,' he complained, 'it's a waste of stationery! It's a census strategy, we interview everyone. This way, people they can't complain. But I don't think it has got the needy this way. But it has eliminated complaints.' Mutuku argued to me that what was widely being interpreted as a 'lucky' form of assistance had headed off complaints, particularly of favouritism and 'tribalism'. He was not the only one with this opinion. At a meeting I attended at the Global Relief headquarters, a foreign consultant went out of his way to praise the NGO for the way in which their algorithmic approach had reduced the number of people complaining about the programme in Korogocho. But when I had spoken to Mutuku he had also ventured another opinion, telling me, 'I think Global Relief did this to keep their reputation.' For Mutuku, a lack of dissent concerning issues of bias along ethnic forms of patronage from within Korogocho was a hardly a sign of success of the grant programme, because he still encountered many people in the ghetto objecting that they had not been included. For him, the surveying strategy had been an exercise in preserving not the biological life of the *beneficiary* but the reputational life of the *benefactor*. Mutuku was the first I heard articulating this point of view, but many of the other ghetto-level bureaucrats to whom I presented his argument did not dispute his interpretation.

As I mentioned at the beginning of this chapter, in some ways Global Relief took on a role that was somewhat dissimilar to what has been identified as characteristic of the world of humanitarianism. That is, their efforts to remain somehow outside of politics, which Peter Redfield has argued means essentially deferring their responsibility to an often 'absent political authority' (Redfield 2005, 330). While Global Relief sought to abdicate political responsibility, they did so both to the Kenyan government as a *specific* political authority deemed by the humanitarian organisation as legitimate, but also sometimes to the wider, global humanitarian apparatus. This, as was the case with UNICEF, can be understood as a form of precedent-setting in which the organisation showed how particular types of lives – that is those of the urban poor – could be saved by the state or others.

However, despite this alternative political work, humanitarian organisations, in reality, do have long-term relationships to particular places and thereby have begun to take on a quasi-state role (Feldman 2012). Take Médecins Sans Frontières. While they may not necessarily establish themselves in existing government healthcare facilities, they do establish and run some over long periods of time. For instance, the organisation established a health centre treating those with HIV/AIDS in Kibera in 1997, only handing it over to the Nairobi City Council and another NGO two decades later, in 2017.

It is therefore understandable that Global Relief wanted to reduce the number of complaints levelled at them by residents and others. Staff needed not simply to reach the most vulnerable, but also to allow themselves the opportunity to do two things. First, to produce a picture of a harmonious grant programme, something vital for their work in precedent-setting. Second, to preserve their relationship with the residents of Korogocho to allow for this specific grant programme but also for the possibility of future humanitarian programmes.

What they seemed to desire, though, was not a long-term relationship thick with their own obligations, or which might establish a sense of entitlement among the ghetto's residents, but a rather more shallow one, that would allow them the mobility to come in and out of the slum on their own terms (or on those of their donors) and save individual lives. As one humanitarian NGO worker working in the consortium of NGOs involved in urban emergencies once told me, 'Donors worried a lot that they could be in the slums forever.' As we shall see briefly next, as well as in the following chapter, this sort of relationship was understood by residents to be a charitable one, and was also understood to have a particular character with far-reaching possibilities for claim-making.

It is Like Somebody's Cow

I have suggested that Global Relief's attempt to 'objectively' cut out the most vulnerable households from the wider social fabric of Korogocho did more to allow the organisation to cut *itself* out of the entangled loops and weaves of that cloth – allowing it to remain unmarred by the complex and messy politics of ghetto life. I want to further argue that this was actually an integral and characteristic strategy within what I have called the charitable economy, which includes both governmental and non-governmental institutions' efforts to assist people in Kenya. This strategy, I suggest, sought to evade the obligations that might pertain in a thicker, more substantive relationship between themselves and the impoverished.

On an overcast and muggy day, I found myself being invited into the shack of Betty, the Women's Representative and chairperson of one of the 'villages', Kisumu Ndogo. Given that it was soon after the end of the targeting process that I had participated in, conversation naturally turned to it. She told me about the selection process of a previous grant programme, saying: 'Last time the selection wasn't bad. The sick and the needy ones were selected. But this time the Elders are not involved, and so now it is charity. The programme has changed to charity.' She paused. 'Whoever shall get it, gets it.' She then argued that people had complained to the Elders, not because the Elders had been involved in the selection, but because they were the 'visible leaders' of the community. Betty's definition of charity as characterised by arbitrariness ('whoever shall get it, gets it') rather than as targeted towards the specific deserving ('sick and needy') was, for sure, idiosyncratic. However, it captures the way in which charity in Korogocho had become opaque and unknowable. Elders and other 'new leaders', such as community health workers, were visible and accountable to the community. I knew of examples in which those actors who were deemed to be 'eating', that is benefiting only themselves and their friends, were forced out from their roles. Charity, in contrast, seem to largely evade these relationships, which were full of morally laden understandings of accountability and obligation.

The *concept* of charity, as something that was largely empty of accountabilities and obligations, could even be invoked strategically. This strategic capacity of the concept was also something not lost on the government in contestations around the child grant that also reached Korogocho. While this chapter has concerned the urban grant, it is productive to turn here, momentarily, to this other grant. A few months after I had spoken to Betty, I was invited to attend one of the meetings, arranged by the government's Children's Officer, for the recipients of the child grant.

The meeting took place in a primary school classroom on the edge of the ghetto's former market, now a playing field that also served variously as a food aid distribution point, music and fashion show ground, and a children's bicycle hire business venue. In the large and airy school classroom, the recipients gathered on benches as they were informed about changes to the programme they were on. Most notable was the change in the way that the grants would be distributed, from cash at the government-owned

Posta to money deposited into a biometrically secured account at a commercial bank. With so few meetings on the grant programme, again owing to the unconditional character of this grant, interactions with the state's representatives in this way were rare. Grasping the opportunity, one brave recipient stood up and asked a question. Ignoring the meeting's main agenda item, the programme's shift to a new payment system, she asked about the problems that plagued the old system, particularly the frequent delays in the disbursement of the grants. The grants were meant to arrive every two months, but they were frequently delayed.

The Children's Officer had little patience for her question. He cut her off and followed with a rebuke, 'You can't complain,' he said, raising his voice, 'This money is not yours. This is just charity.' Such statements seemed to carry far more weight than even the written Service Charter for the programme which said things such as *haki za familia zinazoaidiwa/zinazo-fadhiliwana mradi* (rights of the helped/sponsored families on the project). Even the media commonly interpreted the child grant as charity: a newspaper report in the popular Kenyan newspaper *Daily Nation*, for instance, concerning an increase in the monthly payment of the child grant featured in this book, had in its headline the word 'Charity'. It is therefore understandable how one of my interlocutors, Ann, a mother of four, talked about the grants as, 'like somebody's cow. He can cut you off anytime he wants, and if he cuts you off, we'll just go back to our lives.' Ariel Wilkis has argued that state grants, as a form of what he calls 'donated money', compared to other sorts of money such as loans or money you earned, were viewed at the bottom of a moral hierarchy concerning money (Wilkis 2017, 92). But what she expressed and what the Children's Officer reminded grant recipients of was that *charitable* grants were even lower in such a hierarchy offering as they did no possibilities for a sense of a rightful entitlement to them.

The Children's Officer's reply was just one instance of many attempts to discourage particular forms of relationships, for example, between the state and the citizen, which might allow for the development of a sense of entitlement among the latter. In this way, an actual boundary between what was charity and what was an entitlement was not fixed but instead was part of an ongoing negotiation in the daily life of the programme. The distinction did not map onto another distinction between an NGO and the government, but rather was a political technique for allocating, or indeed avoiding, responsibility.

Conclusion

It is perhaps not saying anything new to declare that everything is relational. In 2008, the French telecommunications company, Orange, ran an advertising campaign in the UK, entitled 'I am everyone'. In one of their television advertisements, a male narrator is accompanied by a series of shots of different people, each in some ways related to him. 'I am my mum, and my sister. I am my best friend Mike who I've known since school,' he says, adding relationships over the course of the short advert before finishing with, 'I am who I am, because of everyone.' This final statement, and crucially the word 'because', preserves the idea of the individual over the dividual; that is, an individual *with* rather than *constituted by* relationships. But it nevertheless comes close to anthropological ideas about relationships and persons. When corporate capitalism is able to deploy the same sorts of arguments as anthropology, one has to wonder if the argument has run its course.

One problem with recognising the relational nature of everything is that it presents us with a vast complex arrangement of connections. Some time ago, Marilyn Strathern (1996) suggested that the problem with Actor-Network-Theory was its apparent inherent drive to account for all of these connections within networks – in their case, networks that bring together more than just humans. But, as she showed, both with conventional social networks and the Actor-Network-Theory variant, certain amounts of cutting must take place. Her own examples, drawn from her research on biological science in Euro-America and from Melanesian kinship, showed the various ways in which this cutting of networks takes place. For instance, the way in which patent law severs the claims of other scientists, in the vast social networks of knowledge, to ownership of a discovery. Strathern also quotes James Weiner, who had argued that 'in a world … that is relationally based, the task confronting humans is not to sustain human relationships … [but] to place a limit on relationships'. But what if, many have argued, we are all living in 'relationally based' worlds in reality, even if not always in ideology (Zigon and Throop 2014)? One task, then, would be to explore the limits around relationships (Candea 2010; Mair 2015). It can also be to show how people and things *place* limits on relationships. In this chapter I have attempted to show this by looking at the work of cutting people away from relationships. Cutting individuals out from the loops and weaves of the ghetto's sociality involved, I argued, also cutting out the relational situatedness and knowledge of others – in this case, ghetto-level bureaucrats.

Penny Harvey and Hannah Knox have shown, however, through their analysis of road building in Peru, that engineers, despite being seen as actors who apply the scientific principles and apparently perform the god trick are, in fact, always embedded within and engage with the relationships, norms and values of social worlds (Harvey and Knox 2015, 9–10). They show that for roads to be built successfully, this sort of engagement is required. Yet projects, engineering or otherwise, often do fail, and as James Ferguson (1994) showed us long ago, this is often down to their own failure to recognise and build according to these social worlds.

In this chapter, my interest has not concerned how successful or failed projects are built. Although I am, like James Ferguson's seminal contribution to the anthropology of development, interested in what failed projects actually do, even though they fail to do what they set out to do. If we listen to the residents' and others' critiques as they emerged from Korogocho, it is entirely plausible that the god trick, that is, the aim to cut out the recipients from the wider relational cloth, was not simply pursued to 'objectively' identify the poorest, but also to build the NGO and its humanitarian work into, yet loosely attached to, the world it sought to intervene in. It was done in a way that would allow it to continue its work unencumbered, by preserving its reputation, while remaining ever mobile and thereby capable of moving in and out of the ghetto when necessary.

PART II

3

Under the Aegis of Mistrust

Anthropologists studying what is often particularly familiar to them, including bureaucracies, have drawn attention to the problems of studying those knowledge practices and forms that are shared between the anthropologists and interlocutor (Riles 2001; Ballestero 2019). Drawing on Maurice Bloch's observation that certain types of more familiar expertise, such as scientific ones, have not been the privileged object of anthropological enquiry, Marilyn Strathern argues that certain more esoteric practices are 'more likely to dazzle than others'. To be dazzled, she suggested, is to be afforded the impetus for further analysis and revelation (Strathern 1999, 10–11). In my own fieldwork, I similarly came across things both in the grants and the wider charitable economy that were overtly familiar: meetings, documents, policies, algorithms, and the other material infrastructures that characterise bureaucratic worlds.[1] Unable to be dazzled by such objects, anthropologists have approached them in different ways. Often this has meant an ethnographic attentiveness to what jars, from the odd invocation of kinship in high finance (Riles 2004) to the ways our interlocutors see the mundane in ways that are unfamiliar to us (Ballestero 2019).

My own fieldwork around the bureaucracy of the cash grants posed a very different problematic. While prepared, because of my familiarity with diverse forms of development and humanitarian interventions, to see the conventional bureaucracies and their knowledge practices, I was taken aback by their relative absence in the cash grants. That is, studying as I was an attempt to build a social assistance system, I was surprised when the bureaucracy I was expecting rarely seemed to materialise. Expecting to regularly sit in on and observe meetings relating to the grants, I was instead met by their sporadic occurrence. The intensive bureaucracy involved in the registration process of the urban grant, explored in the previous chapter, was, as I quickly discovered, somewhat of an anomaly. After the recipients had been identified and registered, on the whole they, along with those on the urban grant, seemed to be left alone by the charitable, bureaucratic apparatus. The cash payments would arrive either, in the case of the urban grant, in the recipient's mobile money account, or, in the child grant, in their Posta account. Repeatedly during my fieldwork, I was struck by the absence of workshops, or training sessions, or even the individual surveillance of grant recipients. This was in stark contrast to activities associated with other programmes that I sometimes encountered during my fieldwork, for instance, the distribution of food in a malnutrition clinic or a legal aid camp for residents at the Chief's Camp.

When it came to the cash grants, the bureaucrats who are conventionally involved in these, and who had been involved, albeit in a minimal capacity, in the survey processes, were effectively stood down. Existing bureaucratic hierarchies within the charitable economy were being flattened out, reversed, and even, by eschewing the intermediary, hollowed out. Missing in the grant programmes, then, were those sites – traditional in the bureaucratic apparatus common to both governmental and non-governmental interventions – in which people are monitored, surveilled, cajoled and formed into new economic, political and moral subjectivities. As I have said earlier, the absence of these processes has often led to the grants being celebrated for treating the poor with a dignity that comes about from trusting them to make their own decisions. In doing so, they cast other, intermediary bureaucrats, as unnecessary, even morally suspect. Indeed, bureaucrats are branded, it is argued by those occupying a variety of political positions, from anarchism to laissez-faire capitalism, as a vestige of an antiquated system, being considered at worst as self-serving or at best as mere cogs in a violent, bureaucratic machine.

Quite predictably, the ghetto-level bureaucrats in Korogocho disagreed with their new-found obsolescence in this new paradigm of institutionalised care. They were already aggrieved at their own relational and situated knowledge being ignored in the identification process for the urban grant. But now, faced with being almost totally removed from the administration of the grant, they sought to assert their vital role and, as we shall see, demonstrated this by taking a keen interest in the behaviour of the recipients. Here was another moment that dazzled. First faced with the loss of bureaucracy, I was then taken aback by its reintroduction.

This chapter turns to the ghetto-level bureaucrats I spent time with during my fieldwork, whom I will describe more fully below. My argument, put simply, is that their attempts to reintroduce certain forms of regulation can be interpreted as a way through which they sought to care for a relationship between Korogocho and the uncertain, and often unknowable, charitable economy. This form of care is one aspect of the ethics of solidarity that I explore in this book. My argument joins with those of others who have introduced an ethical element to understandings of bureaucracy, which is conventionally considered as amoral. As Paul du Gay (2000) has argued, bureaucrats partake in deeply ethical projects in which they strive towards being 'good' bureaucrats, for instance by cultivating dispositions such as impersonality or respect of hierarchy.

My argument in this chapter goes against an interpretation that would see the re-regulation attempts I observed as errors of a technical nature that could somehow be ironed out. Not only were the ghetto-level bureaucrats I knew highly capable, savvy operators but there was also, I suggest, a striking similarity in the patterns of behaviours I observed. Another interpretation, however, deserves more attention, and it is perhaps the more intuitive: the bureaucrat's livelihood and sense of worth depended upon showing their continued value to their actual and potential paymasters, whether the government, an NGO or even an individual benefactor.

This interpretation would consider their roles akin to what David Graeber (2018) has famously called 'bullshit jobs'. That is, a job that is essentially 'pointless, unnecessary, or pernicious' (2018, 3). These particular roles might fall into what he calls the Type 2 'taskmaster', someone 'whose primary role is to create bullshit tasks for others to do, to supervise bullshit, or even to create entirely new bullshit jobs' (2018, 51). Related to this is the common notion, in studies of bureaucracy, that bureaucrats are not only in the business of making distinctions in populations but also between themselves and those populations. These arguments are compelling and persuasive, particularly as many of us are ourselves critical of the demands put upon us by various bureaucracies, and often dismayed at the ways through which they operate to produce forms of neglect (Herzfeld 1993).

While Graeber was reluctant to propose alternatives to a worldwide political economic system that produces 'bullshit jobs', he did suggest the idea of Universal Basic Income. This, he argued, is a cash grant that given to everyone unconditionally, stripping away bureaucracy in a manner far removed from the cash grants that feature in this book.

I am not averse to his policy proposal, and indeed very sympathetic to the idea of seeing unconditional grants in Kenya more closely approximate Universal Basic Income. But there is, as far as I know, still today very little political appetite in Kenya to introduce it. Affordability concerns, morally inflected fears around the production of 'dependency' or 'idleness' among the citizenry, and concerns about state responsibility, drawn from a long experience of state corruption, are just some of the issues that work against any such possible transformation of what already exists in the way of cash grants.

Scholars and journalists have tried to assuage some of these concerns, for instance, by offering the technical evidence that shows that recipients do not become dependent but work harder, or that recipients do not waste the money. In short, to show the importance of trusting the poor to make their own decisions. While these scholarly and journalistic efforts are crucial, they do not examine how other actors are involved in demonstrating to others what are deemed as the necessary virtues of the poor, and thereby showing the poor's trustworthiness. Ariel Wilkis has argued that, in certain situations around what he calls 'donated money' in Buenos Aires, the poor themselves were able to ensure the flow of money if, as he writes, they 'were capable of a public performance that guaranteed acknowledgement of their moral virtues' (Wilkis 2017, 82). This chapter sets out on a journey to show how others in the ghetto, aside from the poor themselves, sought to attempt a similar sort of thing in an experimental cash grant programme that was premised on a trust of the poor.

In what follows, then, I do not interpret the practices that feature in this chapter, which can be understood as a re-regulation of the cash grants as a deregulated form of charitable assistance, as examples of a bureaucracy hell-bent on survival for the sake of itself and its members, and producing essentially worthless jobs that enact distinctions of value between educated bureaucrats and the population they are meant to serve. Such interpretations see bureaucracy as a form of violence or disregard. Instead, I consider how these practices might also, rather than instead, be understood as an ethical form of care for relationships between benefactors and beneficiaries. And it is an ethics of solidarity, I argue, that emerges out of the social relationships, norms, and values of the existing charitable economy.

In this chapter I will show how the bureaucrats' practices involved making visible what they thought was the poor's acceptable behaviour, while hiding what they thought was unacceptable. To make visible the right behaviour required the reintroduction of new forms of regulation. As I shall show, when these ghetto-level bureaucrats mistrusted the individual cash grant recipients, or even when they trusted them but hid their behaviours, they were doing so to care for, and hopefully make trustworthy, the precarious structural relationship between the benefactors and the poor. This is a relationship that characterises the globally oriented charitable economy that reaches into places like Korogocho, an economy which has become increasingly complex (Brown and Green 2017, 48).

While mistrust is conventionally seen as an uncaring, even violent act, it can, I show, be interpreted as a decidedly caring one when its object is a relationship. This interpretation, I believe, is able to build on our understanding of how bureaucrats are part of hierarchical relationships that structure redistribution in Kenya and beyond (Haynes 2012; Welker 2012; Scherz 2014). While not always successful, the acts have a certain logic of care that gestures towards a form of solidarity within the wider relational infrastructure of the charitable economy, where the gaze of donors or the government concerned with alleviating poverty or suffering remains fixed on its subjects, even if the cash grants and their emphasis on trust give the surface illusion of breaking such a gaze.

Trust

In an interview, the chief operating officer of GiveDirectly – a well-established philanthropic institution that experiments with unconditional grants in Kenya – had this to say: 'There's an assumption out there that we need to monitor how poor people spend their funds. We did that to the extent of collecting data for our research, but otherwise, we trust the poor to spend the funds wisely' (Budsock 2016). His statement is not only illustrative of the thinking that laid the foundation for the grants in Korogocho and beyond, but also a particularly revealing one both about the nature of freedom and trust, and their role in the grants. I will show how a separation between knowledge, glossed in the quote above as 'research', and trust in the poor, was logically impossible. To trust the poor was not separate from but relied upon knowledge of the poor. Indeed, for the bureaucrats in Korogocho, looming over the now curtailed bureaucracy was a lingering expectation, expressed by some of the bureaucrats I knew, that the grants might, at some point, require them and their knowledge practices. As I show in this chapter, to stand any chance of making the relationship between benefactors and residents of Korogocho last into the future – that is, to make the relationship itself trustworthy – required ghetto-oriented bureaucratic knowledge practices that would allow this trust in the poor to continue. To make my argument a little clearer, it is helpful to look more closely at the subject of trust.

Trust is a topic not unfamiliar to anthropology (Gambetta 1988; Englund 2002; Sillitoe 2010; Jiménez 2011), or indeed the social sciences and humanities more generally (Fukuyama 1996; Warren 1999; Hardin 2006). But in this chapter and for my argument, I am particularly interested in expanding my discussion of freedom in the introduction, and incorporating it into a discussion concerning trust.

A number of my interlocutors who either designed or helped to manage both grants brought up the concept of freedom. I was sitting with Joyce Kamau, a civil servant in the secretariat for the child grant. We were together in her office on the fourth floor of a rather nondescript building in the government district of Nairobi, in the Central Business District. As we discussed the initiative and the complaints often levelled at it, she seemed to grow impatient, eventually saying to me with exasperation, 'But you see, Tom, the programme is good, because it gives people freedom and choice. People can use the money for what they want.' Joyce's emphasis on freedom and choice echoed the quality of flexibility emphasised by the American NGO worker quoted in the introduction. Both believed that by giving money, and trusting them with it, recipients were also being given freedom, choice, and flexibility to draw on their own knowledge in the market.

Peter Johnson, in discussing the origins of trust, argues that it concerns 'the variety of ways in which agents become conscious of the freedom of others' (as quoted in Seligman 2000, 63). This connects closely to what the philosopher Annette Baier has argued, in a classic piece that has attempted to tease apart the differences between a trusting and a contractarian transaction; that trust is 'letting other persons ... take care of something the trustor cares about, where such "caring for" involves some exercise of discretionary powers' (1986, 240). Baier further suggests that the most important things to be entrusted to people are those which require some action, something more than what she terms 'non-interference' in order to thrive.

Baier offers the example of entrusting a child to one's separated spouse. The trust carries with it the expectation that the spouse will interfere in a positive way in that child's development. Her point is that we must care not only very deeply for the thing that is being entrusted, but also carry with us an expectation that the trustee will work on that thing entrusted in ways that will transform it. We can see something similar in the trusting of grant recipients. The benefactors expect the recipients to use their discretionary powers to transform the grants into something else by utilising them in the market free from the guidance of experts.

While Joyce Kamau may have given the impression that any use of the money was acceptable, in reality, she and others associated with the grants had varied and never stable ideas around what sorts of personal transformations the money should generate. These ideas were largely determined by the benefactors – that is, the 'trustor' in the existing hierarchical relationship around regimes of assistance. The benefactors' trust in the recipients involved expectations about whether the values and strategies of the beneficiaries were proper to their social, political and biological condition. However, these expected values and strategies were not always very clear to those in Korogocho. This opaqueness around the grant programmes made many of the recipients and bureaucrats I knew especially anxious, as they wondered what a responsible use of the money should look like and what sorts of personal transformation should be generated by the money. Later in this chapter, I explore one particular discourse, of hard work and entrepreneurialism, that did seem important to those in Korogocho, and which its bureaucrats believed was integral to the ghetto's relationship to the charitable economy.

The notion of trusting the poor is central to the unconditional cash grants. As we saw with GiveDirectly, however, this does not preclude research practices that seek to generate new forms of knowledge about the recipients. As the chief operating officer said, the organisation *did* monitor them 'to the extent of collecting data for our research'. While this may appear to breach the very notion of trust, it actually goes to the heart of any relationship, whether it is more contractarian or more trust based. Although individual monitoring may cease, thus introducing a certain form of freedom for grant recipients, for the hierarchical relationship between donors or the government and their recipients to continue requires a knowledge of each other. So, even in those relationships in which trust is introduced, like the grants in Korogocho, some verification that this trust is well-placed is essential. Indeed, while trust might preclude close monitoring and control, it *must* include some sort of process or action which would offer confirmation that one was justified to trust in the first place. Otherwise, of course, trust would equate to blind faith. Therefore, with the new ostensibly *trustful* unconditional grants, it is important to recognise the part they play in a wider, long-standing, precarious charitable economy that has formed within certain global, political, and economic relationships; the most crucial of these being between that between the benefactors and their poor. One way to look at this is to examine the concept of charity.

Charity revolves around the voluntary transfer of both material and immaterial gifts from bilateral and multilateral donors, as well as private individuals, through governments, NGOs or partnerships between the two, to those designated as being in need of assistance. This economy is motived by an understanding of a formal identity between a giver and a receiver (Stirrat and Henkel 1997; Wilson and Brown 2008). In an admittedly generalising and idealised understanding, donors consider the recipients of their charitable gifts as being deprived of the same fundamental and universal rights that they themselves possess (Wilson and Brown 2008, 12).[2] As cash enters the charitable economy, it is conventionally transformed through particular regulatory processes into specific gifts that seek to fulfil people's rights. This does not mean, however, that the recipients experience it as a right, as we saw in the previous chapter and we will see again later in this one.

Because the charitable relationship involves an assumption of a common formal identity, as fellow humans with basic rights, and then the subsequent charitable efforts to help achieve those rights, it also necessitates efforts to verify that achievement. These circumscribe a recipient's freedom and have important consequences. In short, the gaze of the benefactor, which characterises the development and humanitarian apparatus across the world, endures in new efforts to trust the poor. But in certain ways, it also becomes more apparent. As regulation is stripped back, the existing contractarian hierarchical relationship is made ever more vulnerable as attempts are made to transition it into a trusting one. This vulnerability is undoubtedly a part of any attempt to build a relationship characterised by trust; trust takes much time to build but far less to break.

The Precarious Charitable Economy and the Ghetto-level Bureaucracy

As we saw in the previous chapter, ghetto-level bureaucrats, many of them more like volunteers, were integral to the identification and registration of grant recipients, even if the scorecard and the algorithm worked to cut them out as relational people, from the fabric of Korogocho. But these bureaucrats have also been integral to the charitable economy in general in identifying, training and tracking recipients of charity, as well as helping in distributing charitable aid. As I have already mentioned, the grants emerged from within the long-standing social relationships, norms, and values of the precarious charitable economy in Korogocho. Bureaucrats who had lived and worked in Korogocho for many years understood grants as just the latest experiment in a long line of development and humanitarian ideas that have come into the ghetto, which have included, among many other things, infrastructural and environmental improvements, food aid, economic empowerment, and HIV/AIDS interventions. I have already introduced the charitable economy in Korogocho as well as the bureaucrats, but a little more needs to be said.

The ghetto-level bureaucrats in Korogocho jostle to secure short-term pieces of work from individuals, NGOs, and government departments on a range of different issues including water and sanitation, HIV/AIDS, nutrition, and human rights. Some of these bureaucrats have been born or educated in Korogocho. Some live within the ghetto proper, where mud and corrugated-iron shacks dominate, while others live in the low-income estates that border it, within houses of slightly better, if still dubious, quality. A few others, such as the manager of a local NGO introduced below, travel from further away for their work.

Whether living outside or within the ghetto, each day they set about their varied work, from measuring babies' weight at the local clinic to cajoling groups of youth to attend an entrepreneurship workshop, to organising local women into savings groups. There were also differences within this loose, informal bureaucracy in regard to wealth, status, and education levels, as well as authority, and bureaucrats sometimes sought to demonstrate these distinctions to those around them. Yet what was also clear was the concern bureaucrats had for the people of Korogocho. For example, as I mentioned earlier, a community health worker visiting a house might often provide the inhabitants with money or food from their own pocket. A local NGO worker might go beyond their day job by giving advice, for instance on farming strategies and current crop prices, as well as helping to connect a slum dweller engaging in some farming with a buyer. In this way, while the bureaucrats featured in this chapter are distinct, they are also part of the world of slum dwellers. In fact, in a place like Korogocho, it is very difficult to say who is an insider or an outsider. Instead, these forms of activity outlined above, as well as the activities presented in this chapter, can be understood, I venture, as a form of mutuality. While there is now a rich literature on this mutuality in Africa, rarely are bureaucrats included within it (Bähre 2007; Shipton 2007; Rodima-Taylor 2014; Rodima-Taylor and Bähre 2014). I contend that the charitable economy's long history in Kenya, since the colonial era, has created a certain mutuality that may be studied on its own terms, and which is revealed through the grant programmes discussed in this chapter.

Moreover, what is important to appreciate is that bureaucrats in Korogocho neither simply implement policies of care, such as in the charitable economy, nor do they care for persons in more informal ways within this economy. They also work to attract what is a precarious, unpredictable, and ever-shifting portfolio of development, humanitarian, and social welfare interventions that have the potential of being absorbed into the slum's own charitable economy. As these workers go about their everyday work, they maintain a vigilance for the new sources of funding and resources that often float in and around the slum.

Mistrusting the Poor

As I have suggested, in the conventional charitable economy, which continued to operate during my fieldwork in Korogocho, funds raised by the benefactors are transformed into particular gifts. They are delivered to identified recipients who are subsequently tracked and monitored. Ghetto-level bureaucrats and recipients alike are therefore brought into these intensive bureaucratic processes. In the grants, however, the hierarchy of knowledge was flattened out, or to some extent reversed, with the poor recipient now given, in the form of a grant, a sort of unmediated gift of cash or 'free money', and henceforth considered an expert. This meant that known bureaucratic and technocratic forms, such as skills training, were dismissed, while ghetto-level bureaucratic intermediaries were stood down, representing a hollowing out of bureaucracy. Yet, facing redundancy, in the broader sense, the ghetto-level bureaucrats curiously began to introduce new forms of regulation.

As mentioned earlier, the examples of the reintroduction of regulation in Korogocho could be readily dismissed as errors of a technical nature, or simply as some form of miscommunication, or even as the self-interestedness of bureaucrats themselves. But I believe the regulatory initiatives pursued by the bureaucrats have a particular significance, and a sort of logic, emerging from the charitable economy's deep and sustained history in Korogocho. The intermediaries, those bureaucrats with a long engagement in, and understanding of, the charitable economy, felt the heavy presence of one aspect: its evidential requirements. For them the gaze of the benefactors never seemed to be far away. And so, despite the best efforts of the policy makers, the grants could not escape the long-standing norms, values, and social relationships within which they were embedded. Therefore, even though the grants sought to instigate a new trustful regime of giving, they could not escape the existing context of the charitable economy.

Ana, a community health worker, was one bureaucrat who had worked for many years in Korogocho. When the grants arrived, she was exasperated. 'We don't know what they're using the money for,' she said. She continued to argue that: '[The institutions] should work hand in hand with us. They should give us information, so we can advise. We should know who is getting the money, so that we can follow up and monitor as well.' Across Korogocho, bureaucrats were expressing similar sentiments. The benefactors behind the grants saw themselves as trusting the poor by allowing them their discretion, and allowing them to pursue their own strategies. But while these benefactors aspired to trust grant recipients by reducing monitoring, for bureaucrats in Korogocho this trust posed too big a danger that the recipients might appear to the benefactors as lacking the requisite wisdom. In short, an attempt to trust seemed to run the risk of jeopardising a hierarchical relationship, itself already precarious. It appeared that bureaucrats recognised that the continuation of the relationship between benefactors and the poor required work in order to make the 'correct' behaviour of the poor visible to the benefactors' gaze. I present two examples, which I argue focused on reintroducing regulation in different ways. The first example sought to make all individuals accountable. The second sought to make certain individuals representational.

June was the manager at Living Faith, the local NGO involved in the administration of the urban grant. She explained to me one day in her office how she understood the grant programme. She began by acknowledging that the programme was not serving everyone who needed it, but expressed confidence that it would over time. She suggested that, through a succession of tranches, the programme would eventually lift all residents of Korogocho out of poverty. While humanitarians often prioritise the 'most vulnerable', June recognised that all in Korogocho needed assistance. It was her belief that what was important was not trusting the recipients, but nurturing a charitable relationship that endured, successively encompassing every person in need. Furthermore, a trust that allowed charitable recipients the freedom to behave how they wanted, she thought, would jeopardise this relationship. The solution was a reinstatement of regulation. She explained to me how, in the previous phase of the urban grant programme, Living Faith had requested that the recipients purchase food with the grant and return evidence, in the form of receipts, to the office. The issuing of receipts was completely alien to the local *maduka* (shops) and *mama mboga* (roadside vegetable sellers) most residents frequented. As a result, recipients were required to travel to a supermarket in an adjacent wealthier neighbourhood. When I spoke to the transnational humanitarian NGO, Global Relief, about this, the manager of the programme explained that this was a misunderstanding on the part of Living Faith. As soon as the NGO had been made aware of this through the complaints of the residents, those residents were informed not only that receipts were not required, but that purchases made with the grant money did not need to be confined to food. Many of my informants repeated similar stories, and some of them, even in the second round of the programme, were still holding on to receipts with the expectation they would be required to present them.

The second example I present looks at the way certain individuals were seen as potentially representational of the larger collective of Korogocho. Let us return to Caroline, a community worker who was particularly well known in the ghetto and who commanded a lot of respect, as well as envy, for her ability to forge and nourish her connections to external patrons and donors. She had gathered an expert knowledge over years of engagement with charities and the government. As one resident once told me, 'All good things, they come through Caroline.' When I had subsequently asked Caroline how she could work on so many different interventions, she had laughed before telling me that she grabs those involved in them at the entrance of the ghetto, before they had the opportunity to visit the Chief. She claimed to have done the same thing to me when I first arrived in Korogocho, assuming I was an NGO worker or donor. These bureaucrats play an important role in looking to represent the people of Korogocho and to make claims on the charitable economy – something that anthropologists have observed in other parts of the world (Elyachar 2006; Welker 2012; Whyte et al. 2013; Scherz 2014).

One day, Caroline was invited to attend a national meeting concerned with orphans and vulnerable children, a strategic priority in Kenya since the onset of HIV/AIDS in the late 1990s. She returned to Korogocho excited and invigorated. Almost immediately, she called a meeting of those enrolled in the government's child grant programme in her own 'office' in the centre of Korogocho. At the meeting, I listened as she informed the assembled attendees that a programme evaluation would be taking place and external consultants would be coming to visit Korogocho to see the impact of the grant on people's lives. Recipients were unsurprised; people from the ghetto and outside of it had often asked them to participate in a survey or other forms of research in connection with other programmes. Caroline spent the next few weeks trying to arrange the recipients into small savings groups with one another. Privately to me, she lamented that none had saved any of their grant money. Had the recipients started to do so seven years ago, she thought, they would now have enough to begin some form of income-generating business. Yet, the evaluation never happened. When I asked the District Children's Officer, who had also attended the national meeting, he told me that the meeting had not described any such process. The meeting had been a broad discussion of the situation of orphans in the country. However, unlike the mistake made by Living Faith above, it was entirely understandable that Caroline would assume an evaluation might take place, because evaluations remain an integral part of any form of policy, even the grants. Caroline's belief that she must impart her expert knowledge through a new bureaucratic process is instructive, though. I regularly heard her talk about the need for the poor in Korogocho to be working harder to make their own income. Part of the reason was that she wanted people to become independent from the grant, particularly as she had a strong sense that the grant programme itself was unreliable and would likely end at some point. With her long experience in the charitable economy, she knew the temporal limitations and unreliability of assistance.

But Caroline offered another reason as we spoke, which illuminates a particular aspect of the bureaucratic work I am highlighting. After complaining about the recipients' neglect of saving strategies she quickly followed up with: 'If we do well, you see, more people will be taken onto the programme.' In saying this she made two important shifts. One was from the individual to the collective. The other was from independence to dependency. Or, put another way, the current recipients' independence success became a collective asset for dependency on the grant programme. In conversations with Caroline during my fieldwork, it was clear that she saw herself as an important intermediary in the charitable economy between potential benefactors and the poor of Korogocho, working to build on existing relationships and generate new ones.

This sort of attitude, and the activities Caroline set in motion, bear some resemblance to what Maia Green has described in neighbouring Tanzania as 'anticipatory development', which, she writes, 'refers to the ways in which agents seeking a place in development orders, and associated resource streams, adopt postures premised on the possibility of this emplacement' (2012, 322). Green's emphasis is on what certain actors do to get access to the development apparatus. However, what I am drawing attention to is what certain actors do to ensure the continuation of the relationship between these sorts of apparatuses and their beneficiaries: in other words, what needs to be done to keep charitable resources flowing into Korogocho. Further, and importantly, this involved not just working on oneself, but working on certain people to transform them into the sorts of exemplars that would demonstrate to the gaze of the charitable economy how the community was 'doing well'. In the next section, I take a step back by looking at what it means to make claims in this charitable economy, but then return to this idea of 'doing well' in the section that follows it.

Making Claims in the Charitable Economy

Surveys and other forms of research were a strikingly familiar feature for residents in Korogocho and were directly connected to the charitable economy. For instance, the African Population and Health Research Center also held regular medical camps. One acquaintance, and also a resident, equated research, even my own when I first started fieldwork, to what he had come to identify as a 'baseline survey' – the research conducted by NGOs with which to later determine the extent of the impact of their intervention. This research and activities, such as those initiated by Caroline, were seen by residents and bureaucrats alike as making visible both their suffering and their successes.

James Ferguson has argued that NGOs in Africa, with their assistance and their surveillance of people, look very much like the 'social' of the social welfare states (Ferguson 2010, 168). We have already seen how they imagined another role for themselves through precedent-setting as a way through which they could insert themselves into democratic political processes. However, on the ground in Korogocho, this sense of NGOs as a 'social' of the social welfare states was experienced quite differently again. Lynn, a community health worker, once told me that, 'It's all the NGO', and how, in contrast to the government, NGOs 'reach people', and perhaps envisaged a quasi-state role for the non-government organisations. But the situation is more complicated than that. In Kenya, as in many other African countries, public health, humanitarian, and social interventions have increasingly been delivered through international partnerships involving nation-states, multilateral institutions such as the World Bank, United Nations and WHO, and NGOs (Brown 2015). This has complicated any efforts to make claims for assistance. A story recounted to me several times by community workers during my fieldwork is illustrative. A large gathering of residents, who had not been enrolled in an earlier phase of the urban grant, funded by an NGO but with government involvement, descended one day upon the Chief's Camp. There they chanted *haki yetu* (our rights). The protest, I was told, came from representatives of the eastern-Cushitic population in Korogocho who have felt historically marginalised by the Kenyan state. They also felt that their members had been excluded from the material flows of the charitable economy. Drawing on an increasingly prevalent discourse of rights and justice in Kenya, they demanded their inclusion in the programme as their entitlement on the basis of citizenship. Caroline remembered the event well. She laughed as she recounted the story to me. Echoing the Children's Officer quoted in the previous chapter, she told me: 'It was not about their rights – this is charity.' Here, Caroline rejected their rights-based claim-making approach as fundamentally unsuitable to the charitable economy.

Raymond Williams (1976), in his *Keywords*, argues that the predominant meaning of charity emerged in the twelfth century from a Christian sense of love between man and God, and between men and their neighbours. Over time it became more specific, referring to help to the needy and, by the seventeenth century, also more institutionalised. It has also taken on negative connotations, seen clearly in the common contrast made between charity and rights, the former being voluntary and the latter embodied in legislation (Williams 1976; Bornstein 2012).

Attempts like this to stage protests on the basis of rights and citizenship were not very common in Korogocho, largely because it was not always particularly clear, even if there was government involvement, that it was an appropriate form of claim-making. Instead, the overwhelming experience of residents was to hope and wait for assistance (see also Auyero 2012). As mentioned in the previous chapter, those residents who had managed to secure some assistance, such as selection as a grant recipient, would often put it down to luck or divine intervention. This sense of luck was linked to the reality of what was, to most people in Korogocho, a largely unknowable charitable economy. Moreover, the relationship between residents and the economy was precarious. Residents in Korogocho never knew when assistance might arrive, when it might transform into something else, or when it might leave. It was the same for the two grants. But this did not make the residents of Korogocho powerless. Instead, they attempted to align themselves with bureaucrats, like Caroline, who worked not only to make the residents' suffering and success visible, as we have already seen, but were also the conduit through which the subsequent resources flowed.

Beneficiaries to Bureaucrat

To get a sense of the way that people sought out opportunities in the charitable economy, we can turn to Mary. Midway through my fieldwork, Jude, my research assistant, insisted that I meet her. Weaving through the alleyways, we eventually arrived at Mary's place, a small concrete structure which immediately set her apart from most others. She was a widow, with seven children. The oldest was in prison, but two others were artists, who through their vocation had even managed to travel abroad. One of her daughters ran a hair salon, while the three youngest were still at school. Mary was on the child grant, but she was also well embedded in the wider charitable economy. Even knowing the lingo, she at one point referred to one child as an 'orphan' and another child as 'vulnerable'.

Mary had joined the 'Secure Shelter' movement, a group of 500 people who were saving in order to access a loan through which they could buy land and construct housing. When I met her, she had already secured the land, which was along Mombasa Road, and only needed to save 20 per cent more before she could get a loan to start the house construction.

Mary had also managed to secure other opportunities, however, both in and as a result of the charitable economy. I met her near her house one day as she returned from Living Faith church. There she had been talking to Martin, the social worker whom I had shadowed during the survey process for the urban grant. Mary explained how he had told her of the low price of maize being sold outside of Nairobi, in Limuru Town, and had taken her there one day, introducing her to the traders. The prices, she agreed, were good and she had been able to purchase around four sacks which she then sold within Korogocho. While aligning with patrons is an important form of claim-making in the global health regime, something that has been termed 'clientship' in contrast to 'citizenship', these relationships go beyond material resources and incorporate epistemological and social ones (Whyte et al. 2013).

In the two grants' attempts to eschew bureaucracy, they also risk these sorts of encounters. The idea behind the grants – that the poor are experts – ignores the fact that people very often seek out the expertise of others, who may provide further connections and knowledge, as Martin did for Mary. They also ignore the way that the lines between beneficiary and bureaucracy are blurred. In an interview with Mary, she had told me about her trips to South Africa, and even Canada, as part of her activist work in HIV/AIDS. 'After I went abroad, I came back here to Korogocho, but people thought that after being abroad I would move to Buru Buru or Lavington,' she laughed, as she referred to the two middle-class estates nearby.

> 'What are you gaining apart from going up in a plane?' they asked me as they saw I was still here in Korogocho. But I told them that I am doing it for our people, and I cannot fulfil what took me to Canada if I move away.

As a recipient of the child grant, trips abroad and the support of the social worker, Martin, she was a beneficiary. But as a globe-trotting activist, she was now part of the ghetto-level bureaucracy. At least, people frequently tried to place her in that latter category. She would often, she told me, remind people that she was still a beneficiary, that going to Canada had not made her rich, and she was still in need of support. Her work for 'our people' was not about economic redistribution but about supporting people in other ways, pointing them to where they could get further support, and advising them. It was the same way that Martin was helping her.

The Hard-working Poor and Their Entrepreneurialism

Let us return now to Caroline, the grants, and what I am describing as her effort to re-regulate them. This re-regulation can be understood better by looking more closely at the expectations embodied in grant programmes – that is, the sorts of transformations that the grants are expected to generate. As I have been suggesting, while the grants might offer the poor the freedom to pursue their own sorts of strategies and values, this freedom is not unbound. Indeed, as anthropologists of ethics have argued, freedom can only ever be understood in relation to historically constituted social relationships and discourses (Laidlaw 2013). Yet, I am drawing attention to a more specific instance of this, showing how the attempt to build a relationship characterised by trust required making behaviours visible. In relation to cash grants in Kenya, to understand what behaviours needed to be made visible, we need to look more closely at the idea of work and the informal economy.

One good place to start is a prominent publication titled *Just Give Money to the Poor*, that has drawn attention to grants in the global South (Hanlon et al. 2010). It is important to note that this publication is not simply an academic commentary on the emergence of unconditional cash grants in Kenya and beyond but, as I found out, also part of performing the grants. On several occasions, I saw NGO workers reading the book in cafés, and it was also sold in some of the bookshops frequented by both the Kenyan middle class and expatriates. In the book, the authors extol the virtues of the poor. In one passage they write:

> The poor really are different from the better off. If you give money to a person who is relatively well off, such as one of the writers of this book, he or she is likely to take an extra holiday or buy better wine. The poor, on the other hand, find that the cash encourages them to work harder, because they are no longer caught in the poverty trap and can now see a way out. (Hanlon et al. 2010, 173)

But the grants in Korogocho combined this idea that they encouraged the poor to work hard and escape from their poverty with another one concerning how they would nourish existing forms of care in the household, particularly in regard to nutrition, health, and education. In total, the grants are seen as apparently fostering the poor's existing virtues of working hard, fighting their way out of their own poverty, and caring for the household – the same poor who presumably do not think about leisure. A global constituency of 'the poor' and their now-positive characteristics is constantly reaffirmed in publications like this aimed at a worldwide audience.[3] This brings to mind Jacques Rancière's (2003) critique of philosophers and sociologists who have defined the virtues of those at 'the bottom'. In much philosophy and sociology, he wrote, 'One who is a shoemaker by nature should make shoes and nothing else' (Rancière 2003, 27). Drawing material from nineteenth-century France, Rancière (2012) showed that workers engaged in many other activities, besides those often assumed of them, including writing poetry, letters, and diaries.

But when those behind the creation of, and those connected with the grants emphasised how the poor simply strive to escape poverty or care for those household members in poverty, they stay close to the idea of only shoemaking for those at the bottom. Any wider extra-work activities, such as leisure, are assumed to be undesirable for the poor.

In reality, recipients in Korogocho regularly used the grants for non-work-related activities in order to make their lives in poverty worth living, as I will show in more depth in the final chapter But, as we saw earlier, the particular discourse of hard work remained an important part of ghetto-level bureaucrats' own regulatory work.

The emphasis on the hard-working poor also taps into a quite specific vision of work when it moves to places where formal employment is the exception rather than the norm. This is exemplified by Caroline's attempt to organise the women into savings groups. There she sought to present them to the gaze of the benefactors as exemplars of self-reliance and entre-preneurialism, discourses which are widespread and deeply ingrained in Kenya, as they are elsewhere (Elyachar 2002; Lazar 2004; Rajak 2008). The Kenyan government has long promoted these values, establishing schemes such as the Youth Enterprise Development Fund and the Women Enterprise Fund. At the same time, a number of banks and NGOs have increasingly, since the 1990s, offered microloans to budding entrepreneurs. These schemes have their own history in Kenya, but also join a global social and economic policy which considers that the latent entrepreneur inside every one of the poor might be unleashed only by granting them access to finance (de Soto 2000). They also join a much more long-standing trend towards entrepreneurialism in public life (D. Harvey 1989).

Furthermore, they connect more closely to ideas around dependency that surround the charitable economy, as well as the grants themselves (Fraser and Gordon 1994). For instance, the urban cash grants were designed to support the recipients' consumption in the market, for the formation of caregiving subjectivities. But nearing the end of the eight-month period, when the grants were coming to an end, recipients were taken to a series of workshops where they were instructed to develop business plans. Many of those plans centred around establishing some form of small business that they could sustain in Korogocho, or injecting an existing business with money as a form of investment for the future. After submitting them, and waiting for a number of weeks, some of the recipients received the *pesa ya biashara* (business grant). In contrast, the government's child grant had no similar financial provision for business. 'People are just eating the money,' I was told by disconcerted community workers.

A few miles away in his office in the grounds of the Living Faith church, I sat with Mutuku, the programme manager of the urban grant. Talking about the cash transfer, Mutuku grew animated:

You see, there is a dependency syndrome here, but with adequate knowledge, well, you can do a lot with little resources. One day, I'll have my own NGO, and in fact, I want to register one soon. You see, Tom, you need to recognise people's talents and build upon them. The cash transfer, it's just 10 per cent of the issue, and without education and training, it's rubbish. We need to look ahead and think, 'What will the cash transfer programme look like?' Those in the west, those that are in welfare programmes, they are garbage now. Relief, you see, is easier than development, and this cash transfer programme is relief, but it's not good enough.

In some ways this is reminiscent of Polanyi's reflections on the Speenhamland welfare system in Britain from 1795 (Polanyi 2001 [1944]). He wrote how this welfare system produced people whose self-respect sank to the point where they 'preferred poor relief to wages' (Polanyi 2001, 84). Mutuku was similarly worried about what kinds of people the cash grants would produce. Then, in contrasting 'relief' with 'development', Mutuku mirrored the common distinction between short-term humanitarian solutions and longer-term strategies of development. Neither, he believed, should allow for dependency on aid. His emphasis was on education and training, to prevent dependency and avoid producing persons, who, he argued in strong moral terms, were 'garbage'. Such pronouncements are part of, feed into, and expand, existing fears among Kenyans of a 'culture of dependency' in the country, and, even more so, a dependency on foreign aid.[4]

John, another of my research assistants, a married father of two and resident of Korogocho, was also an urban grant recipient in a programme that was a precursor to the one that was implemented in Korogocho during my fieldwork. He believed that the entrepreneurial discourse reflected a misunderstanding of his needs and those of his fellow slum dwellers. A necessity, he argued, was being disguised or, perhaps more accurately, being misunderstood. As he described it to me once, NGOs tend to observe the multitude of small businesses operating along the roadsides in the ghetto as conclusive evidence of the entrepreneurial proclivities and desires of slum dwellers. Those running small businesses found wage-labour in Nairobi and elsewhere in Kenya rare, uncertain and often unreliable, and thus turned to self-employment in the informal economy as a response. But this was itself uncertain and unreliable. One woman

I knew, herself caring for a malnourished infant, described running a business as like 'having a baby. You never know if it will survive or not.'

Some sort of office work, whether for an NGO or the government, was often most desired, but far out of reach for most people. Construction work was physically demanding, and worse, very unstable. Factory work in the nearby Industrial Area would be steady and pay well, but owners and managers, I was told, often expected payments from applicants in order to secure a position. During my fieldwork, John had bowed to pressure to harness his apparently latent entrepreneurial self, despite little enthusiasm for it, and was working with some of his peers to start their own water standpipe business. He told me often that he would have much preferred help obtaining a steady, reliable job working for someone else. Four years after my fieldwork, John did manage to secure a job, working on commission selling health insurance, but today, exhausted by the insecurities of this precarious employment, he longs for a chance to escape from Kenya where Covid-19 has exacerbated the precarities of an economy that has already offered him so little.

We have already seen how Caroline worked to create exemplars for an evaluation that never happened. But I also noticed during my fieldwork how ghetto-level bureaucrats directed evaluation consultants and other visitors to the same particular individuals within Korogocho who appeared to be running successful businesses. There are two further key points to be made about these exemplars. First, these were exemplars not of the suffering of the poor, but of the success of the poor. Anthropologists have frequently shown how such things as biological vulnerability might form the basis of claims (Petryna 2002; Nguyen 2010), but less often remarked has been how claims might also rely upon the character of the poor. It could be said that philanthropists rely upon communities to give them not just stories of Agamben's (1998) *bios*, but tales concerning their *zoe*. The second point to be made is that the bureaucrats saw these exemplars as tools to help build enduring relationships between benefactors and beneficiaries, not just to contribute to a particular image of the abstract category of the poor. David Neves and Andries du Toit have argued in their study of the informal economy in South Africa that: 'Economic activity is neither understood, nor is its viability judged, simply in relation to the maximization of profit' (Neves and du Toit 2012, 145). Indeed, as anthropologists know too well, a range of values beyond the creation of profit characterises economic life. But we might also consider that certain types of economic activity might be oriented around profit but also cultivated as a way through which to allow other sorts of resources to flow. In Korogocho, Caroline considered a specific form of economic activity to be important, not for profit, but to access the resources of not-for-profits.

Mobility: Allowing for but Hiding Discretion

While the reinstatement of regulation by the ghetto-level bureaucracy in Korogocho associated with the control of recipients or the creation of particular exemplars was perhaps most striking, it was not the only bureaucratic work involved. Also involved was work, as mentioned much earlier in the chapter, to trust the poor, allowing them discretion yet hiding this discretion. This was required because a kind of regulation still lingered around the grants. One prominent discretion concerned residents' strategies of mobility that challenged the spatial assumptions built into the grants.

Unconditional grants sometimes offer new visions around work and welfare. But, as we have seen, they emerge out of and do not always challenge long-standing social relationships, norms, and values around redistribution, such as those within the larger charitable regime out of which the grants emerged. Yet even though Korogocho's bureaucrats have witnessed, been part of and benefited from this flow, many of them remained critical. They viewed the grants as part of a long-standing and perverse situation in which NGOs depend on the maintenance rather than the elimination of poverty in Korogocho. One community health worker, Rose, once told me that NGOs come, take photographs of the poverty, and leave. '*Wanawatumia watu kama daraja*' (literally: 'They are using people like a bridge'), she said. It was the NGOs, she further explained, that depended on the poor of Korogocho. In turn, the residents of Korogocho devised strategies to tap the pipes of assistance that were precariously attached to the ghetto. Stories abounded among the ghetto's bureaucrats of people attempting to convince them that they resided in Korogocho and that they were suitably impoverished; one story had a woman attempting to convince a bureaucrat that an outdoor *choo* (toilet), which was the norm for the rented shacks in the ghetto, was actually her home. The poor, it appeared to the poor and their bureaucrats, were required not only to be impoverished but to be rooted in places that many of them believed to be a major factor in the continuation of their poverty.

The grants in Korogocho had, for a long time, relied upon these existing spatial-oriented assumptions in their regulations. To legitimately receive a grant, one had to be a resident of the local area. But bureaucrats looked for ways around this. It did not escape Caroline's knowledge that many of the child grant recipients had moved out of Korogocho, returning every few months only to pick up their payments. Others arranged for a trusted friend or family member to collect them. One day I stopped by Caroline's 'office' – as I've said before, simply a corrugated metal shack on the ghetto's main artery road. I often popped in on my way somewhere else, but I usually ended up staying longer than I had anticipated, particularly as she was always ready to share the ghetto's latest gossip with me. That day we talked about the child grant recipients, some of whom, she told me, had begun the process of properly establishing themselves in their rural homes. Her eyes lit up as she described, excitedly, how some of these recipients would pay her a visit in her office, pulling out and showing her photographs of the houses they had built in their rural areas. She also confided in me that she encouraged their plans and did not reveal them to her superiors. While those behind the grant expected the money to go to the children in the household, for Caroline, it made sense for the people raising them to establish a permanent presence in the areas, in what she, as we saw earlier in this book, believed to be their proper and legitimate home. This would offer them a place of security – a need they were acutely aware of as a result of the hundreds of thousands of fellow citizens forced from their homes after the post-election violence.

Caroline often urged residents in Korogocho to go back to their rural homes. I saw this once when she became embroiled in an argument with a young man. The argument came about after she had outright refused to include him in the survey, dismissing his claims that Nairobi was his home. Spinning around the logic, she argued that if he could not support himself *here* in Nairobi, and he had not been forced to come because of violence, he should go back to his rural homeland. Turning to me, and using a term common in Kenya as a result of the displacement caused by the recent post-election violence, Caroline had said: 'Are people really IDPs [internally displaced persons] or are they migrants? Are they forced to come here? People here, they shouldn't live here, they should go back to their homes.' Of course, few people had homes in their rural areas to go back to and her statement seemed, at the time, cruel. But it must be remembered that Caroline had been working hard for years among people blighted by the problems of crime and alcoholism in Korogocho and she was, as she once told me, tired of it all. Moreover, the argument with the young man had been good natured and he gave back as good as he got from her.

Although the IDP acronym might have been the one most easily at hand, given its wider public circulation, she tapped into understandings that had longer historical continuities. During the late colonial period, the Voluntarily Unemployed Persons Ordinance, while ultimately impossible to implement, gave power to the police to arrest the unemployed and return them to the native reserves or to find jobs for them. Upon independence, President Jomo Kenyatta urged Kenyans to *rudi mashambani* (return to the farms) as a means to build the nation. Today, suggestions, like Caroline's, that residents return to their rural homes were less about making the national collective and more about maintaining the household one.

It was not only bureaucrats in Korogocho but also higher-level civil servants who shared Caroline's sentiments. They had begun challenging the way in which the child grants, in particular, rooted the poor in Nairobi, by allowing them only to be physically collected at one place where the recipient was registered. Eventually, the challenge by the Kenyan bureaucrats succeeded, and a policy change was implemented that would allow grant payments to be withdrawn from any part of the country. James, a bureaucrat in the secretariat for the child grant, told me that now:

> You can get the cash and then you can move out of Nairobi back to your rural area. The cost of living in Nairobi now is too high and money doesn't go that far, and Nairobi, it's too congested these days.

The challenge had been a hard one to mount because, at the time, debates were raging around placing conditions on the grants. For those in favour of unconditional grants, a broad benefactor gaze was sufficient, yet existing audit cultures asserted themselves, creating a tension that continues today. High-level Kenyan bureaucrats faced these global audit cultures that remained within the charitable regime and challenged them to allow strategies of mobility. While these challenges raged on, ghetto-level bureaucrats like Caroline continued to work to hide mobility from the benefactor gaze and any lingering audit policies that sought to root the poor in a fixed location.

Conclusion

Ghetto-level bureaucrats in Korogocho have for many years been part of the development and humanitarian apparatus. They have carried out a broad range of work involving finding recipients, channelling resources, such as food or medicine, to them, educating them, and monitoring them. But then came the grants, which, as we have seen, advertise themselves as both trusting of the poor and suspicious of regulation and expert knowledge. Joining a broader movement that has been labelled as post-bureaucracy (Heckscher and Donnellon 1994) they also remain connected to a long history of social and humanitarian assistance that has similarly sought to disrupt the form and textures of hierarchy, from recent calls for a Basic Income to earlier ideas proposed by Thomas Paine (2000 [1795]).

The motivation behind this chapter was to address the puzzle of why bureaucrats responded to these attempts by seeking to reintroduce paternalistic regulation. I have argued that they doubled down on what they had already been doing, working as intermediaries to translate between the two broad categories, benefactors and beneficiaries, the expectations and values of each. I have resisted the more conventional interpretations that the reintroduction of regulation was either the mechanical response of bureaucracy, or that the bureaucrats themselves were concerned simply with self-preservation or distinguishing themselves from those they served. I have also diverged from the interpretation that sees bureaucracy and its related practices as a way in which subjects are disciplined and made. Instead, I have argued that the bureaucratic response can be understood as a form of care, particularly in regard to a relationship, that forms what we might see as an ethics of solidarity. This involved attempts to transform, and show the expected transformation, of the gift recipients, while at the same time hiding behaviours and values that might seem antithetical to those expected by the benefactors.

These behaviours by bureaucrats were a response to efforts to transform hierarchies of expert knowledge and bureaucracy. For those behind the grants, a utopian world free of red tape is sometimes imagined, in which people's creative capacity and their ability to flourish is only held back by the twin evils of paternalism and poverty. Yet, red tape might sometimes form into a red carpet, something welcoming rather than entrapping. Similarly, bureaucracy might not need to be thought of as a Weberian iron cage.

Erik Bähre's (2017) recent discussions concerning this are instructive. Through Talcott Parsons, Weber's (2001 [1930]) thesis was that the impersonal rationality brought on by modern capitalism was so extensive that it confined everyone in what he famously – in Talcott Parsons' translation – called an iron cage. Yet, as Bähre argues, drawing on Peter Baehr (2001), a better English translation of the original, *stahlhartes Gehäuse*, is actually something closer to a 'shell as hard as steel'. Bureaucracy, in other words, is not just constraining but protective. In Korogocho, most people surviving in the informal economy had only a precarious relationship to the bureaucracy of the charitable economy. This might be welcomed by those influenced by Parsons' translation of Weber, who see bureaucracy in the form of an iron cage. But if we consider that bureaucracy and its formal rationality may actually be protective, we might be prepared to be a little more cautious. It is possible to see that the activities of the street-level bureaucrats were not only about working on the relationship between the benefactor and beneficiaries, but also about bringing people into their protective shell as a route to the larger, or at least more resourceful one, of the wider charitable economy.

The new efforts to trust the poor with grants posed a problem not only regarding bureaucrats' own livelihood, but also in relation to what they believed to be an existential risk to relationships within the charitable economy, and, we could hazard, the ability of the poor to be enclosed by the protective shell of the bureaucracy of the charitable economy. A form of re-bureaucratisation may then, perhaps, be considered a form of care, a deeply ethical effort in the face of equally ethically-infused attempts to disrupt bureaucratic hierarchies, without disrupting the wider political and economic relationships within which the charitable economy is embedded.

4

Detaching from Others, Surviving with Others

It was late afternoon in Korogocho. I was sitting with my friend and research assistant Jude, in her two-roomed shack, resting after a long, particularly hot and sticky, day of fieldwork. As we talked over the day's events, I brought up a topic that Jude was by then very familiar with me broaching. With the grants offering people money as a way to support the work of care, whether for oneself or for others, as opposed to the more familiar debt-based development, I wanted to continue to explore what this care might look like. On this day, I had been badgering people with questions about the care that took place outside the household, particularly with those neighbours to whom people often lived in such close proximity. I had been pestering Jude for some time with these questions, and she had been as heroic in her patience at hearing them as she had been indefatigable in her attempts to answer them. In what appeared to be a final push to help me understand what many people, I later realised, had already been telling me for some time, Jude said, 'Here, a good neighbour is not one that gives.' Her statement expertly articulated the ethnographic puzzle that forms the basis of this chapter, which moves away from bureaucrats and towards neighbourly, conjugal and what, in Korogocho, people referred to as 'come we stay' or 'come we try' relationships.[1]

Giving, since Mauss (2002 [1925]), has been widely considered by anthropologists as a significant means of establishing and maintaining relationships, including both egalitarian and less than egalitarian ones. But giving is also often seen by anthropologists, as well as their interlocutors, as a morally approved behaviour within these relationships. In some parts of Kenya, for example, people often boast of giving to kin and neighbours who are in need (Shipton 2007, 112). Furthermore, in many documented instances, the refusal to engage in these practices runs the risk of causing resentment and thereby positioning oneself outside social life (Ross 2010, 125). With this in mind, how might we make sense not only of Jude's statement that being a good neighbour is not reliant upon giving, but also of the ways in which her statement pointed to the moral acceptability, even praiseworthiness, of modes of detachment and disengagement in Korogocho?

In the previous chapter, I argued that mistrust among bureaucrats, conventionally seen as something uncaring, can be interpreted differently if we look at it as a part of the way in which relationships are cared for. In this chapter, I continue to travel along this line of thought by arguing that detachment and disengagement between neighbours, and between women and men, in Korogocho should be interpreted as another form of care for relationships that highlight a tentative ethics of solidarity. In other words, detachment can actually be seen as a process of attachment. Furthermore, I show how this ethical practice must be interpreted through a recognition of economic relationships and the distribution of resources within them. By this I mean not only in the sense of the very material everyday forms of support and care that are part of the constitutive relationships, but also in the way that what is considered morally approvable behaviour is formed within the socioeconomic circumstances into which my interlocutors had been forced.

While in the previous chapter I focused specifically on the charitable economy, in this chapter I widen the lens to the broader economies within which my interlocutors were embedded. I particularly consider the ways in which my interlocutors, as first-generation migrants, were precariously and marginally connected to kinship-based, as well as other redistributive flows, and to a state-organised capitalist economy. They were no longer able to take for granted the rights and obligations of existing kinship relationships or new potential arrangements of friendship with others in the ghetto. Yet, crucially, because their very survival as selves depended upon their constitutive relationships, a central ethical task was to care for them. In this chapter, many but not all of the people that feature were grant recipients. However, the grants, as I claimed in the introduction, proved to be an interesting laboratory, in the imaginative sense, which both revealed and facilitated the sort of care that I am exploring. My own concerns and interests around the cash grants drove my questions but, as people drew me into their wider life experiences, they were able to show that these questions often made little sense.

While in this and the previous chapter I consider relationships as things that need to be cared for – and this is at once both ethical and economic – it is in this chapter that I develop much more thoroughly the idea of relational selves. As I argued in the introduction, by relational selves I mean something quite similar to what Jarett Zigon has called 'relational beings'. Rather than counterpose the 'individualized self of Western societies' and the 'relational self of non-Western societies', he argues that *all* humans are 'always beings-in-relationships' (Zigon 2014, 20–21).

Interestingly, Zigon's arguments resonate in some ways with Marshall Sahlins' (2011a, 2011b) influential discussion of kinship. It is today well established, not only in the narrow confines of anthropology but also among people in many different societies, that kinship is not simply a biological but also a social construction. This construction is often made through shared practices such as eating together, living together, working together and so on, becoming what Marshall Sahlins phrased as a 'mutuality of being'. Following Victor Turner, Sahlins understands such a mutuality as a 'participation in one another's existence' (Sahlins 2011a). But just because these shared practices are a distinctive element of kinship does not mean they are not characteristic of other sorts of relationships, such as those my female interlocutors had with people outside their home, including with men and with their neighbours. As for kinship, for Sahlins these relationships are ones in which people not only participate in a variety of aspects of each other's existence, but are indispensable because of that very existence.

In this chapter, I similarly see relationships as integral to people's selves, their moral experience, and even their biological survival. I refer to this amalgam of the aspects of people's lives as *relational selves*. What I aim to show is that these selves were under threat in Korogocho, forcing women to confront this problem in their own unique ways.

Relational Self under Threat

In chapter 1, I introduced Lucy. A singular story, but one that sought to place her in a wider and historically deeper story concerning the production of differentiation and marginality in urban and rural Kenya. But Lucy's is also a story that highlighted an experience that was shared by many of my other interlocutors in Korogocho. While much has been said and discussed of men's experience of marginality in urban Africa, there is still far too little said of the experience of people like the women I knew in Korogocho (but see Ross 2010). From here on, therefore, I draw further on these experiences.

The women I knew in Korogocho were well aware of the fragility of their attachments to their kinfolk, neighbours, and even their customers, colleagues or bosses in the informal market economy. At times these attachments were experienced as an outright sense of exclusion – perhaps, for example, seeing a neighbour crossing the street to avoid bumping into you. At other times these attachments felt to my interlocutors like the wrong kind of attachment, particularly when it felt they had become over-dependent upon someone else, in a place where independence, often expressed as the capacity to hustle and survive on your own, is considered a virtue.

When it came to their encounters with men, many women I knew had had painful, sometimes horrific, experiences with men who were violent and neglectful. Some women had been widowed by HIV/AIDS, others were second wives but with little support from their husband, others were *mpango wa kando* (lit. a side plan – a popular Kenyan Kiswahili term for a lover), and still others were in 'come we try' relationships. Many women I knew struggled to find within themselves the hope of a better, more loving and respectful relationship with a man. Some older women even declared they were no longer interested in having a man around, arguing that they would often prove to be more trouble than it was worth.

Their experiences of struggling on the margins, with the delicate threads that connected them to others constantly at risk of breaking, or frankly, hardly existent in the first place, meant that the women I knew were also enveloped by a sense of uncertainty about the direction of their lives. As one woman once put it to me, 'Here in Korogocho, we don't know where we are going.'

Women's sense of self, their very vital physicality, their personhood, and their hopes for a future were continually threatened when their relationships with others were marked, as they were, by fragility. This fragility around relationships and the threat they pose was, of course, entangled with people's economic circumstances. For some, but certainly not all, women, for example, the very fact that they were forced by circumstance to take responsibility for hustling for whatever they could, struck powerfully at their own visions of themselves as modern, urban mothers. A 'modern mother', a *mama ya kisasa*, in the city should, they believed, leave the hustling, or even better, the stable employment, to the husband, while they assumed responsibility for the home, ensuring children were clothed, fed and the house was looked after.

Their economic precariousness and positionality loomed as an ever-present threat. Rural relatives expected them to return home to their *ushago* (rural home) for Christmas, even if they were landless themselves. But in Korogocho, it was prohibitively expensive to do so. A largely unregulated private bus service in Kenya had seen companies inflate bus fares in the Christmas holiday period to astronomical heights, far out of reach of most of the urban Nairobi poor. Some of my interlocutors had not seen their own parents in years, relying instead on mobile phones and via messages sent through others to keep in touch.

Kin and conjugal relationships were hard to maintain among those in Korogocho who were sometimes referred to, although rarely would identify themselves, as *maskini wa mwisho* (the poorest). The poorest women were not defined simply by income levels but rather by markers such as livelihood or the kind of house they rented. Most of my interlocutors agreed that the poorest women were those who washed clothes for others and who lived in the worst-constructed mud shacks often closest the river.

Wealth, as has long been noted for Africa, also lies in people themselves (Guyer 1993). In other words, the wealthy are those who have accumulated not necessarily material resources, but people, through the strengthening of their relationships with others. I am not convinced, however, that we need to draw on a regionally specific idea of wealth in people to make sense of the fact that for my interlocutors, the poorest were those who lacked key relationships. Most notable were widows, who were treated without *heshima* (respect). Here, one missing key relationship had wider relational ramifications.

I spent a lot of time talking to my interlocutors about the connections between their economic precariousness and the fragility of their relationships with kin and, related to that, of their own selves. Some articulated how their relationships affected them physically and psychologically. Take Mama Mugi, who once told me falteringly about her own life before she had begun receiving a grant:

> You didn't see me earlier, I was thin like a dog. I was very stressed, when I think that I have a husband, that is stress, the children were also stressful. Then I think about my people, they already abandoned me because I don't have anything. When I put all that together, I should be in a hole now.

Here, 'my people' referred to her kin, and Mama Mugi's experience was similar to that of so many others I knew in Korogocho. Relationships with kin faltered under the weight of poverty. One woman I knew complained to me about how her brother, living in another part of Nairobi, would no longer see her, and would instead hide in his house when she visited. 'He thinks that when I come to see him I am coming to ask for something', she explained to me. It was a form of what Sisel Kusimba has called 'strategic ignorance' in Kenya, in which people deliberately try to avoid knowing much about a person in need (Kusimba 2021, 117). In Mama Mugi's case, an expectation of her own dependency was fraying the already fragile threads that connected her with her brother.

Detachment and the Care for Relationships

In Korogocho, with kin often physically far away or no longer able to be depended upon and men unreliable, a woman depended upon relationships with neighbours and friends for love, companionship, as well as physical survival (see also Hart 1988). While many of these relationships were with those from the same ethnic group, others were often not. With existing rights and obligations of those ethnic groups under jeopardy, women's own selves necessitated new ways of relating. One form of relating was termed, in Korogocho, *kuzoeana* (lit. to be accustomed to one another), and brought into their relational matrix connections with neighbours and others. It was by attending to these relationships that the individual survived. Those who sought to form such relationships would often provide each other with encouragement and emotional support. At times they might incorporate something more material, such as responding to a particularly pressing need to pay school fees. The relationship might involve other sorts of practical support: taking a child to the clinic, letting someone know of a job or business opportunity, or even guiding someone to assistance offered by the government or an NGO. Furthermore, with people's kin often far away, to be accustomed to another might allow for some care in the event of an illness.

While this form of relating was important, what was especially interesting was the prominence of warnings of the danger of giving and expressions of the desire to seek even more separation from others. This is not to say that people did not want to help another in need. However, these, and the related practices of detachment, were, I am arguing, part of caring for the relationships that constituted the self. In other words, efforts to repair relationships, including with kin, and to form new ones, were part of efforts to repair and remake the self. It was these sorts of expressions, and related acts, of detachment that might be seen as uncaring but which I see as deeply imbricated in the care for relationships. That is, what might be seen as uncaring or even selfish acts from the perspective of another person, even the anthropologist, can be seen as caring ones when considered from the perspective of the relationship that joins two persons together. Care, then, is directed not towards other *persons* but rather towards the *relationships* between these persons.

Anthropologists interested in ethics and morality have recognised that the ethical domain cannot be divorced from social relationships: for example, the way that we routinely hold others to account. However, I believe that we can go further by examining how those relationships might be the explicit object of people's ethical practices. Because of the importance of relationships, my interlocutors were only too aware of the need not to take them for granted. They were fragile and had been gently cultivated over long periods. Acts of giving and receiving in such a context were never undertaken lightly, with parties attempting to work out exactly the strength and the limits of each relationship. There were no certainties and these fragile relationships had to be treated carefully. To be clear, this work of caring for relationships should not be understood as the building of 'social capital', as if there can be a coherent self isolated from its relationships. Instead, the self – including its physicality, its spirituality, and its deeply ethical nature – is damaged and can dissolve when its constitutive relationships have deteriorated.

Anthropologists have in recent years been drawn to the concept of care, but as Clara Han (2012) has argued, we may need to be careful about how we approach it. Drawing on her research among poor Chileans, she has argued that attempts to counter ideas of the atomised individual with those of care, love, and interdependency run the risk of ignoring the boundaries and uncertainties around relationships, as well as the problems people face of being separate (Han 2012, 28). However, I suggest that we do not need to assume that separateness is necessarily a problem. Indeed, my own informants were hardly condemning of it. But there is no reason to fall into the trap of counterposing atomised individuals with those who are caring and interdependent. Rupert Stasch (2009) has made a related argument. He has challenged the idea that the strongest social bonds need necessarily be based upon 'identification and shared face-to-face experience' (2009, 2). Even close relatives among the Korowai of West

Papua relate by constantly seeking to separate themselves from others, for example, by 'keeping their bodies, articles, and food apart' (2009, 58). In Korogocho too, people tried to keep themselves apart from others in particular ways. As I have already noted, detachment in Korogocho can be understood not as a mode of relationality but as an ethical act of care towards a relationship – part of the formation and maintenance of broader solidarities. Through separating in regard to certain dimensions of their relationships, my interlocutors sought to strengthen these affiliations by reducing the burdens that coalesce around them.

Central to the desire for detachment was personal autarky, a concept which in Korogocho has a strong morally positive valuation. For women themselves, it was understood that this self-sufficiency was about not being overly dependent upon others and about having one's 'own plans'. In this they extinguished any simplistic depiction of African collectivism. Indeed, anthropologists of Africa have, for some time, similarly highlighted the importance of individuality (Lienhardt 1989), modes of strategising (Guyer 2004, 25), and economic separateness (Englund 1999). Common to these anthropological contributions has been the recognition of the moral legitimacy among very many different people in Africa to pursue economic gain and to retain an element of separateness from others.[2]

Many in Korogocho, men and women alike, saw some sort of business as a desirable route to personal autarky. As I have explained earlier, permanent wage-labour was often out of reach, and rarely compatible with important domestic and childcare responsibilities. People would often judge themselves and others they knew in relation to the highly visible successful entrepreneurs in the ghetto.[3] During a casual chat I was having about business one day with one woman who prepared and sold food along Korogocho's main artery road, she gestured to the other side of the road at another food stall. She explained the success of that rival stall, which had allowed its owners to purchase their own *matatu*. While she speculated that malign powers may have aided their route to prosperity, she nonetheless made clear that she held their entrepreneurial capacities in high esteem.

Others I knew who were receiving a monthly cash grant attempted to use them to initiate or expand a business. Similarly, during fieldwork, I was regularly approached for assistance, but this was always accompanied by a narrative, spoken or written, of how the money would be transformed through a small-scale business. In Korogocho such endeavours were desirable partly because they provided freedom from a dependence upon ultimately undependable bosses. This is not to say, of course, that businesses did not require their own interpersonal relations for success, but these were qualitatively distinct.

Bounding Generosity and Being Separate

As well as seeking to be economically self-sufficient in regard to income, women would refrain from asking others for help, and thereby retain an element of economic separateness. Let us return to Lucy. As we have already learned, she came perilously close to death after contracting HIV/AIDS. As she told me, 'the disease had multiplied' in her body, leading her to contract tuberculosis. So convinced was she of the proximity of her own death that she had telephoned her parents to ask them to take her children. She was worried that after she passed away they would become street children, referred to in Nairobi, as I have said, as *chokora*.

Lucy described to me the pain of seeing her children carrying and eating rotten *ugali* (Kenya's staple stiff maize porridge). But when one day I asked about how her neighbours or other friends might have helped her, she told me: 'Here people in Korogocho are behind ... it's not like in the States where somebody can check for another. Even your children they can't go and eat at the neighbours.' It is better, Lucy told me, to go to sleep with hungry children than it is to request food from a neighbour. This contrasts with reports from some rural areas in Africa, for example among the Luo in Western Kenya, where, according to Parker Shipton, food exchanges are said to 'bind neighbours together' (2007, 111), although it is much closer to what others have reported in urban areas (Ross 2010). In Korogocho, Lucy explained, hunger will pass, and the next day will hopefully bring an opportunity to earn some money to eat again.

Lucy was not alone in worrying about dependence. I was once offered a Kiswahili proverb, *Akufukuzaye hakwambii toka*, which translates literally as: 'The one who chases you away does not tell you to leave.' It means, he explained, that a guest should not wait to be asked to leave but should recognise the signs that indicate they might be outstaying their welcome. But while this proverb instructs others about the limits of hospitality and generosity, another phrase, more integral to everyday life in Korogocho, worked to discourage it from the outset. As I mentioned before, as a response to requests for assistance, people would often ask, 'Why should I help you? I didn't ask you to Nairobi.' Nairobi was widely considered not to be a legitimate home, particularly for those who had not been able to achieve the necessary social and economic resources to survive independently.

That there was a conventional response to requests for assistance demonstrates a sense in which obligations between kin or others, while strained and always at breaking point, still remained, at least as an ideal. Indeed, the patron position was considered to be one particular ideal. A young mother of two, Bina, once explained this to me like this:

> I have no friends. I don't get visitors because I am poor, even if I cook something and take it to them, they cannot eat. It's not just unique to me, but others like me. Since I moved here, nobody has come to visit me. If you have money, you have a lot of friends … you see, money brings a family. I have been sitting here the whole day and nobody has knocked on the door. If I had money and was a well-known person, people would be knocking at my door asking for help.

Bina had reversed what I see as a more conventional or intuitive understanding of kin-based redistribution, by showing that it is not simply kin that should assist with material resources, but that it is only by accumulating these resources that one may even have kin. Without these resources, there are no kin. But Bina was at pains to make clear that receiving a grant did not transform her into a wealthy person. Indeed, she saw it as precisely a sign of her poverty. Others I knew took a different view by hiding the grant from others, including kin, in order to head off the implications of wealth and its obligatory consequences around redistribution. This was the flip side of Sibel Kusimba's aforementioned idea of 'strategic ignorance'.[4] In Korogocho, the poor often tried to avoid other people potentially in need of finding out about their own apparent wealth. If the ideal of the wealthy benefactor remained important, the immediate and practical task was often to avoid such a status, lest one was expected to redistribute what few economic resources one had. For there is little chance of reaching the ideal of being a wealthy person if one is seen, erroneously, as already being wealthy. Thus, for women in Korogocho, it was accumulation, not giving, that was considered essential to a journey in which one becomes a wealthy benefactor, and might then be brought more fully into the intimate social fabric of the slum.

There were some women who found that their economic situation had dramatically improved and who could not hide it. But while they recognised the importance of giving, they also understood its limits. This was articulated well by Ida, a woman who had managed to develop a thriving *duka* (small convenience shop). Her change of fortune came after many years of struggling to both educate and feed her children. Sitting in her *duka*, she once spoke to me about the difficulties of becoming successful when previously having been seen in a state of deprivation. The morally correct behaviour in these situations could be explained as: 'As you go up, don't show off and give a helping hand if you can.' Yet at the time, as soon as she told me this, she qualified her statement with, 'But it's not just about giving, it's the way you communicate with people still, the way you are with people.' Ida was indicating that giving was not necessarily how interdependencies were maintained. The 'way you are with people', she went on to explain, involved stopping by and speaking with them, listening to their concerns and offering advice.

While Ida suggested that giving was not necessarily a mark of good neighbourliness, Jude, in the conversation I pick up from the beginning of this chapter, suggested that it could actually be detrimental to it. Despite only having a primary level of education, Jude had been successful in securing various short-term contracts with NGOs as a community health worker within Korogocho, as part of what I have previously called the ghetto-level bureaucracy. Because of my interest in the new grants that had arrived in Korogocho, I had become interested in the flows, blockages, transformation of money. While Jude had humoured me for some time in my quest to understand this movement of money outside the market, her statement that a good neighbour is not defined by his or her munificence challenged my assumption that neighbourliness, even in the city, would require one to give to others. Fiona Ross has written about care and support among the urban poor in South Africa, arguing that 'Friendships cannot easily withstand the anger and resentment that result when expected help is not forthcoming' (Ross 2010, 125). She argues that this leads people to become wary about asking for help. But what Jude pointed out to me was a little different. After telling me that a good neighbour is not one who gives, she further explained why:

If you give all the time to that mama in your plot, then she is always expecting you to give to her. So, after some time, you maybe want something back, and then she starts quarrelling with you. No that's not good. What happens some time when you need her?

This, I believe, runs counter to some of the more familiar narratives in anthropology that concern the limiting not of generosity but of acquisitiveness. For example, Jonathan Parry and Maurice Bloch (1989) posited two transactional orders, one short-term, based around acquisitiveness, and with the money often associated with it, and the other long-term, concerned with the reproduction of the social and cosmic order. Parry and Bloch argued that the former was mostly morally subordinated to the latter. Other anthropologists have followed by highlighting how acquisitiveness is often kept within certain bounds lest it come to damage the long-term order which is seen to be based on the value of relationality and the virtues of generosity (for example Elyachar 2005). However, less appreciation in social scientific thought seems to have been given to how generosity, too, may need to be bounded.

In Korogocho, giving, in normal circumstances, seemed to obligate reciprocity. But too much giving led to an imbalance which carried with it a threat that it might never be returned. In this way, the danger was that the relationship might move to one of hierarchy, which, as David Graeber (2011) argued, has a logic in opposition to reciprocity, although, of course, not necessarily in contradistinction to the Maussian idea of gifts, which I will return to. Graeber suggested that giving in these types of relationships does not result in the obligation to reciprocate, but rather sets a precedent for the giving to continue flowing in the same direction. He writes: 'The moment we recognise someone as a different sort of person, either above or below us, then ordinary rules of reciprocity become modified or are set aside' (2011, 111). In Korogocho, the threat that one, or others, might become that different sort of person existed in a context in which one had to be extremely attentive and responsive to the dangers of dependency. Another common reply to those asking for assistance from another person was: 'You don't have, I also don't have.' In effect, it worked to reassert their common social and economic positionality on the margins of Kenyan society. Giving, then, according to Jude, was not indexical of good neighbourliness. In fact, it was worse than this. It could even be detrimental to good neighbourly relations because it encouraged what might become an ultimately unsustainable dependency. Potential interdependency ran the risk of being transformed into real dependency.

Again, to be clear, the issue for my interlocutors was not that dependency or assisting each other was considered beyond the bounds of morality. Far from it. The dependency of children upon their parents, for example, is the most obvious example of an acceptable form of such relationality.

Furthermore, as we saw earlier with Bina, being a well-known person with money who could distribute it to those in need, and thus transform into a patron figure, was considered an ideal. Similarly, as I mentioned earlier, everyday forms of caring for each other and each other's family, such as sharing childcare burdens, ferrying others to the clinic or hospital, and so on, were as omnipresent as they were incontrovertible. Yet they existed alongside an imperative not to care in a way that might risk the production of dependency. In Korogocho, dependency posed dangers to relationships that were considered integral to survival. It was not that people wanted to escape relationships; rather, they wanted to avoid a particular aspect of the relationship that might eventually risk its own destruction. Therefore, as Jude argued, this form of support could only be sustained through a willingness to refuse a mutuality in the domains that anthropologists usually consider important in sustaining relationships.

Relationality and Reputation

An unreciprocated gift, as Jude told me, can lead to quarrelling between persons. But quarrels were significant beyond the quarrelling partners. They generated *mjadala* (literally, a discussion, but meaning gossip). In the conversation I had with Lucy, she had explained how frequent attempts to ask neighbours for food would result in *mjadala*, and eventually, in Lucy's words, make them 'despise you'. The problems that this would generate were considered far riskier than those which might emerge from not giving. I was once reprimanded by an Elder when I mistakenly downplayed the significance of gossip in the ghetto. 'Talk is not cheap here in Korogocho', he had told me sternly.

Lucy also articulated this for me. Despite her ill health and looking after her children alone, she had managed to secure a livelihood, albeit a precarious one, on the roadside for her chicken offal business. She had been having problems securing a place along the roadside and had had disagreements with the shops that sat behind where she set up her stall. I asked her if she was losing money, but she brushed off the question by saying, 'Ah ah, you don't lose money, it's your *sifa*' (reputation). After asking her what she meant, she replied: 'That will give you a bad name. So for you to avoid those things. No one will help you, if you have a bad name, something terrible will happen to you. Who will take action if you are quarrelling? The one who is always quarrelling on the road?'

Her point resonates with that made by Jude about the danger of quarrelling. By affecting one's reputation, the impact of quarrelling went beyond a particular relationship and incorporated still unknown others who potentially could come to one's aid in a time of need. Furthermore, we can see here how the economic domain of the market is closely intertwined with issues of care and mutual aid: while customers might not come to one's aid in times of need, others around might.

At another point, Lucy and I had discussed giving credit to customers. She explained to me that she rarely offers this, and when she does it is only to friends whom she has known for a long time and whom she deems trustworthy. Lucy invoked the term *kuzoeana*, which as I have said means to be accustomed to one another. However, these sorts of relationships take time, and in Korogocho, in order to make any sort of profit, traders must rely extensively on those whom they do not know. The risk for Lucy was not that these customers might disappear. Instead, it was that the relationship would cease to be one based upon the expectations of exchange and pass to one of unreciprocated debt. She explained to me how offering credit would always run the risk of non-repayment, and how one would spend much of one's time quarrelling with debtors as they passed.

It is clear that debt and credit relations, based on long-standing relationships, do exist, as Lucy noted. But it is important not to conflate their existence with their importance. Such relationships would be entered into with trepidation, for fear that they would cause public conflict, and again affect one's reputation. Indeed, it was only through the absence of quarrelling and because of one's public reputation that one became visible to others as somebody worth knowing. Nobody goes near those who quarrel, I was often reminded in Korogocho. In this way, traders like Lucy often worked to avoid economic relationships based on credit and debt because of the risk that such an entanglement might lead to the damaging of their own relational selfhood.

A Gift that Detaches

I have so far examined how, in Korogocho, there was a reluctance – although not to be mistaken for a refusal – to give to others and to ask from others. I have suggested that this reluctance was not because people did not want to form relationships with others, but precisely because they did. I finish this chapter by returning to the anthropological mainstay of gifts to explore a case involving a conjugal relationship, in which giving did attempt to maintain a relationship, but only via a process of detachment. In this way I propose that there may be a non-Maussian form of gift, in which reciprocation is not expected, or indeed obligated, but which still attempts to maintain relationships.

I met Joy early in my fieldwork. She lived in a one-roomed shack with her six children. Her possessions were few: a thin mattress, a small table, a broken wooden bench and a stool. She had previously been married, but her husband, who had been born out of wedlock, had left her with no land up-country in Nyanza, Western Kenya, when he died. When I knew her, Joy had what she termed a male 'friend', a man married to another woman but who visited Joy periodically before returning to his wife. She was acutely aware of the perils of unduly pressuring this friend for money. Considering he was already married, she worried that he might easily abandon her. Joy was, like Lucy, a self-proclaimed and proud businesswoman, selling various foodstuffs on the roadside and innovating where she could in order to gain an upper hand in the fierce competition which characterised trade in Korogocho.[5]

As mentioned, many women I knew in Korogocho held an idealised image of urban life as shaped around the differing male and female roles; the male being responsible for income and the female for the domestic realm. The reality, people were quick to realise once they arrived, was far different as both men and women now needed to earn some kind of income. Once, Joy had spoken to me about a couple, a woman married to a pastor, whom she thought had become stable and close (she used the phrase, *hapa kwa hapa*, a popular one among young Kenyans). This relationship, Joy believed, had emerged after the woman had begun a charcoal-selling business. She was apparently now valued because of the income she brought into the household. Joy used the couple as an example of the sort of relationship she would like for herself. However, as it stood, her domestic situation was quite different. Some men in Korogocho, including Joy's own friend, were worried about their partners conducting businesses on the roadside. In particular, they were threatened by the opportunities it offered their partners to expand their field of sociality that might incorporate other men. The road as a space for relational growth was for many people, as we will see in the next chapter, a constant source of anxiety.

Joy worked along the main road, sitting on a small stool with her products laid out on a small piece of cloth. She described to me one day how her male friend would sit near to watch her, keeping an eye on her male customers as she worked. She despaired at this surveillance. Occasionally, he would wander over to her stall and argue with male customers he deemed were spending a disproportionate amount of time with her. This had the effect of frightening away these customers, thus hindering the immediate transaction as well as any potential future ones. Joy received a business grant from an NGO at the end of the urban grant programme, which, as already mentioned, was designed to 'graduate' her out of poverty. Because her male friend had previously trained as a tailor, she decided to allocate some of the grant towards purchasing a sewing machine, which she then gifted him. She told me:

> I invested the money in business and I even bought him a sewing machine, cloth materials, everything; and we began working from our house. I was shocked one day to discover he has taken the sewing machine and all the business stuff and sold them. I had been avoiding to buy anything for the house myself until I was well established in business so that as my business grows I buy items slowly by slowly. Before I knew what was happening the money was gone. The sewing machine was sold and I never saw a cent from the materials.

Because I felt a sense of loyalty to Joy, and also because Joy's male friend was rarely around when I was with her, I only spoke to him once, and then only briefly about other matters. My aim, though, is not to attempt to grasp all the perspectives in play in what was a complex and fraught situation, but instead to understand Joy's own intentions. My argument here entails an admittedly rather unusual interpretation of gift-giving. Gifts are often seen either in the Maussian form (Mauss 2002 [1925]), as an exchange which maintains relationships, whether egalitarian or more hierarchical, or as free, in which the aim is to create no relationship (Laidlaw 2000). The sewing machine, however, I suggest, was a free gift which worked to create distance between two persons in order to maintain the relationship. In accordance with my overarching argument, Joy, like others in Korogocho, was looking to reduce the burdens of a relationship to allow that relationship to endure.

The specificity of the object being exchanged has always been crucial to making sense of ceremonial gift exchange, whether blankets in potlatch, mwali (shell armbands) or soulava (shell necklaces) in kula, or pigs in moka. In the more intimate domain of the home, the sharing of food has often been felt to be paradigmatic for the making of kin (see for example

Carsten 1995). In Korogocho, women regularly prepare meals for their male partners, often using their own resources to procure the food. However, in the preceding case with Joy and the sewing machine, a gift from a humanitarian NGO was transformed into a very different sort of gift: a gift that aimed to produce detachment. The importance of the sewing machine for Joy was that it embodied the potential for a form of detachment. It was not simply an object that would generate income and thus ease the anxieties within the household. If that was the case, then Joy could well have kept the sewing machine for herself, or invested all her money in her own business. While Joy says that they began working together, her main aim, she told me, was to allow her friend his own independent business so that she could actually continue hers on the roadside. There, as she noted, her friend was too close to her, straining the potential relationships which were necessary to her own business success. Seen in this way, the giving of a gift was not a simply direct way of maintaining a relationship but was rather an attempt by Joy to detach herself from a particular burdensome aspect of her relationship with her friend to allow their continued attachment. Joy never articulated to me exactly how she imagined her relationship would eventually turn out, but there is no reason to exclude the possibility that it might entail a form of dependency or interdependency. However, the pressing issue for her was about ensuring that the threads of their relationship remained intact, and to allow for this possibility a level of personal autarky and detachment was required.

Conclusion

It is often tempting for anthropologists, when studying development or humanitarianism, to point out that in the midst of these efforts to improve and save lives, those lives already have their own unique, and different, histories, trajectories and dynamics. As important as it is to highlight this, it should also be recognised that it is not a move made only by anthropologists or allied disciplines but also by policy makers and practitioners. The two cash grants studied in this book were an exemplary embodiment of such a move, yet they sought to not just highlight but to allow, even facilitate, the activities and particularities of people's lives.

I believe that some of our received ideas concerning mutuality in anthropology are unsuited to capturing certain, but of course not all, dimensions of my interlocutors' caring lives. This is because the focus of theorising sometimes is on a comparison between 'them' and 'us', rather than on the differences within these categories. For instance, the persistence of a redistributive kinship system in contrast to a state-centred one. Or the importance of an urban informal market-based economy in contradistinction to a formal one. Such a form of comparison seems to have much less applicability for my interlocutors, raising their children either alone or with limited support from male partners, who existed on the margins of both such forms of redistribution and production. Therefore, what we need to understand is how kinship, or for that matter, neighbourliness, or the informal economy, is experienced differently. On the margins of both, my interlocutors worried they were, or might become, a burden on others around them – but, at the same time, they were concerned that others would continue to be, or threaten to become, a burden on them.

This resulted, as I have explored, in desires and practices to detach, in particular ways, from others. While both refusing to give and giving in a non-Maussian form can be considered as types of detachment, the central argument of this chapter has been that these forms of detachment can be productively studied ways in which relationships are created and maintained. This is not the opposite but a form of solidarity.

It does seem to be the case that much less attention has been placed on the forms of detachment and distancing that I have examined in this chapter which are integral to the continued existence of these constitutive relationships. A notable exception is Rupert Stasch's (2009) work, which has shown how bringing people together can also mean keeping them apart in other ways. While my findings have similarly challenged this opposition between detachment and attachment, I have found it particularly productive to consider detachment as an ethical practice of the self. Joining Zigon (2014), as well as echoing certain approaches within moral philosophy (e.g. Held 2006), my starting theoretical position that selves are constituted by their relationships has led me to consider the ethical care for those relationships.

Furthermore, I have sought to show how dimensions of relationships interact. While Jonathan Mair (2015) has argued that actual relationships consist of ongoing efforts to manage distance and proximity in their different dimensions, I have argued that distancing in certain ways can mean being closer in others. For example, the refusal to give to others was precisely practised to achieve a certain form of proximity to those same others, which was essential for the survival of the self. Moreover, I have tried to convey how this careful work directed towards relationships cannot be easily traced back to some sort of coherent cultural order, whether associated with kinship or associated with the capitalist market economy. Instead, my (mainly female) interlocutors laboured to piece together some form of coherent self while living on the margins of both. The detachment I have explored showed the ways in which women cared for their existing relationships and looked for others that were nascent, allowing for the self to emerge, tentatively, amidst the precariousness of everyday life.

5

A Mother's Care

Every other Wednesday, mothers with their children clasped to their backs, would make their way through Korogocho's alleyways and tarmacked roads to reach Grogan neighbourhood. A few more minutes' walk would bring them to the blue-painted steel gates that separated Provide Health Centre and its pleasant grassy compound from the surrounding neighbourhood. Within the gates, volunteer community health workers and health centre staff moved around quietly, registering patients, putting children in weighing harnesses and recording their weights, weighing out flour, and counting out packets of Plumpy'nut, a ready-to-use therapeutic food. The World Food Programme-funded nutrition clinic not only offered mothers respite from the hubbub of Korogocho; it also held the possibility for survival for the malnourished children it treated amidst the quiet violence of urban hunger.

It was during one of these clinics that I first met Mama Joseph and her 4-year-old daughter, Faith, who had made the 10-minute journey from their corrugated-iron shack in Highridge. Mama Joseph and her children were known to governmental and non-governmental agencies. Their names, ages, weights and other vital statistics, were in a range of databases. The family was therefore enlisted in their politics of counting and measuring suffering. But such counting does not get us very close to actually understanding how the family experienced hunger, nor how hunger was not the only problem they faced.[1]

After that first encounter with Mama Joseph, she had invited me to her home, and I had since visited the family a few times. Mama Joseph lived with Faith and her four other children together with her husband, Godfrey, on a plot adjoining the one he had been born and brought up on, and where his mother still lived. Mama Joseph had joined Godfrey, and her mother-in-law in Korogocho in the late 1990s, relocating from Muranga, an area just under 100 kilometres north of Nairobi, looking for work. Godfrey was a travelling knife sharpener: one among those who can be seen dotted about the streets of Nairobi, sat atop their ingeniously modified bicycles – the bicycle's rear wheels elevated from the ground by a kickstand and connected via an auxiliary bike-chain to a spinning grindstone. Godfrey was often away from home working most of the day, but since he sustained injuries in the violence following the 2007 presidential elections, he had struggled to match the intensity at which he had worked previously; such work, pedalling relentlessly – not to mention cycling between customers – is strenuous.

Mama Joseph was taking Faith to the World Food Programme-funded clinic in the hope that it would address both Faith's acute malnutrition and a severe case of rickets, caused by vitamin D deficiency. Faith's physical condition was obvious upon seeing her, but was even starker when I met her twin brother Paul. I found it hard to believe that they were the same age. Whenever I was at their home, Mama Joseph would often look on chuckling as Paul ran around giggling, mischievously grabbing my hand or hiding behind furniture. Faith, in contrast, was unable to stand. Her legs were bowed, and, when I first knew her, she did not have the strength to sit up on her own.

Rickets is a serious but, lamentably, not a rare health issue in Nairobi's slums. One principal cause of the condition is a lack of exposure to sunlight. The ghetto's shacks are generally dark places. The decades of governmental neglect in providing or facilitating decent housing conditions for the urban poor that I have attempted to articulate, has left them at the mercy of landlords who have built, in the cheapest possible way, shacks that could barely be closer to one another. Any sunlight that does succeed in reaching inside does so only through the door opening – of course, only when the door is open – in slivers that make their way through cracks in the poorly constructed mud or corrugated walls, or in tiny quasi-window spaces.

In Korogocho, mothers told me, very young children are sometimes left alone during the day inside the shacks, the doors usually locked. In order to scrape together a semblance of an income, parents often must travel for work within the ghetto or to other parts of the city, and when they do, some reason that it is safer that their children are kept inside. If parents can afford daycare for their children, it is more often than not inside another shack, giving little chance for the children to be exposed to sunlight. Living in precarious economic circumstances, Mama Joseph had, in the past, few opportunities to earn an income and had travelled to town to beg, which had meant leaving her children at home when no alternative childcare was available. As I have mentioned, her husband Godfrey was also out all day hustling, as Kenyans often call it, for customers. He was only able to earn around KSh150 (£1.02) per day for his knife-sharpening work, which compounded the family's problems, preventing them from eating enough or buying the nutrient-rich foods that young children most need. Mama Joseph had once reeled off to me the list of food she had been advised by health workers to feed Faith, including *omena* fish,[2] green vegetables, chicken or cow's liver, avocado, and passion fruit. 'We can't afford to feed one child all of those sorts of foods,' she had told me dejectedly.

Faith was receiving Plumpy'nut from the nutrition clinic, but this only addressed the wasting of her delicate body. There was nothing in the programme to address the rickets itself, apart from the recommendation for her parents to give her access to sunlight as much as possible. But when Mama Joseph tried this, she once told me, neighbours would taunt her, asking why she was so fat when her child was so thin.

The last time Faith was given medication for the condition was many months before that day in the clinic when I first met her. It was on that same day that Mama Joseph became an urban grant recipient, in a grant programme that was a precursor to the one that I explored during the time of my fieldwork in Korogocho.

Careful Triage

In the previous chapter, I explored care as it pertained to relationships between adults, particularly between women and their neighbours and husbands and lovers. In this final chapter, I turn inwards, into the household, to look at a mother's work of care both within and for its constitutive relationships. Here also is an ethics of solidarity. As I have tried to show throughout this book, many households in Korogocho lived precarious lives, frequently skirting the very thresholds of survival, and on the margins of the ghetto's sociality, wider networks of kinship, and the informal, market economy. Mothers, even children, would sometimes go to sleep hungry, particularly during the period in which I did fieldwork, which was a time when the food crisis affecting the Horn of Africa in 2011, and the lack of any food price controls, had pushed food prices in Nairobi to dramatically high levels. The rising cost of living also meant that it was not uncommon to be unable to pay for life-saving drugs or to delay attending a health centre or hospital. As women I knew in Korogocho would often tell me, life in the ghetto was a distinctly day-to-day affair that involved piecing together what work was available and at hand, while living with an almost continual threat of violence both inside and outside their compounds.

In the first section of this chapter, I turn to a critical event in which Mama Joseph fought to save Faith's life. This event, however, turned out to reveal something even greater than a singular life. Through the rest of the chapter, I explore some of the ways in which mothers in Korogocho sought to keep themselves, their children, and the relational unit of the family alive into a future that was as imagined and hoped for as it was indeterminate. It is this sense of individual and familial, relational futures that I explore in this chapter, as I connect Mama Joseph's experience with those of other mothers I spent time with. Drawing from literature concerning suffering and hunger as well as literature that concerns kinship and morality, I pay close attention to the ways in which mothers in the midst of uncertainty attended to the existence and quality of their intimate relationships by making often disquieting decisions, which I call careful triage, that revolve around care in and for the family. As in the previous chapter, these also, I show, involve gestures of detachment and distancing as mothers seek to maintain the nuclearity of the family. But they also embody a sort of hopeful care, not only in keeping a family together but also around the bonds that connect them into the future. Engaging with the idea of filial piety, via the anthropologist Meyer Fortes (1949, 1961) I argue that while the cash grants, particularly the eight-month-long urban one, exhibited only a short-term horizon, mothers had to live in the now, the day-to-day, while creatively imagining and retaining hope for a future life for themselves, and for the very obligations that were seen as tying them together with their children.

A Critical Event

One morning Kamau and I were sitting in the café near the Chief's Camp. Mornings were often quite crisp in Nairobi, and that day we were sitting on hard wooden benches in the corrugated-iron shack, warming our bodies by drinking hot chai from colourful Chinese-made plastic tumblers. Kamau reminded me that we had not seen Mama Joseph for a few weeks and that we should drop by to see how she and Faith were getting along.

It was the afternoon by the time we visited her. She welcomed us into her shack, but it was immediately clear that things were not good. Faith was lying on the packed-dirt floor, her breathing rapid and shallow. Mama Joseph explained to us that she had taken Faith to an NGO health centre in the neighbourhood earlier that day, a different, better equipped one than the one she normally went to for the World Food Programme nutrition clinic, and had been sent away with some drugs. She grabbed the little folded paper pocket of drugs from a side table and thrust them towards us. The clinician's hand-written scribbles on the paper pocket were legible, but neither Kamau nor I had the necessary medical qualifications to know what they meant. Mama Joseph did not seem to know either. We all agreed we should go back to the health centre to speak to the clinician. With Faith's weak body in Mama Joseph's arms, we set off. The health centre, aptly or perhaps hopefully, called *Tumaini Clinic* – in Kiswahili, *tumaini* means hope – was located only a few minutes' walk away. Upon arriving we were quite promptly able to intercept a rather harried-looking clinician to ask about Faith's diagnosis and treatment. She explained that Faith was suffering from pneumonia and had been prescribed antibiotics. There was not much else she could advise, apart from keeping a close eye on her. As we walked back to Mama Joseph's home, we discussed what we thought would be the best course of action. While I had met Faith numerous times before, I had been under the false and naïve assumption that her inclusion in the World Food Programme nutrition clinic meant she was in safe hands. My naïvety would not end there. By the time we arrived back I was reassured that her breathing already seemed to be improving somewhat. The clinician had advised us to let the antibiotics take their course but the three of us resolved that if Faith's condition worsened, she was to be taken straight to hospital. Kamau and I left Mama Joseph with enough money to get there; I did not have a car and no ambulances would come into Korogocho. We also left money for some medical fees, knowing that even if she went to a public hospital, there would still be fees to pay before Faith would be properly and promptly treated.

Faith's condition did worsen that night. Mama Joseph took her immediately to Kiambu District Hospital. This is about two hours travel on public transport, but Mama Joseph, like many others I knew, trusted this hospital more than the closer Kenyatta National Hospital. Many people had experienced long queues and rude reception from healthcare workers at the national hospital and tended to avoid it unless it was absolutely necessary to go there. Over the following days, I spoke to Mama Joseph regularly on the phone. My relief on hearing that Faith was starting to make some improvement felt a little less shaky knowing that she was now in safer, professional hands. Not wanting to be an additional burden during this critical moment, Kamau and I waited a few days before visiting them both at the hospital. When we arrived, we were taken aback: Faith's eyes were bright, and she was sitting up on the ground, playing with a discarded plastic spoon. The contrast to how she was a few days before was unmistakable. She was still drastically underweight: a typical 4-year-old weighs 15 kg and Faith weighed 6.4 kg. But she had put on half a kilogram since she had been admitted into hospital.

Mama Joseph was exhausted but relieved. During the few days she and Faith had been in hospital, eight children who had been put on oxygen, like Faith, had died. The doctor had told Mama Joseph that had she waited any longer, Faith would have certainly passed away because by then her lungs would have become too weak. Both a sense of guilt, for not helping and insisting Mama Joseph take Faith to hospital the moment I saw her, and relief at the fortunate outcome washed over me.

We kept in touch by phone as Faith continued to make good progress and it was not long before she was discharged. But it was a couple of weeks before I was next able to visit Mama Joseph, Faith and the rest of the family at their home. I had only wanted to greet them and see how they were. I did want not to take up too much of Mama Joseph's time. When I arrived, I noticed that Faith was showing signs of recovery, but she was still visibly ill and substantially underweight. But when I tried to ask about her health, Mama Joseph brushed off my enquiries. It seemed that her concerns were not concentrated where I had imagined they would be.

Abruptly changing the topic of conversation, she said, 'It's my two boys,' referring to her sons, the eldest, 14-year-old Joseph, and his brother, Paul, who was 11. 'They are turning bad. They are not bad children, it's just the company they are keeping. I gave 5 bob [KSh5, equivalent to 3 pence] to Joseph to fetch some water and he just answered me back,' she told me. She continued, 'I've managed to borrow KSh2,000 [£13.54] from one friend, and KSh1,000 [£6.77] from another friend, and I've heard about these approved schools they can go to.'[3] I was surprised at her seemingly sudden shift in attention away from Faith, but I wanted to know what lay behind it. Mama Joseph had been able to get both into Boma Rescue, a nearby Catholic rehabilitation centre for boys who had been rescued from *boma*, the landfill site that ran along the border of Korogocho. Here she had hoped they would be protected from the attractions of the landfill site as well be able to start learning again.

Joseph had already been held back several years at his school and had now become Mama Joseph's priority. While Boma Rescue was providing free education, it was located literally along the edge of the landfill site, and for Mama Joseph this was not a good place for her strong-willed children. Not only were they close to the very place that was causing so many problems, but they were also too far away from the house, meaning the walk to and from the school offered the kids plentiful opportunities to earn a little money. For a bit of *mandeng'a*, scrap metal, they could collect KSh20 [£0.14], enough for a bag of *anyona*, the scraps of bread waste described in chapter 1.

Mama Joseph had also been able to forge some connections earlier through Boma Rescue. That day, she discussed with me how she had been told at the centre about a boarding school in Nairobi that her two boys could go to. 'They need to be away from Koch. If they stay here, they'll go back to *boma*.' We talked through the details. While the offer was for free schooling at this boarding school, she needed a small amount of money to pay for registration. I gave her a little towards this amount as she told me that she would be able to get more from her friends.

Relationships and the Triaging of Care

The decision-making power Mama Joseph had over Faith, and specifically her decision to shift her attention to her other, older, children, while Faith was still so close to death, is certainly disconcerting. Seen in a certain light, some might even consider it a form of parental neglect practised under conditions not of her own making. But to do so would require ignoring what we already know about the distressing decisions that must be made about life, family and its temporalties in situations of chronic hunger and famine.

In a footnote in the economist Amartya Sen's possibly most well-known work, *Poverty and Famines: An Essay on Entitlement and Deprivation*, he wrote that 'people sometimes choose to starve rather than sell their productive assets' (Sen 1982, 50 fn 11). He later modified this assertion, claiming that this behaviour was characteristic not of famines but of chronic hunger (Devereux 2009). But further research concerning life in famines has shown that 'coping strategies' in these situations are 'preoccupied with avoiding asset depletion rather than with maintaining consumption levels' (Devereux 2009, 71). The anthropologist Alex de Waal (1989) argued, from evidence collected during the 1984–5 Darfur famine, that this should be seen less as choosing to starve, but as choosing to suffer in order to preserve life in the long-term.[4]

Around the same time that Alex de Waal put forward his arguments, the anthropologist Nancy Scheper-Hughes (1993) was reaching similar conclusions from her time spent with mothers living impoverished and precarious lives in Brazil, where almost a third of children died before they had reached their first birthday. She argued that these mothers were forced by their circumstances to neglect their infants. Drawing on the ecologist, Garrett Hardin (1974), perhaps better known for his 'tragedy of the commons' argument, Scheper-Hughes argued the Brazilian mothers she knew practised a 'lifeboat ethic'. Within this 'ethic', mothers deem it nonsensical to invest considerable mental, emotional and material resources in infants who have little chance of survival.

Mama Joseph, like many other mothers I knew in Korogocho, was bombarded with what Ben Penglase (2009) has called 'everyday emergencies'. Much of daily life was about responding to them in the best way she could. Again, I believe this can be productively understood as careful triage. It was the anthropologist Vinh-Kim Nguyen who argued that the flow of foreign aid resources to those suffering from HIV/AIDS in West Africa depended on triage, 'procedures that separate the more vulnerable patients from those who cannot be saved' (Nguyen 2009, 208). But careful triage in Korogocho was different. It was a dynamic process rather than a one-time decision, in which mothers directed resources in one direction to make the situation 'good enough', before shifting them elsewhere. This gave a certain fluidity and flexibility to their own decisions that shaped 'who shall live what sort of life and for how long' (Fassin 2009, 53).

Nancy Scheper-Hughes further wrote of her interlocutors in Brazil that:

> survival of any one child is generally subordinated to the well-being of the entire domestic group, especially to that household core made up of adult women and their older, and therefore more dependable, children. In a world of great uncertainty ... it makes no sense at all to put any one person ... and certainly not a sickly toddler or fragile infant – at the centre of anything. (Scheper-Hughes 1993, 403)

Those in Korogocho similarly lived in 'a world of great uncertainty', and some, like, Mama Joseph were faced with heart-wrenching conflicts of careful triage. Yet, Mama Joseph did not place Faith at either the centre or the edge of her motherly care. Instead, she dynamically moved all her children between the core and the periphery of her attention. This was because none of these 'dependents' were in any way dependable. If, as we know, the vulnerability of infants is a social phenomenon, so too is the apparent dependability of older children.

Keeping Children

Let us return to Lucy, whom we have met several times, and what she described as her 'black' period. As the reader may recall, as her body was being ravaged by HIV and she lay bedridden, Lucy's children were forced to fend for themselves. While her condition and her inability to mother was a critical factor in her children's new circumstances, so too was the wider environment of Korogocho. In fact, many mothers often attributed the cause of *chokora* to Korogocho's wider milieu, which they often compared, nostalgically, to an idyllic rural life they were raised in. It is worth quoting at length what one middle-aged mother once told me:

> You know, in our rural home there is nothing like this *mandeng'a*, there's no *chokora*…. A child wakes up in the morning, washes and goes to school, then he returns to do his work, which is helping his mum to go and collect water in the river. Then he returns to look for firewood. At night, he arrives, the child hasn't gone for scrap metal like here, you see. That one, he will be good if he studies, and that one, he will be bad if he even goes *ng'ambo* [lit. the other side, but meaning outside of Korogocho itself]. Later, he will even be a thief.

Summing up, she said, '*ni vile Korogocho watu wanaishi*', it is this Korogocho that people are living in.[5] Idealisations of the rural homeland as a moral heart and perceptions of the city as fundamentally immoral are not new (Mayer and Mayer 1961; Ferguson 1992), yet they continue to shape narratives in Korogocho in the twenty-first century. The mother quoted above saw the rural environment as conducive to the creation of 'good' children, even if it did not guarantee it when she said, 'that one will be good if he studies'. But Korogocho, as well as the wider environs of Nairobi, mothers understood as setting up their children for an almost inevitable failure.

To be a mother in the ghetto, as my interlocutors taught me, is to practise an attentive, even if never constant, vigilance over one's children. It requires a keen attention to signs that might indicate that a child is flirting with the first steps of a dangerous path that, once started on, will be difficult to escape from. As every mother in Korogocho was well aware, one of the first steps was a child's truancy from school. A boy, often hungry, would skip school in order to collect *mandeng'a* or go to *boma*, enabling them to earn a little money. He might enlist the help of his schoolfriends, copying their work into his schoolbooks before he returns home. Truancy would generally mean time on the streets, inevitably falling in with others out of school and, before too long, with what people in Korogocho called *wezi wakubwa*, big thieves; in other words, thieves engaged in more serious crimes from robbery to carjacking, often in Nairobi but sometimes further afield. One of my friends Eric, for instance, a talented footballer from a neighbouring ghetto, had in a previous period of his life travelled abroad to countries such as Uganda, to help smuggle stolen goods and drugs. Because small children in Korogocho can more easily evade the attention of police, *wezi wakubwa* will often enlist them to run errands delivering stolen goods. Mama Ida, a landless Luhya with three children, had given me a particularly clear explanation of what happens next:

> There is a day he will realise that these things these people steal sell at a higher price. So, he would say, 'If these guys can steal this thing and I can transport it from this place to another, why don't I get involved with them so that we can steal together?' You find the next step, the kid is starting to steal.

For mothers, when a child begins to steal, they have become 'bad'. And as another of my interlocutors, Alice, who I will return to later, told me, 'If your child goes bad, he is killed.' When she said this to me, she was not only drawing from her own painful experience with her teenage son, but also from that of her neighbour, whose son was killed during my fieldwork.

Parents were gravely concerned for their daughters for other reasons. While they feared for their daughters' physical safety, they were often more worried about them falling pregnant. I knew several parents who felt burdened with living and supporting both their daughters and grand-children. Their grandchildren's biological fathers had often disappeared, usually into one of Nairobi's other ghettos. When they did stick around, they often provided very little. One mother, Joan, complained about the amount she had struggled to put her daughter, Sarah, through formal schooling, even managing to get her into secondary school. But while at school, the girl ended up in a relationship with what Joan called an 'uned-ucated man' without a stable income. Sarah moved out of her mother's shack to stay with him. Soon after, when she was only 17, Sarah fell pregnant by the man. Without a decent income, he was unable, and did little, to support Sarah and their new child financially. Eventually Sarah was forced to return to her mother's house, now burdening Joan with a further mouth that needed feeding.

Proximity and Distance

As Mama Joseph's desperate endeavours showed, mothers in Korogocho hardly see the loss of a child through death or the addition of another mouth to feed as a result of pregnancy to be a fait accompli. In intervening as their children seek to navigate a risky path, their practices of care can be understood both as something that happens within mother–child relationships, and as something that works for them. Within a relationship, a child's life and future is cared for, but at the same time these sorts of care attempt to maintain the 'proper' form of the household unit's social relationships. In other words, the proper form entails maintaining the relational unit of the nuclear family by keeping their children alive and inhibiting the arrival of new lives. It is not that new lives cannot produce experiences of intense joy, affection and emotion, but to say this is to trade in banalities that my interlocutors would likely have little time for. For them, new lives, or the loss of existing ones, jeopardises a family's chances of survival, as well as their plans and dreams for the future. In this section, I explore this form of care by drawing on what my interlocutors taught me in regard to practices of both proximity and distancing, particularly in the ways in which these involved keeping the household core from others outside it.

Across East Africa's many different populations and their modes of living, there have often been powerful expectations that children fulfil the requests of their elders. Likewise, in Korogocho there are particular responsibilities placed by parents on their children. Children are often obliged to queue up for water from the standpipe, to fetch *unga* or other items from the nearby shop, to look after younger siblings, to go to church or the mosque, as well as to attend school. But the social fabric of Korogocho, as I have already shown, is more than a collection of individual households; it is instead a bundle of, always contested, expectations woven together. One's neighbour, for example, may, in your absence, instruct your child to carry out a domestic chore. Such circumstances worry parents, challenging their capacity to know and to keep track of the movements of their offspring. Allowing children to play a normative and legitimate role, in which they respond not only to parental authority but also to that of others senior to them, even other older children, sits in tension with its risks. Carrying out any sort of task outside the compound would often situate the child in the dangerous space of 'the road'. For this reason, parents I knew sometimes discouraged their children, albeit often reluctantly, from carrying out domestic chores on behalf of neighbours.

The literal road was inherently dangerous for several reasons. As a result of the slum upgrading programme, some of the main roads had been tarmacked and accompanied with raised pavements.[6] This tarmacking had led to an increase in both the numbers of *boda* (motorcycle taxis) and the speed at which they travelled. A few years ago, Lucy was on the roadside selling maize when she heard that a child had been knocked over. 'Whether it was good luck or bad luck. It was my own child who had been knocked over but not killed,' she told me. Lucy was even able to claim an informal compensation payment from the driver, which not only covered the child's hospital treatment but also helped Lucy set up her chicken offal business. Many people also experienced more intimate violence on the road. Mama Joseph lived very close to the main road. One early morning I had seen her near her home organising for a young boy she did not know to be taken to hospital. She found him lying in the gutter by the side of the road, having been beaten up and left there overnight. It was not that others would not have helped, but she was the first to do so, even though her life was interwoven, perhaps more than others I knew, with the everyday violence and impoverishment of the ghetto. I do not know the back-story of the young boy, but muggings, including armed ones, were not uncommon. Given that the safest strategy to avoid muggings is to walk in the centre of the road, residents were amused when the slum upgrading programme included raised pavements. Walking on the edge of the main roads in Korogocho is tempting both fate and its thieving accomplices who can easily escape into the ghetto's maze of alleyways.

But 'the road' was also considered perilous because it expanded children's field of sociality that moved them, as we have seen, onto a dangerous descent into crime. It similarly brought girls into contact with men congregating on the roadside who offered them gifts, often food such as chips or fruit, that they or their parents were unable to afford themselves.

One way, then, to keep children from becoming lost to, or indeed adding to the family, jeopardising its own survival, was for parents to encourage a form of uncaring between the household and those, like neighbours, outside it. Discouraging what I understood to be acts of care embodied within expectations of mutuality, such as fetching water for a neighbour, allowed parents to keep their children close, limiting their access to this wider field of sociality. If then, in the previous chapter, detachment was considered a way to make those attachments stronger, here I argue it was a way of attending to the strength of other attachments within the nuclear family. Here forms of uncaring, a pulling of children away from others and from normative expectations of mutuality, was a way to hold the household together by policing its dangerous borderlands.

But children also need to be drawn into the household itself. This was revealed to me most conspicuously by the cash grants themselves. As we saw in chapter 2, surveys conducted in preparation for giving the grants do not enable people to express the particularities of their own circumstances. Similarly, formal evaluations, even when deploying qualitative methodologies, often do not allow people the space to express themselves adequately. Moreover, such evaluations are loaded with their own expectations that weigh heavily upon those who experience them not as an analysis of an intervention but as a judgement on them as the subject of these social interventions. Deploying ethnographic methodologies, in contrast, along with a certain level of rapport that had developed over time with my interlocutors, earned me a particular privileged position that revealed things that rarely appear in formal reports. Mothers who received the grants, for instance, would often tell me that instead of buying staples, such as maize, that would provide predictable sustenance to the family over the month, and which they knew would be looked favourably upon by those in charge of the grants, they would look to the grant as a way of offering the household *vitu vizuri* (nice things). An elastic term, it could mean some cow's liver to be eaten as a family on the day the grant came in, or it could be special items that responded to a child as an individual. One mother had explained to me that when a recent grant had arrived, she used some of it to buy make-up that her daughter had been asking for. An understanding of such gift-giving hardly needs to be reduced to a rational logic or strategy in which such acts of care work to maintain relationships. They might constitute a way in which a mother seeks, through her love and attentiveness, to help make a modern, city life available to her family and its members. Yet the mother herself deployed her own strategic thinking in this situation. If she did not offer the gift, she reasoned to me, then a man meeting her daughter on the street would. Here the mother was not only concerned with the making of her daughter's modern life, but also drawing her into the security of the nuclear family. An interpretation of gift-giving through a calculus of strategic rationality might be reductive, but a denial of such rationality in our interlocutors is its own form of violence. One dimension, then, of *vitu vizuri*, which included things like special family meals and different sorts of gifts, in combination with attempts to regulate access to the sociality of the road, was its role in securing the safety of the family and its continuity in a nuclear form.

These gestures and practices often kept the family as physically close as possible, while working to weave their lives together both socially and economically. A form, perhaps, of making what Sahlins (2011a) has called the 'mutuality of being', or the concept of relatedness that Janet Carsten (1995) developed, drawing from her time spent in a Malay home, eating and engaged in household activities with its members. But in Korogocho another way to strive for personal security and to achieve familial continuity was to separate the family geographically, moving children much further away. Here, as I will show, a particular physical mode of detachment was a way to work on its social attachments.

Although some mothers sent their children to their rural home areas, they knew the chances of education there were limited. An alternative was instead to send them to boarding school. We saw earlier how Mama Joseph sought to move two of her sons to an approved boarding school. Approved schools originated in the colonial era, when they were managed by the Department of Approved Schools, intended for children engaged in crime or other activities who needed some sort of correction (Okello Weda and Mwangi 2015). Today, a number of these schools still operate for juveniles who have committed a crime or who are considered in need of protection.

Many readers are likely to associate boarding schools with a private education that is largely only accessible to the wealthier segments of society. However, lower cost private schooling in ghettos such as Korogocho has plugged the country's yawning gaps in state public education. Moreover, private education is generally considered by the ghetto's residents to be of a higher quality than what the state offers, something parents put down to the basic and simple fact that they are paying for it. This means that teachers tend not only to turn up regularly but also appear to take a keener interest in the children they are teaching. Private boarding schools are, of course, more expensive, and out of reach for most in Korogocho, but some parents have been able to make great sacrifices to get their children into them.

Take Glory, a mother in her forties who lived with her husband and three children. Her husband hustled a little, carrying loads in a nearby market, but suffered from alcoholism and therefore contributed very little to the family's income. Glory had turned to domestic work, washing clothes for better off Nairobians, something considered not without some shame as I have already mentioned, and which earned her very little. But the family had been enrolled onto the urban grant, which had eased their problems a little, even if only temporarily.

A few years before I met her, Glory had been approached by a man, purportedly representing an NGO, promising to enrol her eldest daughter, Florence, in a boarding school, and to pay her fees. 'Boarding school is good,' she told me one day, fiddling with the small *jiko*, in order to prepare the morning *chai*, 'there's no mingling. Here, if you just have *chai* for breakfast, the boys will buy you chips.' But, Glory told me, the NGO turned out to be a swindle. The representative asked her to pay an initial fee, with assurances that the NGO would pay the remaining boarding school fees. But after paying that initial fee, Glory never heard from the man or the NGO, and her phone calls went unanswered. A time-consuming and ultimately fruitless search for the NGO's office in nearby Huruma estate followed. She realised that this was a 'ghost NGO', a phenomenon that is unfortunately not uncommon in Kenya (Mkawale 2015). However, it transpired that the boarding school itself had more of a material reality; it was only the middleman who had proved to be a ghost. Moreover, the school had accepted Florence – this much was true – so Glory decided to see if she could pay the school fees herself. When I met her, because she was on the grant, payment of the fees had become a little easier. But she remembered vividly the earlier, pre-grant period. The family had stopped eating lunch altogether, and on some evenings they would only have enough for a handful of *anyona* and a mug of strong sweet chai. When it seemed that the youngest son at primary school was suffering, they struggled to make sure that at least he would get something that resembled a proper evening meal. Teachers also helped, buying him *chakula cha barabara*, fast-food on the street.

Others I knew had been able to find opportunities in the same way Mama Joseph earlier had been trying. Monica was a mother of six children, and married with a husband who worked in *majengo* (the construction industry). Before I met Monica, her first-born son, Emmanuel, used to go to *Mukuru* (the dumping site, also often called *boma* as we have seen earlier), when he was around 13. There was a period when he did not go to school for two terms, even hiding his school shoes behind the toilet and then changing into his old shoes. Monica and her husband were leaving in the morning to go to work, and he was taking advantage of them. They only realised how bad he had got when Monica beat him after finding out what he was doing, and he then pulled a knife on her as if he was going to stab her. After that he disappeared. He only returned after being scared by a devastating fire, caused by a burst petrol pipeline, that ripped through a neighbouring ghetto, *Mukuru kwa njenga* killing over one hundred people. He had explained to Monica how he had joined a group of *chokora*. In this group, senior children send out the younger ones to steal and if anybody came back empty handed, nobody was allowed to sleep. When he was successful, much of that money was stolen by them. So he had to ensure that he was stealing enough money to feed himself and pay his contribution. He told his parents when he returned that he wanted to go boarding school, '*napenda kuishi*' ('I'd like to live') he told them. Monica and her husband were able to organise his acceptance at an approved school in Ngong where, when I met them both, he had been for four months. She was still waiting for permission to see him but the school told her she would have to wait a year.

Both stories illustrate the lengths to which parents will go to move their children out of Korogocho. Few people in Korogocho wanted to live there, and while it would always be better if they were able to leave, the cost of living in Nairobi was prohibitively high. Instead, in order to keep the family together as a relational unit, some of the most impoverished families sought to break them physically apart. Glory even tried to ensure that her daughter would remain out of Korogocho during school holidays, anxious that her additional free time would be spent in the wrong company. Keeping the family apart, as long as its constituent members were safe, was a way through which families would be able to hold onto the always hopeful possibility of a better life in an unknowable future.

The Value of Children

In order to think further about the caring work that mothers undertake towards their children, and about the relationships that connect them, I am interested in why they *want* to do that work. One way to look at this is to ask how parents value children. I offer an interpretation that might be read as almost utilitarian, or at least subscribing to a rational, economic calculus. But my interpretation tacks closely to my interlocutors' reasoning, with the caveat that it should not be understood as exhausting it. Nor should be it be read that a mother's explicit, articulated reasoning has the definitive, final word, as this would be to deny not only actions but also the implicit, the implied and the unsaid. To say motherly care is not *simply* a utilitarian gamble does not mean it might *also* be so.

Since the historian Philippe Ariès' (1965) influential account of the history of childhood since the sixteenth century in Western Europe, historians and social scientists have increasingly understood childhood as a contested category (for instance Zelizer 1994). These studies have shown not only that ideals of childhood vary across time and space, but that practices rarely conform to these ideals. As Zelizer has argued, ideologies of childhood in many Western cultures see it as a place of pure, virtuous, space free from the 'corrupting' force of the market and yet, in reality, childhood and the market are often mixed in different ways. Anthropologists similarly have routinely explored the way in which different 'modern' cultures might idealise, but frequently contradict that idealisation, the separation of domains from politics and kinship (Lazar 2017) to love and the market (Cole and Thomas 2009).

The importance of kinship within the domain of politics and the economy has, of course, also been a long-recognised feature in East Africa (Evans-Pritchard 1987 [1940]). Children specifically have been considered in the region as important for the lineage (Stambach 2000), and the nation (Cheney 2007). As such, reproductive issues have been deeply political, as well as material and moral, matters in the region (Thomas 2003). In postcolonial Kenya, fierce public debates emerged when sexual reproduction appeared to be occurring more frequently outside of marriage as a result of urbanisation. Lynn Thomas (2003) has documented how, soon after independence in 1963, women's organisations held seminars to discuss the apparent confusion that single women were experiencing in the cities. At the same time, the Kenyan government passed new laws that sought to support the many single mothers appearing in the cities as a result of what was argued to be both growing urbanisation and the breakdown of tribal traditions (Thomas 2003, 143). While government attempts to support single mothers were always piecemeal, more concerted – and ultimately more successful – efforts throughout the postcolonial period were made to reduce the number of children altogether. In the early 1990s in Kenya the fertility rate stood at 6.7 births per woman, but by 2008 it had dropped to 4.6 (Emina et al. 2011).

As seen across the world, a range of factors – including changing forms of livelihood, particularly with urbanisation, and access to contraceptives – also transformed demographics. In Nairobi, the fertility rate dropped to 2.8, but in Korogocho it stood higher, at 3.4. In Korogocho, motherhood also started early. A report from 2014 has shown that by the age of 22, around three-quarters of women have had sexual intercourse, and of those, around four-fifths have become pregnant (Beguy et al. 2014).

As mentioned in the first chapter, formal marriage is rare for young people in Korogocho. Yet a certain amount of moral opprobrium continues to be reserved for young women who become pregnant outside of marriage, particularly for those who are still of school-going age. Beatrice, whom we met in the prologue of this book, tried to hide her daughter's pregnancy and subsequent child, partly because they anticipated, with good reason, that her school would exclude her were they to know. I also knew a young woman, Joan, on the urban grant whose parents had demanded she terminate her pregnancy, throwing her out of the house when she refused. She and her baby moved in with a friend, joining her in a shack that was now even more cramped. The woman had put some of her money towards trying to establish a business, first selling charcoal and then selling second-hand shoes on the side of Nairobi's Juja Road. But she struggled to make this business venture profitable.

Disapproval of pregnancies considered early or illegitimate, should not ignore the fact that motherhood often conferred a certain type of moral personhood upon women. To be a mother was often to *be* someone. This was most strikingly exemplified through the naming practice – particularly prominent among my Kikuyu interlocutors – of mothers as Mama followed by the name of their first-born child. Indeed, it was the case, as Tuulikki Pietila has also shown for the Chagga of northern Tanzania, that mothers in Korogocho drew upon their moral worth as mothers in other domains, such as the market (Pietila 2007).

Many of the mothers I knew in Korogocho recognised the importance of their moral status as mothers. But they also valued children for other reasons, particularly for the way they considered the intertwining of their socioeconomic fates. Mothers harboured hopes for the way in which their own economic and social futures might be shaped by their children. This was particularly the case for younger mothers. Margaret, a mother of three, considering herself at the lowest rung of Kenyan society, deployed her own hierarchical metaphor, when she talked about the importance of formal schooling. 'I have to struggle for them to go to school,' she said, then, without missing a beat followed this up with, 'I hope one day, even one of them will raise me up.' For Margaret, it was not children as a contribution to the growth of the lineage, or the nation, that interested her, but her own individual growth and upward mobility in Kenya's urban capitalist wage economy.[7] Also noteworthy is how young mothers, including Margaret, considered the temporality of children's contribution to her life course. On the one hand, while children played an important domestic role in the family, many mothers did not look to them for an economic contribution in the present moment. As we have seen, in a place like Korogocho, a child sent out to earn money was considered by many mothers as a child that was, or would be soon, lost to the family. On the other hand, a young mother in Korogocho looked to her children as a way of offering her upward mobility in her nearer, yet still temporally unspecified, future, rather than as a contribution to her care in older age.

Some older mothers I knew, particularly those who had managed to retain stronger connections to the rural areas which are, as I have mentioned earlier, often the moral heartlands, did keep in mind both their retirement but also their obligations to their patrilineage. Let us turn back to Alice, whom I quoted earlier in this chapter saying that 'If your child goes bad, he is killed.' Alice was a middle-aged Luo, widowed and a single mother of four children. She had been a beneficiary of the child grant since 2005, but had tried as hard as she could to keep it a secret. She was the second wife of her husband who had died in 1993, but when I knew her, she herself had an *mpango wa kando*. Unlike many other women in Korogocho, Alice had land from her husband's patrilineage. She also had a business selling *anyona* that seemed to be doing fairly well, and while she lived in a corrugated-iron shack like everybody else in Korogocho, hers offered her a little more space than those of other people I knew. One day we were sitting together in the dim light of her shack. It was a few months after her teenage son, Simon had been shot, an event that I turn to at the end of this chapter. While his illegal activities were not news to Alice, Simon's latest scrape with the authorities had set off a train of thought about whether her efforts to care for and educate her children had been in vain. She was also at an age when her mind was turning to her possible retirement back in her rural home. This meant a deeper consideration on her part about the ways in which motherhood was constituted not only by, and with corresponding obligations to, children, but also her affines. Among people like her in-laws, who elevated children to a high status, motherhood cannot be grasped without a consideration of kinship beyond the matrifocal household unit. Her ample weight splayed across the sofa, she leaned forward, 'So, when you are now old you cannot make any money, you cannot even have any more kids and your kids are all dead. So, you just go to *ushago* with nothing.' I waited for her to continue. 'Let's say all my kids were thieves and they were all killed', then gesturing to the furniture in her shack, she raised her voice, 'I cannot carry these ones to *ushago*. Even my in-laws will not welcome me with the chairs.' Fixing my eyes with hers she asked rhetorically, 'Did I come to Nairobi to look for chairs?' At the time, I had naïvely asked Alice why her in-laws would not welcome her, perhaps assuming that they would not blame her for the death of her children, although, of course, cognisant that a set of chairs was hardly a replacement. She had chuckled. 'They wouldn't be happy with it; they want the children. Like in Luoland, we really look at the kids as some of our heroes.' For her in-laws, she argued, going to Nairobi was about the growth of the patrilineage, not the acquisition of the material trappings of modern, city life.

Alice drew attention to her own obligations towards her parents, but she also drew attention to how they stood in tension with her personal ambitions. As she made clear, fulfilling obligations to one's parents in Kenya involved providing them with grandchildren. Yet, striving for and assembling the things needed for a good life (the 'chairs') meant moving to the city, and for mothers in Korogocho it meant making a home as much a sanctuary as was materially possible. The quality of relationships and the obligations that existed between parents and their children were fraught with material limitations and conflicting wills and ideas.

Filial Piety

As we have seen so far, motherhood in Korogocho requires mothers to deploy considerable vigilance as they watch out for their children. It also requires difficult decisions to be made around the distribution of care in order to keep children alive, preventing them from either being lost, or adding extra mouths to feed and expanding the nuclear family. I have suggested that dynamically both keeping children close and moving them away are key aspects of Korogocho maternal strategies that strive to ensure the family's relational futures. In this section, I argue that formal education is not simply about maintaining familial relationships but speaks to their moral quality. To look at this, I turn to the concept of filial piety, a subset of wider, morally infused, kinship obligations.

Filial piety is an idea, originating in Chinese philosophical thought, that refers to reverence for one's parents, elders and ancestors. While today it is deployed most prominently in the social scientific literature concerning the East Asian region (for instance Ikels 2004), in the 1960s, the anthropologist Meyer Fortes (1961) found it useful to engage the idea in making sense of the intergenerational obligations among the Tallensi of Ghana. Finding no specific word in the Talni language for filial piety, he nonetheless argued that the concept would be readily understood by his Tallensi interlocutors. He offered an example from his fieldwork, a discussion he had had with a young man who had just returned from an argument with his father. The man told Fortes: 'Is it right, the way he treats me? Yet how can I leave him since he is almost blind and cannot farm for himself? Would he not starve to death? Can you just abandon your father? Is it not he who begot you?' This conversation demonstrated to Fortes that filial piety for the Tallensi was a moral obligation that emerged from the sheer facts of biological reproduction (Fortes 1961, 174). However, Fortes was actually inconsistent on this point. He elsewhere argued that the extent and nature of filial piety varied according to the degree of attachment a child had to the parents (Fortes 1949). This attachment, he said, was connected to how dependent the child was on the parent. This has inspired some readers, such as Harri Englund (2008, 43), to interpret Fortes as pointing towards the 'hard work that generated kinship obligations'. Similarly in Korogocho, I observed that filial piety, as a reverence and care for parents, did not always exist simply from being born. It was a contested and precarious relational achievement between parent and child. One way of looking at it, I argue, is to think not about dependents but about the creation of *dependable* dependents in the urban slum milieu.

Because I spoke mostly with mothers rather than children, my focus remains on these adults. But because mothers are their own parents' offspring, it becomes possible to begin to explore ideas around filial piety. The drawback of this, of course, is that it may miss important generational changes and debates around the nature of obligations. However, my contribution is not intended as the definitive word on filial piety in urban Africa, but rather to serve as an opening to a conversation around it. Indeed, while I cannot attest to knowing how widely shared this sense of conditional filial piety is, what is interesting is not whether it is representative but the fact that obligations are routinely scrutinised. Obligations, and not only between children and their parents, precisely because they are so important, often become the subject of debates.

Debating and Hoping for Filial Piety

Discussions around filial piety in Korogocho stood in stark contrast to those identified by Fortes among the Tallensi. Quite understandably so, considering the time and space that separates them. Let me offer one example to illustrate the difference; a conversation which took place as Jude, one of my research assistants, and I rested at her two-roomed shack in Highridge in the middle of a particularly frantic day of fieldwork. I had been trying to get a handle on some basic sociological facts concerning the networks of kinship relationships that cash grant recipients might, with the grant, be animating and maintaining. While some aspects of the economy in Koro-gocho are more visible – for instance *chama*, the merry-go-round saving groups – remittances were one of those economic flows and activities that were much less obvious. Therefore, I would often try to draw people into conversations about them. Such conversations, along with my own obser-vations, not only revealed the presence of remittances but also showed the difficulties that people had with them. None of the Korogocho residents I knew had friends or family who lived abroad, so remittances were within the city or between urban and rural areas.[8]

I already knew by that point that some people in Korogocho would receive a few *gorogoro* of maize from relatives up-country if the harvest season in the rural area had been particularly good.[9] But rural kin often expected that their urban-based kin would be in a socioeconomic position that would facilitate some sort of return outside of harvest time; usually payments of cash, these days usually made through mobile money services. Urban dwellers sometimes did little to quell such expectations for fear that they would be viewed as a failure, an attitude that persists among migrants across the world. But increasingly attitudes have changed, and Korogocho slum dwellers have played their part in this. Some have sought to describe to their rural kin, in telephone conversations, the living con-ditions and circumstances of ghetto life. Other have relied upon visitors from their home villages and areas to pass on the message.

But the making of remittances among kin does not merely map onto the ability, or not, to make them. Asking Jude to explain why some people were not sending money, apart from their obvious lack of means, she recounted a conversation she had had with her own friend a few days earlier. The friend, Jude recounted, had chuckled. 'What have they done for you?', she had asked, 'They didn't even give you an education. What do you owe them?' For the friend, filial piety was itself born not from beget-ting but from giving. And remittances here were less about material means than moral obligations. While the 'gift' of education from parent to child was seen as an important cultivator, even a prerequisite, of filial piety, it was also seen as a facilitator to a better life in which this piety could be exercised. Clara Han (2012) has contrasted the views of a social assistance programme in Chile that viewed dignity as the escape out of poverty with acts of kindness among the poor that enabled a dignity *within* poverty. However, for my friends and informants in Korogocho, their shared understanding of a dignified life was a life out of poverty which conformed to 'modern' urban aspirations.

Of course, if I had had a chance to speak to Jude's friend, I cannot imagine she would have denied any obligation between her and her parents. In Korogocho, people recognise and respect the obligations between themselves and their parents in life and in death. But she was emphasising, I think, how obligations are not an 'unquestioned and inalienable right' but rather a precarious achievement. What is considered an achievement is structured by prevailing social norms and cultural values that existed within a particular Kenyan political economy. While Jude at that time had a reasonable level of regular income from her work with NGOs, and a masterful grasp of English, she only had a primary education. This level of education was hardly considered an education at all in an economy that was inundated with young people with higher education qualifications but without work. But, importantly, Jude's friend felt an entitlement to formal education not from the state but from her parents. The responsibility for formal advanced education required for moral personhood and economic well-being emerging from modern Kenyan statecraft had been fundamentally moved into the realm of kinship.

Finally, as I mentioned earlier, parents who often wanted to provide formal education to their children did not see it simply as generating obligations for relatively simple things like remittances, but as creating possibilities for the transformation of both child and parent. Here, then, the *value* of children for a transformed future was also understood by parents as an *obligation* that the child owed.

Hope's Fragility

Although mothers in Korogocho held onto a hope of a better life that was dependent upon their relationships with their children and their transformative potential, mothers' own experiences of urban life meant they were only too aware of the fragility of this hope. The material realities of Korogocho life put a strain on the possibilities of mothers either cultivating any resemblance of filial piety in their children or fulfilling the same in their relationships to their own parents. Let us turn, finally, to Alice and her 18-year-old, son, Simon.

I bumped into Alice outside her shack washing clothes, but she was not her usual self. She appeared distracted but, as she normally did when I passed, she invited me into her shack, ushering me into her cramped living room. I did not see him at first. But, as my eyes became accustomed to the dark, I realised a man, who later turned out to be Simon, was lying on her sofa. He was flitting in and out of sleep and I could make out beads of sweat across his face. A blanket had been draped over his legs. Alice shook him awake roughly, pulled away the blanket, and turned to look at me. Just above Simon's knee was a small but obvious wound. She told me that he had broken his leg nearby after falling down the stairs of a road-bridge when running from thieves. Trust takes a lot of time to build in Korogocho and, while I had known Alice for a while, she did not know me well enough to immediately tell me the truth. A few days later, when I was back at her place, Simon was looking better, and his leg was now bandaged up. Alice now confided in me, saying the wound was a result of a gunshot from the police. Going to the hospital, she explained, was out of the question. It would have meant doctors removing the bullet from his leg and handing it over to the police who would have traced it back to one of their own officer's firearms. If that happened, it was common knowledge that Simon would have been quickly arrested. Fortuitously, Alice's daughter was a nurse, and she was able to arrange for him to be treated here in the shack, allowing the bullet to be discarded discreetly. If Alice had slightly better material circumstances than others I knew, partly as a result of the regular child grant but also because of her access to cultivable land, it seemed to offer very little to help protect her son from his descent into Nairobi's criminal underworld, even if it did help, on this occasion, to keep him out of prison.

This event, as I mentioned above, had led to Alice contemplating her own life and its struggles and considering what she had sacrificed. In our conversation, before she had complained about the possibilities of returning to her rural area, and the heart of her patrilineage, with just chairs, she had also said something else. With Simon on her mind, whom she had struggled hard to educate, even helping him become a car mechanic for a short while, she said:

In Korogocho you can educate your child. Those who will accept your education will prosper and continue with their lives. But there are those who don't like going to school, they just like going beyond the ghetto. They might even turn to be thieves. So, even if they are killed it is OK. As a parent you can try but the child just refuses to hear. So, you have sacrificed a lot, you have educated them, they have gone to school and you have taken them to some college – and then they turn out to be thieves.

Mothers struggle to offer education to their children and to provide them with whatever opportunities and care that is possible, but there are few guarantees these efforts will be reciprocated given both the individuality and separateness of the other, and the draw of collectivities of crime.

Conclusion

In the two previous chapters, I showed how what might appear on the surface as uncaring practices could in fact be interpreted as caring when the object was relationships. I opened this chapter with a lengthy discussion of Mama Joseph and the disquieting decisions she was forced to make in allocating care between her children, showing how navigating multiple relationships will always necessarily mean practising both care and uncare at different stages and in different registers. In the previous chapter I showed how forms of uncaring relational work might help to strengthen a relationship, but in this one I have steered closer perhaps to a point made long ago by Marilyn Strathern. In drawing from her experience with the Hagen of Papua New Guinea, she argued that gifts 'sever[ed] and detach[ed] people from people' (1990, 191). In giving to one party and forming attachments to them, one necessarily separates oneself from another. Similarly, for Mama Joseph, caring for one child might mean momentarily uncaring for, or perhaps detaching from the needs of, another child.

In Korogocho, and to echo Nancy Scheper-Hughes, such decision-making had a 'reasonableness' and an 'inner logic'. I have sought to more closely consider her logic by drawing from both conversations with, and observations of, other mothers and their children that I knew in Korogocho. Understanding the logic has meant grasping the context in which action takes place and, in the case of Korogocho, it means recognising its violent nature. This has allowed me to explore some of the ways in which mothers endeavour to keep their children safe, in many cases through the ideals of distancing the child from Korogocho and its harms.

Understanding why children are kept safe has also meant understanding the value of children themselves. Children are valued in many ways, but in Korogocho two values were emphasised which exhibit different forms of temporality and spatiality. On the one hand, children are valued as important for the long continuity of wider kinship relationships in the rural moral heartland, and on the other hand, children are valued as important for the future of the household in the urban milieux.

Finally, we have seen how mothers not only seek to navigate their different relationships of care concerning their children, but to work on the quality of these relationships. I have focused particularly on the work that was required to generate moral obligations between children and their mothers. I am not suggesting that these moral obligations are straightforwardly conditional; my more modest contribution is to pose the question that obligations are subject to debates that include conditionalities.

Conclusion

In September 2020, as the second wave of the Covid-19 pandemic hit the United Kingdom, the city of Leeds, where I was born, requested permission from the national government to pilot a Universal Basic Income scheme. This city joined others including Hull, Liverpool and Sheffield, in vying to be the first in England to trial such a scheme. According to one national poll, the majority of the UK's population agreed that the ongoing pandemic was an appropriate time for the government to make sure 'everyone has an income, without a means test or a requirement to work'.

The sea change in opinion had been dramatic; it was down to a few factors, but particularly the rapid and indiscriminate way in which the pandemic created a vast swathe of newly unemployed or furloughed people. But the attraction to the idea of giving people cash grants was growing even before the pandemic, from across the political spectrum and in different countries: from the billionaire class of Silicon Valley's so-called digerati, including figures such as Elon Musk and Mark Zuckerberg, to inspirational fighters against economic inequality such as the late David Graeber.

In truth, it is probably not the ambitions of these schemes that we should be paying attention to, but the words that lurk within their description: trial, pilot, experiment. This is no less the case for countries in Africa. If countries like Kenya were once sites for the transfer, from the global North to the global South, of technology and ideas, they are now more sites of experimentation in these technologies and ideas (Fejerskov 2017). The charity GiveDirectly has continued with their work in the western part of Kenya, initially experimenting with giving quite targeted cash grants but then experimenting with giving them to all the adults of certain villages. The urban grant that reached Korogocho in 2011 finished as I was completing my fieldwork. In 2020, the Covid-19 pandemic brought a cash grant, funded by the European Union, to the ghetto again; this time just for three months. Other grants had likely arrived, in similar circumstances and for similar aims, since the time I carried out my fieldwork.

Perhaps something will come of these experiments within Kenya, and they will scale-up to a national level. We have already seen some scaling-up of both of the targeted cash grants that feature in this book. While much remains funded by foreign donors, the government's budget allocation for social protection has nonetheless increased since the beginning of the century (Ikiara 2009). This evidence might suggest ownership at an economic level rather than legal one. But there have also been important legal developments in the last decade or so. One is the ratification of a new constitution in 2010, which in its ambition has sometimes been seen as one of the most progressive in Africa (Onyango-Obbo 2010). This constitution has returned to Article 25 of the Universal Declaration of Human Rights to include social and economic rights in its constitution. Article 43 of Kenya's Constitution states that:

> Every person has the right to the highest attainable standard of health, which includes the right to health care services, including reproductive health care, to accessible and adequate housing, and to reasonable standards of sanitation, to be free from hunger, and to have adequate food of acceptable quality, to clean and safe water in adequate quantities, to social security, and to education. (Government of Kenya 2010)

Similar promises to these were made immediately following Kenya's independence in 1963, but the promises back then turned out to be empty, leaving the expectations of its citizens unrealised. Both this enshrining of social and economic rights in the 2010 Constitution, and the growing governmental budgetary allocation, seem to gesture back to the promises made in the 1960s post-independence years. Yet, despite these important developments, caution is important. Jean and John Comaroff have talked of the 'fetishism of constitutionalism' characterised by an 'enchanted faith in constitutions' when countries remain gripped by lawlessness (Comaroff and Comaroff 2006, 24–5).[1] Moreover, recent efforts in Kenya such as the attempt to introduce Universal Health Coverage have faltered, becoming mired in the problems of privatisation, as well as corruption and mismanagement (Prince 2022).

An experience of lawlessness was also, as I showed in the opening of the book, something that characterised Korogocho. Yet amidst this lawlessness, the introduction of cash grants seemed to be welcomed not by everyone, but certainly by many of the women I came to know. In this book I have sought to explore these cash grants in their particular concrete contexts (Olivier de Sardan and Piccoli 2018).

Peculiar Things

At the beginning of my research, I was particularly intrigued by the unconditional sorts of grants that had generated among many different actors an
optimism that they represented a better tool for economic redistribution,
even if such grants failed to challenge the structural nature of poverty. For
many people of varying political persuasions, it is difficult not to be, in
principle, supportive of the idea of offering cash to people already situated
in a market economy, and allowing them to use it how they see fit, while
reducing surveillance of them, and not burdening them with the endless
trainings, workshops and meetings that are so characteristic of schemes of
human improvement.[2]

In Kenya, the grants seemed to run up against older and still existing
attempts to relieve suffering and extreme poverty. They appeared qualitatively different to the traditions of giving people the things that the
experts *think* they need, usually discounting any consideration of what
people actually *want* (Trapp 2016). The grants are different from other
schemes of economic empowerment. Debt-driven development in Africa
has been, and continues to be, an enduring and attractive poverty alleviation strategy, as well as, it turns out, a way for the rich to get richer
(Elyachar 2005; James 2014; Donovan and Park 2019). But the grants also
appeared to take us further away from what has been called the 'tyranny of
participation' (Hickey and Mohan 2004). In many development schemes,
new spaces are created, designed to bring to the fore aspects of 'local
knowledge' as a solution to local people's problems. As Mosse has argued,
local knowledge is something not discovered but created through project
activities, strongly shaped by dominant local interests and project objec-
tives, and therefore a process through which people learned new kinds
of planning knowledge (Mosse 2005, 95). But in the unconditional cash
grant programmes, it was often argued that it was unnecessary for local
knowledge to be discovered or created by policy makers in order to inform
experts. Although, in reality, as I showed in chapter 3, it remained integral
to the charitable economy and its precarious relationships.

But the cash grants should be, and regularly are, looked at critically.
It is clear that the grants in Kenya, in being directed to particularly vulnerable women, continued particularly European social democratic ideas,
extended through colonialism, of what James Ferguson has called a 'kind
of photographic negative of the figure of the wage-earning man' (2015,

40). Moreover, in Kenya, they maintained the globally networked and distributed charitable relationships, ideas and values that have characterised the country's regimes and activities of assistance for decades. They may not quite be a minimalist biopolitics (Redfield 2005), but they are, as critics argue, a bolder biopolitics that continues liberal capitalistic political economies that view poverty and inequality as states that are to be addressed voluntarily rather than from the standpoint of a legal duty (Ballard 2013). In this way, the grants embrace a market, and combine it with hierarchies of redistribution, but in the process seek to flatten, invert, and hollow out these very hierarchies. In doing so, and in seeking to trust the poor with cash, advocates for the grants at times seem to ignore the wider hierarchical social relationships in which they are enmeshed, leaving instead a residual and somewhat romantic view that trusting the poor is a simple act that can be detached from highly unequal political and economic relationships.

In fact, some of these often-predatory relationships are arguably what has contributed to the very inequality and poverty that humanitarians and development experts aspire to alleviate in Korogocho. As I have detailed, from the colonial period onwards ordinary Kenyans have been forced from their land, 'voluntarily' or otherwise, ending up in slums like Korogocho – places in which nobody wants to live. From the moment they arrive, their lack of secure tenure offers them only permanent insecurity. As I was finishing writing this book, in the midst of the pandemic lockdown in Kenya, the authorities razed to the ground the shacks of thousands of people in a ghetto adjacent to Korogocho. Cash grants are clearly impotent in the face of such threats.

Cash grants, then, are peculiar things. They neither destroy existing ways of life through economic violence, although they certainly shape them (Bähre 2011), nor do they simply transform lives for the better. They are variously cast as being the best thing we have in the alleviation of extreme poverty – or the worst. Some praise them as allowing the poor to escape their situation on their own terms, while others dismiss them as simply giving the poor the illusion of doing so. Some see them as perhaps the building blocks of what could be a better and potentially more expansive redistributive system, while others consider them a woefully inadequate sticking plaster attached to a haemorrhaging capitalist world system.

As I have grappled throughout my fieldwork and today with a sense of both optimism and disillusionment – perhaps better described as naïvety or cynicism – towards the grants, I have also been drawn in other directions, beyond the appraisal of their political or economic opportunities or limitations. This has rested on what might be the only incontrovertible aspect of cash grants: they help to keep people alive.

During my fieldwork I followed various actors who became embroiled in the grants' material flows, inversions of hierarchy of expertise and arguments for the epistemological sovereignty of the poor. As I did so, I was also pulled into their concerns about what it means to keep bodies, persons and hopes alive. The very nature of unconditional cash grants created spaces, still circumscribed, of freedom for the poor within which they could enact, and tell me about, their own, often painful struggles, their values, ideas and hopes for the future – all of which exceeded the particularities of the grants themselves. Ethnographic methodologies allowed me to dwell with these interlocutors in these circumscribed and momentary spaces of freedom, but they also showed me the dilemmas cash grants posed when they remained part of long-standing political economies.

I began my research with an interest in understanding what happened when cash grant experiments landed in a particular place. I suspected, from my own reading and assumptions, that people probably already cared for, as well as disregarded, each other in some way, and that the grants might nourish or transform these cares and the inequities. But what emerged from my fieldwork, and as I have grappled with my material, is a sense, I believe, of a slightly different understanding of care.

If reports of the death of solidarity and care that the cash grants were premised upon have been greatly exaggerated, what I have been led to see is not that they are simply actually alive, but that we might even have been looking at the wrong thing in the first place. We do not just need to see how grants continue, animate or transform existing forms of care, whether based on romance, friendship, kinship or neighbourliness, but also how they might help us to *think* about care.

My own interlocutors would complain that 'these days' people no longer help each other like they used to in the old days. As anthropologists, and simply as people living in our common, increasingly damaged world, we often hear these sentiments; that everyday forms of mutuality and solidarity have been destroyed, or are breaking, down. But often when anthropologists dig under the surface of these proclamations and observe actual behaviour, they typically find all sorts of ways in which people help each other. David Graeber, for instance, wrote of 'everyday communism', something he argued existed in all societies, and particularly when people are working together on something. He wrote, 'If someone fixing a broken water pipe says, "Hand me the wrench," his co-worker will not, generally speaking, say, "And what do I get for it?"' (Graeber 2011, 95–6). This sort of behaviour, he argued, was the minimal baseline behaviour for human societies. We may also see resemblances to this behaviour in what Clara Han has referred to as 'silent kindness' (Han 2012, 54–91). This form of kindness, which she has identified in the poor urban neighbourhoods in Santiago in Chile is a mode of care people do for each other without remarking upon it. It could be, for example, quietly and simply responding to the cry of another person's child.

Both these cases show us how anthropologists often remark upon what is often unremarkable for the people whose lives they study. Care for, and cooperation with, others is simply done without remark. Therefore, what they make clear is that while it is important to listen carefully to our interlocutors when they lament the lack of care, mutuality, or solidarity, it is also possible, as an outsider, to see how care endures in other ways.

While it is therefore imperative to continue looking at unremarkable, unremarked upon and everyday forms of care, I have tried, in this book, to highlight something different. That is, the everyday forms of care that exist not only for each other but for the relationships themselves. It has meant seeing relationships as things that connect, but also as things that might involve different acceptable forms of proximity and distance. A neighbour, for instance, should not be too close for the relationship to continue. A bureaucrat might need to get close to those she or he serves in order to help relationships between benefactors and beneficiaries to continue. A mother might need to juggle proximity and distance, care and disregard, between her children. If we only look at care for persons then we might misunderstand that people act in different ways to maintain the relationships so that they endure into the future. This is what I have alluded to as an ethics of solidarity. But, as I have shown, it is a solidarity that is very much *not* solid but rather fragile and often unreliable.

Seismic Isolators and Elastic Fabrics

The assumption underlying my argument is that the people of Korogocho are constituted by their relationships. This is less an argument concerning their 'culture', whether Kikuyu, Luo, Kalenji or of any of Kenya's other ethnic groups – although the patrilineal aspects of these groups did sometimes make an appearance as people thought about and debated their relationships and obligations. It is also not an argument that only focuses on people's 'moral experience', although people's work on their relationships was deeply moral. Rather, my assumption has been that people and their full range of experiences are made up of relationships with other people; their ability to survive, to exchange in the market and out of it, their ways of pursuing the good life and the obligations this sometimes entails are all fundamentally relational.

The approach I have taken, then, has emphasised looking at what can keep this relational life possible. I have shown that it must have the qualities of dynamism and flexibility.

To finish, I suggest what I believe is a helpful, albeit peculiar, analogy of what I have been describing. It concerns the design and construction by engineers of earthquake-resistant buildings. One method of construction is to use what engineers call a 'seismic isolator'. The physics are far more complicated than I can describe, or for that matter understand, but the basic principle is simple: to allow a building to move without causing it to break up and fall down. Like a seismic isolator, a relationship needs flexibility. Just as the isolator allows the ground and the building to move, so too does a relationship that allows the persons it connects to move closer or further away. I do not, of course, mean geographically, although, as we saw in chapter 5, this can also be the case. In short, the relational fabric in Korogocho cannot simply be seen as intact or torn, but rather should be viewed through its elasticity.

I have argued throughout this book, and particularly in Part II, that this flexibility and elasticity, this pushing and pulling, is what characterised the relational fabric of Korogocho. Fabric is generally fragile, and this was the case also for the relational cloth in Korogocho. Yet, a fabric that is flexible and elastic is far less likely to be torn than an inflexible and rigid one.

Seeing elasticity in the warps and loops of the relational fabric has meant recognising how acts that may appear uncaring might actually be caring, as people themselves work on the multidimensional aspects of the relationships that constitute this cloth, bringing people closer or pushing them away in some respects. This was, as I have shown, a care for relationships. What is more, this all takes place in a context in which the wider political and economic relationships that make life so tragically hard for people in Korogocho are not simply uncaring but cruel. The cash grants did not produce this context – but neither did they transform it. They did reveal, though, the form of care that has been explored in this book.

Notes

Prologue

1. I use the terms 'ghetto' and 'slum' interchangeably in this book. There are also other popular terms such as 'informal settlement', and in Kenya, *mtaa*, Kiswahili for neighbourhood or street, but used officially in Kenya to denote the administrative section of the Location.
2. They were also hoping to be supported in the future by Kamau who had just succeeded, in spite of his inauspicious circumstances, in graduating from the prestigious University of Nairobi. To have a university degree in Korogocho was very unusual, but Kamau from an early age had worked hard and, as he recognised, also got lucky. From when he was of primary school-going age, he had been sponsored through his education by a Christian transnational NGO.
3. The Chief not only had an administrative responsibility for the Korogocho *mtaa*, but also for the much-feared Administration Police. The Provincial Administration, which includes the Administration Police, has now been dissolved as a result of the 2010 Constitution.
4. Both Kamau and I attended the resultant protest about Nyash's murder, as young men and women marched the streets to complain about the insecurity in the ghetto, and we later attended his funeral. Kamau and he knew each other well, and not only because they were both youth workers and activists who had been born and raised in Korogocho – but because they were friends.

Introduction: Grants and the Care for Relationships

1. While NGOs are a diverse phenomenon (Hilhorst 2003), the focus in this book is largely around those that aimed to address issues relating to development, humanitarianism and global health.
2. That is, a one-way transfer of money from an institution to poor and vulnerable people.
3. Both sorts of cash grants, though, have grown in popularity in recent years and have become scattered across the fields of development, humanitarianism, and as part of proposals that frame themselves as a form of redistributive justice, such as Basic Income.
4. The African Population and Health Research Organisation has its origins in the 1990s as part of the international Population Council, a biomedical, social science and public health research institution based in New York. Now an independent organisation, it receives a vast array of funding from most of the major health funders, including WHO, USAID, the Gates Foundation, Global Fund, as well as a range of universities. In 2002, it began conducting its Demo-

graphic Surveillance Survey in Korogocho and another settlement, Viwandani, following a total population of 60,000 people. Every four months a visit is paid to the participating households, probing into almost every aspect of respondents' lives.

5. The child grant constituted a large part of it, but although the urban grant was initially included, it was subsequently dropped. The other grants included the Older Persons Cash Transfer, the Persons with Severe Disabilities Cash Transfer, and the Hunger Safety Net Programme that targeted the traditional famine-stricken areas in the north of the country.

6. Programmes such as Bolsa Família in Brazil, as well as Mexico's Opportunidades, declared as important success stories, have become symbols for those attempting to implement similar programmes in other countries. Foreign donors, such as such as Britain's former Department for International Development, have organised and funded visits of policy-makers from African countries to observe programmes in Latin America, complicating simplistic, often rhetorical, arguments that the rise in social assistance is a success story from the global South. Yet the prominence of such 'success stories' also raises concern about the ways in which social policy is being pursued through projects rather than reforms at a much broader level (Tendler 2005).

7. It is notable that much discussion around the design of cash grants is oriented around what is termed 'graduation', in which it is argued that recipients should be transferred to other programmes, such as microcredit, or be given lump-sum business grants to prevent them staying on the grant indefinitely.

8. The Cash Transfer Learning Partnership was at the forefront of advocating for and researching the increasing role of cash transfers in the humanitarian aid industry, as well as coordinating the programmes during the large-scale drought affecting the Horn of Africa at the time.

9. But the minimalistic nature of bureaucracy should not be understood necessarily as 'government from a distance' (Miller and Rose 1990), in which people are required to check themselves in order to reach particular targets (Strathern 2000).

10. The same criticism was put forward by activists when reacting to the World Bank's strategy to eliminate extreme poverty by 2030. In their view, by concentrating on the problems of the poor, rather than tackling the problems of the rich, the World Bank avoids any more radical approach which would emphasise social justice (Roberts 2013).

11. These are what are called Basic Income rather than *Universal* Basic Income. There is little political appetite in Kenya to offer grants to the rich, despite arguments that the rich are, first, unlikely to want to be recipients, given the nominal value of the grant and, second, that they are likely to pay back the value of the grant anyway through taxation. In certain ways, the cash grants I studied in Korogocho are therefore dissimilar to what are often seen as more encompassing types of grants, those considered under the umbrella of Universal Basic Income. This is because while the cash grants in Kenya are offered to groups of the 'needy' or 'vulnerable', and often rest on traditional ideas of the male-breadwinner and dependent wife and children, Universal Basic Income is given to everyone, regardless of perceived status. Yet it is nonetheless impor-

tant to recognise the particularities of claims to universality (including in the also recently popular Universal Health Coverage agenda), which carry with them certain assumptions, as well as involving significant negotiation both in policy and practice. For instance, arguments for Universal Basic Income to include children rarely grapple with the ways in which childhood is a contested category (Ariès 1965). In arguing that payments would be made to parents or guardians responsible for children, proponents ignore how various populations might have different ideas about responsibility and how it is distributed across kin.

12. Economists would also agree, considering that their understanding of rational, maximising individuals was only ever intended to be the basis of their simplified, predictive models rather than a description of life in all its diversity.

13. In *Caring Cash*, I am similarly concerned with relationships running from the abstract and impersonal to the concrete and more personal and intimate. Some scholars have sought to differentiate between these two ways of looking at relationships. Gregory Feldman (2011), for instance, has referred to the former, abstract form, as relationships and the latter, more personal type, as connections. In this book, however, I find the elasticity of the term 'relationship' to be useful and do not differentiate between these different forms of attachment. This allows me to consider the abstract connections that constitute social life; relationships that can and are routinely pointed out by both ourselves and our interlocutors, such as the relationship between the state and the citizen. It also allows me to extract the rather more abstract conceptualisation of a relationship from my observations of the more personal, intimate connections between, say, a particular governmental worker and a citizen.

14. Death does not, of course, constitute the end of a relationship. While relationships between the living and the dead are sustained through memories and ancestorship, this is not the focus of this book.

15. Along with locations in Kwale on the coast, and Garissa in the north.

16. Korogocho certainly had a violence and roughness that was, both for me and my interlocutors, sometimes disconcerting and other times downright scary. As the reader has already seen, gunfights and murders are not uncommon in Korogocho. Through my fieldwork I met people who had been shot either by police or a rival gang, and heard many stories of others who had died at their hands. Even my first introduction to the slum was touched by violence. Deep in conversation – or if I'm more honest, flailing as I tried to convert my book-learnt, formal Kiswahili into the fast-changing Nairobi street language of Sheng that was being fired at me – I initially missed it. But the eyes of the others soon alerted me. Just in front of us, a man pulled a large knife on another, relieving the victim of his mobile phone and a bit of cash. I was later told that it was lucky that the man actually had something to give him; he might not otherwise have escaped unharmed. After that, on the constant instruction of others, I always carried something to give to a mugger, although nothing too expensive.

17. After a day of fieldwork, we would usually sit together and go through the day's research, discussing people we had interviewed, and raise issues that we had questions about.

18. It is not possible, she argues, for people to base their decision on whether to have children upon rational decision-making; for instance, weighing up the costs and benefits. This is because these decisions will be made by our current selves, with our current knowledge, experience and priorities, not our future ones that have been dramatically transformed by the experience of parenthood.

19. In contrast to many of my interactions with men, establishing and building relationships with my female interlocutors was often slower, and required considerably more patience on their part.

1 The Ghetto: A Place of Refuge and Charity

1. I owned a smartphone but when, earlier in my fieldwork, I had pulled it out to take a photograph, I was advised to leave it at home unless I wanted it to be stolen. The advice was as for much my benefit as it was for the potential thief. As we saw in the introduction, high-value items are attractive to young men struggling to make ends meet and they could well meet a tragic end were they to be caught stealing them. This is also the reason why I have not been able to provide my own photographs. Moreover, those foreigners who do take photos in the slums, often as part of 'slum tours', have often been accused of profiting from the poverty of slum dwellers.

2. The railway was originally being built by the Imperial British East African Company but financial difficulties meant the British government took over control in 1895.

3. These would soon be replaced by stone buildings that still stand in Nairobi today, although they are currently at risk of demolition.

4. The anthropologist James Holston (2008), speaking from his experience in the peripheries of São Paolo in Brazil, has discussed the way in which the urban poor there developed a form of 'insurgent citizenship'. Belonging and claims to the city resulted, in part, from their contribution to it in the form of building their own houses upon the land they had squatted upon. Holston's arguments concern a particularly situated political movement in Brazil, but policy makers interested in a more top-down, economic, and universalist approach have also imagined ways in which to connect the energies of the urban poor to land. Most famous, perhaps, were the policy suggestions of Peruvian economist Hernando de Soto (2000), known widely for his support for neoliberal oriented economic policies, which proposed formal state land-titling as a way of unleashing not just the vitality of the poor but also their latent entrepreneurial spirit. Through land titles, he argued, and influentially so as his proposals have been taken up across the world, the poor may be able to access formal capital, in the way of credit/debt, that would allow them to escape poverty. This formal security of tenure argument, which was an even more hopeful version of the 'sites-and-services' schemes, gained traction and became a major World Bank policy. It was taken up by the Kenyan government, which attempted to apply it to some urban slums in the cities. But it met with little success, particularly as in places like Korogocho, land rights and ownership issues are far more complex than the policy would allow for.

5. The General Service Unit is a paramilitary wing of both the Kenyan military and the police force. It was established in the colonial era and was used in the fight against Mau Mau.
6. While many have used the category of 'youth' as relatively unproblematic, Deborah Durham, drawing on discourses of 'youth', has shown how the category should be seen as shifting. In this way, she views it as a lens through which to understand aspects of the 'moral configurations of society', rather than a fixed population of people (Durham 2004, 589).
7. The region is the country's historic heartlands for the Luo, an ethnic group that has perennially been in political opposition despite the best efforts of a string of leaders, including Tom Mboya, Oginga Odinga and his son Raila Odinga. It was called Nyanza Province before the 2010 Constitution dissolved the province system, replacing provinces with counties.
8. These had, by the 1980s, been banned by government in an apparent attempt to foster a Kenyan unity.
9. The term *harambee* has been traced back to a shortening of a phrase, 'haluma jarraa', used by unskilled Arabic workers on the coast of East Africa who would chant the phrase as together they pushed heavy loads in carts (Orora and Spiegel 1980, 94).

2 Scoring the Poor

1. Jude herself had also once assisted in the search for the missing child belonging to a friend, Sarah. One day Sarah's child did not return home from school. Despite putting up posters and organising for announcements to be made on the local radio station, as well as endless searching of the slum, the child could not be located. A year later, Sarah received reports that a child resembling hers had been spotted in Mathare, a neighbouring slum. Jude and Sarah spent a week traversing the alleyways of Mathare to no avail. Close to giving up, they were told to visit the shack of an elderly *shosho* (grandmother) who was known to take missing and otherwise homeless children into her home, and who apparently had a child who had been staying with her for some months that fitted the description of the child. Upon arriving, the *shosho* listened to their story but told them that they must return with the Chief of Mathare, and also a letter from their own Chief in Korogocho. She was suspicious of people who would come to steal these children. They came back with the Chief and the letter, and the *shosho* brought out the child, who, miraculously, was Sarah's. The *shosho*, still reluctant to let the child go, asked Sarah to visit every day until the child became accustomed to her, and was eventually allowed to leave with her.
2. Because of the emergency situation, the targeting actually involved three rounds, allowing households to be recruited onto the programme in a staggered fashion before the census of the whole population was completed.
3. See note 5 of the introduction.
4. Based on the exchange rate (August 2011) of £1 GBP = KSh147.7. I use the same exchange rate throughout this book unless otherwise stated.
5. In the same year, 2004, the first version of the National Action Plan for Orphans and Vulnerable Children was also produced by the committee.

6. Which itself relies upon a problematic assumption that practice follows policy (Mosse 2005).
7. This low-cost method of managing and transferring money across and beyond Kenya through mobile phones has attracted significant media and academic, even anthropological, attention (Maurer 2012; Kusimba 2021). Even a decade ago, when I did fieldwork, it was already processing more transactions in Kenya alone than Western Union does globally (*Daily Nation* 2011).
8. This made it different from the category of poverty, that embodies a synchronic temporality, and which Georg Simmel (1965 [1908]) understood as emerging from the very act of identifying and assisting suffering individuals.
9. See also Kristin Cheney (2010) for a discussion of the importance of vulnerability as a category.
10. *Kwashiorkor* is a protein-energy form of malnutrition, recognised particularly by the symptom of oedema, or fluid retention. The name originates from Ga, a language from coastal Ghana, and means 'the sickness the baby gets when the new baby comes', recognising the loss of protein as the older child is weaned from breast milk. *Marasmus*, a general, not just protein-energy deficiency, manifests itself most often in muscular wasting and loss of fat. The word comes from the Greek, *marasmos*, meaning withering.
11. The slum and constituency of Kibera, on the other side of Nairobi to Korogocho, politically represented by the Luo Raila Odinga, was one of those affected by the violence. If there was ever any doubt the violence was politically orchestrated, one young man I knew quashed them, explaining how he was paid to buy up many *mapanga* (machetes) across town.

3 Under the Aegis of Mistrust

1. But also, based on my own life experience and upbringing, things that were decidedly unfamiliar including hunger and physical insecurity.
2. While donations of non-monetary gifts form an important part of the charitable realm, the institutionalised charity sector in Africa relies on donations of cash generally from foreigners, although in Kenya, a growing middle-class has also become increasingly interested in charitable giving.
3. Taken together, the idea of 'the poor' as being morally superior and therefore worthy of trust differs from other forms of philanthropy. For instance, Erica Bornstein has documented how some argue that the Hindu *dān* (donation) does not need to involve monitoring *if* the 'donee is carefully selected' (2009, 625).
4. Indeed, at the same time as the Kenyan government accepts interest-free loans via overseas aid to support welfare programmes, its leaders are also proclaiming how independent Kenya is, compared to its East African neighbours such as Tanzania, Uganda and Rwanda.

4 Detaching from Others, Surviving with Others

1. Kenyans are familiar with the term, 'come we stay' relationships or 'marriages', which refer to cohabitation arrangements between sexual partners. Those in

Korogocho might also use this term, but many I knew, with tongues-in-cheek, would laugh and say that their cohabitation arrangements were so precarious that 'come we try' was a more suitable moniker.

2. The argument, made by Parry and Bloch, that 'the maintenance of the long-term order is both pragmatically and conceptually dependent on individual short-term acquisitive endeavours' (Parry and Bloch and Parry 1989, 26) is also relevant here.

3. Max Gluckman long ago considered the way that judges among the Barotse of Northern Rhodesia (today Zambia) made their judgments through the use of precedents that included 'actual instances of upright behaviour, to show how people ought to behave' (Gluckman 1973, 197).

4. This strategic ignorance also cannot be described as a neglect of the poor (Procupez 2012, 175).

5. She once said to me, 'Women build the home. They pay rent, buy food, pay school fees. Men just go and get other women. I don't know for other estates, but in the ghetto, women here work so much and to do business is to be sharp' – here she used the Kiswahili, *kufungua akili* which means to open the mind – 'You get that from other women, who have done business.'

5 A Mother's Care

1. People also had memories of others' hunger. One woman once told me this: 'I have known hunger because my mother, she used to tie a *kanga* (cloth) around her stomach. When it got to that time, we knew no, our mother she is not going to cultivate for others, but she will go and be given porridge, and carry it coming to bring to her children, and she will just stay without eating.'

2. Silver cyprinid, a common fish from Lake Victoria and widely eaten across the country.

3. The term 'bob' is a colloquial term to describe a Kenyan shilling.

4. His arguments built upon the work of historians and anthropologists who have provided careful accounts of famines, hunger and poverty (for instance, Iliffe 1987; Vaughan 1987; Moore and Vaughan 1993).

5. Hers was a common refrain. A young rapper, Batata, hailing from the Mathare slum, had once played me one of his tracks. Taken with the tune and what I could interpret of the lyrics at the time – they were in the Sheng street language I did not know well – I uploaded it during my fieldwork to YouTube. It can be found here: (https://youtu.be/yQrGkQ-hfME). The chorus includes these lyrics, '*Ghetto, ghetto, ndio maisha ambaye si tumezoea*' (Ghetto, ghetto, this is the life we are used to).

6. In the humorous irony that typifies urban life in Nairobi, the English term of tarmac is used to refer to looking for work, while the Sheng term, *walami*, which has its origins in the meaning of 'tarmac', came to be used for referring to a foreigner.

7. To be clear, I am not suggesting that parents purely valued children in a util-itarian sense *qua* their future, economic capacity. They recognised children as people in their own right and appreciated their individual futures in the context of the family's relational ones. Take Samuel, a casual labourer and a

father of five. In a conversation with him about why he was trying to get his children to attend school regularly he did not talk about their contribution to the family, but referred simply to their status as children, saying, 'We as parents are dying. That's what happens doesn't it? When you have children, they are living and you are now dying.' In other words, for him, it was now the child's life that was important.

8.   Although everybody seemed to know stories of the young men who had married foreign aid workers and volunteers.

9.   A *gorogoro* is a measure used commonly in Korogocho which roughly equates to 2 kg of maize flour. The name *gorogoro* is linked to the 1981 *gorogoro* famine, when government policy did not allow households to buy more than one 2 kg tin of maize flour.

Conclusion

1.   I was to experience a very concrete example of this. The beginning of my field-work coincided with the signing, by Mwai Kibaki, of the 2010 Constitution. I joined the crowds of Kenyan citizens at Uhuru Park on the 27 August 2010 to watch the process. After a few hours, I realised that I had been pick-pocketed, and no longer had my mobile phone.

2.   In their approach, the grants are also interesting in their attempt to ostensibly rework existing epistemological and ontological hierarchies, joining other phenomena including the internet, blockchain technologies and peer-to-peer exchanges, which promise, in utopian terms, how exchanges, both economic and social, can take place by minimising the need for intermediaries.

References

Agamben, Giorgio. 1998. *Homo Sacer: Sovereign Power and Bare Life*. Stanford, CA: Stanford University Press.

Alviar, Carlos, and Roger Pearson. 2009. *Cash Transfers for Vulnerable Children in Kenya: From Political Choice to Scale-Up*. Social and Economic Policy Working Paper. New York: UNICEF.

Amnesty International. 2009. 'Kenya: The Unseen Majority: Nairobi's Two Million Slum-Dwellers'. London: Amnesty International.

Anderson, David. 2001. 'Corruption at City Hall: African Housing and Urban Development in Colonial Nairobi'. *Azania: Archaeological Research in Africa* 36–37(1): 138–54. https://doi.org/10.1080/00672700109511704.

Anderson, David. 2006. *Histories of the Hanged: Britain's Dirty War in Kenya and the End of Empire*. London: Phoenix.

Appadurai, Arjun. 2002. 'Deep Democracy: Urban Governmentality and the Horizon of Politics'. *Public Culture* 14(1): 21–47. https://doi.org/10.1215/08992363-14-1-21.

Ariès, Philippe. 1965. *Centuries of Childhood: A Social History of Family Life*. New York: Vintage.

Auyero, Javier. 2012. *Patients of the State: The Politics of Waiting in Argentina*. Durham, NC: Duke University Press.

Baehr, Peter. 2001. 'The "Iron Cage" and the "Shell as Hard as Steel": Parsons, Weber, and the Stahlhartes Gehäuse Metaphor in *The Protestant Ethic and the Spirit of Capitalism*'. *History and Theory* 40(2): 153–69. https://doi.org/10.1111/0018-2656.00160.

Bähre, Erik. 2007. 'Reluctant Solidarity Death, Urban Poverty and Neighbourly Assistance in South Africa'. *Ethnography* 8(1): 33–59. https://doi.org/10.1177/1466138107076136.

——. 2011. 'Liberation and Redistribution: Social Grants, Commercial Insurance, and Religious Riches in South Africa'. *Comparative Studies in Society and History* 53(2): 371–92. https://doi.org/10.1017/S0010417511000090.

——. 2017. 'The Enchantment of Weber's Iron Cage: Financialisation and Insurance in South Africa'. In *Magnifying Perspectives. Contributions to History, A Festschrift for Robert Ross*, edited by Iva Peša and Jan-Bart Gewald, pp. 254–72. ASC Occasional Publications 26. Leiden: African Studies Centre Leiden (ASCL).

Baier, Annette. 1986. 'Trust and Antitrust'. *Ethics* 96(2): 231–60.

Ballard, Richard. 2013. 'Geographies of Development II: Cash Transfers and the Reinvention of Development for the Poor'. *Progress in Human Geography*, January. https://doi.org/10.1177/0309132512474739.

Ballestero, Andrea. 2019. *A Future History of Water*. Durham, NC: Duke University Press.

Bayart, J.-F. 2000. 'Africa in the World: A History of Extraversion'. *African Affairs* 99(395): 217–67. https://doi.org/10.1093/afraf/99.395.217.

Bear, Laura. 2015. *Navigating Austerity: Currents of Debt along a South Asian River*. Stanford, CA: Stanford University Press.

Beguy, Donatien, Joyce Mumah and Lindsey Gottschalk. 2014. 'Unintended Pregnancies among Young Women Living in Urban Slums: Evidence from a Prospective

Study in Nairobi City, Kenya'. *PLOS ONE* 9(7): e101034. https://doi.org/10.1371/journal.pone.0101034.

Biehl, João. 2012. 'Care and Disregard'. In *A Companion to Moral Anthropology*, edited by Didier Fassin, pp. 242–63. Chichester: John Wiley & Sons. https://doi.org/10.1002/9781118290620.ch14.

Bierschenk, Thomas, and Jean-Pierre Olivier de Sardan. 2014. *States at Work: Dynamics of African Bureaucracies*. Leiden; Boston: Brill Academic.

Bornstein, Erica. 2003. *Spirit of Development: Religious NGOs, Morality and Economics in Zimbabwe*. Abingdon: Routledge.

——. 2009. 'The Impulse of Philanthropy'. *Cultural Anthropology* 24(4): 622–51. https://doi.org/10.1111/j.1548-1360.2009.01042.x.

——. 2012. *Disquieting Gifts: Humanitarianism in New Delhi*. Stanford, CA: Stanford University Press.

Bornstein, Erica, and Peter Redfield. 2011a. 'An Introduction to the Anthropology of Humanitarianism'. In *Forces of Compassion: Humanitarianism Between Ethics and Politics*, pp. 3–30. Santa Fe, NM: SAR Press.

——. 2011b. *Forces of Compassion: Humanitarianism Between Ethics and Politics*. Santa Fe, NM: SAR Press.

Bowker, Geoffrey C., and Susan Leigh Star. 1999. *Sorting Things Out: Classification and Its Consequences*. Inside Technology series. Cambridge, MA: MIT Press.

Branch, Daniel. 2011. *Kenya: Between Hope and Despair, 1963–2011*. New Haven, CT: Yale University Press.

Branch, Daniel, and Nicholas Cheeseman. 2006. 'The Politics of Control in Kenya: Understanding the Bureaucratic-Executive State, 1952–78'. *Review of African Political Economy* 33(107): 11–31. https://doi.org/10.1080/03056240600671183.

Brand, Russell. 2013. 'We No Longer Have the Luxury of Tradition'. *New Statesman*, 24 October.

Brown, Hannah. 2015. 'Global Health Partnerships, Governance, and Sovereign Responsibility in Western Kenya'. *American Ethnologist* 42(2): 340–55. https://doi.org/10.1111/amet.12134.

Brown, Hannah, and Maia Green. 2017. 'Demonstrating Development: Meetings as Management in Kenya's Health Sector'. *Journal of the Royal Anthropological Institute* 23(S1): 45–62. https://doi.org/10.1111/1467-9655.12593.

Budsock, Andrew. 2016. 'Unconditional Cash to the Poor: An Interview with GiveDirectly'. *Impakter* (blog), 25 October. https://impakter.com/unconditional-cash-poor-interview-givedirectly/.

Candea, Matei. 2010. '"I Fell in Love with Carlos the Meerkat": Engagement and Detachment in Human–Animal Relations'. *American Ethnologist* 37(2): 241–58.

Carrithers, Michael, Steven Collins and Steven Lukes, eds. 1985. *The Category of the Person: Anthropology, Philosophy, History*. Cambridge: Cambridge University Press.

Carsten, Janet. 1995. 'The Substance of Kinship and the Heat of the Hearth: Feeding, Personhood, and Relatedness among Malays in Pulau Langkawi'. *American Ethnologist* 22(2): 223–41.

Chant, Sylvia. 2006. 'Re-thinking the "Feminization of Poverty" in Relation to Aggregate Gender Indices'. *Journal of Human Development* 7(2): 201–20. https://doi.org/10.1080/14649880600768538.

Cheney, Kristen E. 2007. *Pillars of the Nation: Child Citizens and Ugandan National Development*. Chicago: University of Chicago Press.

Cheney, Kristen E. 2010. 'Expanding Vulnerability, Dwindling Resources: Implications for Orphaned Futures in Uganda'. *Childhood in Africa* 2(1): 8–15.

Cole, Jennifer, and Lynn M. Thomas, eds. 2009. *Love in Africa*. Chicago: University of Chicago Press.

Collier, Stephen J. 2011. *Post-Soviet Social: Neoliberalism, Social Modernity, Biopolitics*. Princeton, NJ: Princeton University Press.

Comaroff, Jean, and John L. Comaroff. 2006. 'Reflections on Youth'. In *Frontiers of Capital: Ethnographic Reflections on the New Economy*, edited by Melissa Suzanne Fisher and Greg Downey, pp. 267–80. Durham, NC: Duke University Press.

Das, Veena. 2006. *Life and Words: Violence and the Descent into the Ordinary*. Berkeley, CA: University of California Press.

——. 2015. *Affliction*. New York: Fordham University Press.

Davis, Mike. 2006. *Planet of Slums*. London: Verso.

de Soto, Hernando. 2000. *The Mystery of Capital: Why Capitalism Triumphs in the West and Fails Everywhere Else*. New York: Basic Books.

de Waal, Alex. 1989. *Famine that Kills: Darfur, Sudan*. New York: Oxford University Press, USA.

Devereux, Stephen. 2009. 'Sen's Entitlement Approach: Critiques and Counter-Critiques'. In *The New Famines: Why Famines Persist in an Era of Globalization*, edited by Stephen Devereux, pp. 66–89. London: Routledge.

Di Nunzio, Marco. 2019. *The Act of Living: Street Life, Marginality, and Development in Urban Ethiopia*. Ithaca, NY: Cornell University Press.

Diouf, Mamadou. 2003. 'Engaging Postcolonial Cultures: African Youth and Public Space'. *African Studies Review* 46(2): 1–12.

Donovan, Kevin P., and Emma Park. 2019. 'Perpetual Debt in the Silicon Savannah'. *Boston Review*, 20 September.

Du Gay, Paul. 2000. *In Praise of Bureaucracy: Weber – Organization – Ethics*. London; Thousand Oaks, CA: Sage Publications.

Durham, Deborah. 2004. 'Disappearing Youth: Youth as a Social Shifter in Botswana'. *American Ethnologist* 31(4): 589–605. https://doi.org/10.1525/ae.2004.31.4.589.

Elyachar, Julia. 2002. 'Empowerment Money: The World Bank, Non-Governmental Organizations, and the Value of Culture in Egypt'. *Public Culture* 14(3): 493–513.

——. 2005. *Markets of Dispossession: NGOs, Economic Development, and the State in Cairo*. Durham, NC: Duke University Press.

——. 2006. 'Best Practices: Research, Finance, and NGOs in Cairo'. *American Ethnologist* 33(3): 413–26. https://doi.org/10.1525/ae.2006.33.3.413.

Emina, Jacques, Donatien Beguy, Eliya M. Zulu, Alex C. Ezeh, Kanyiva Muindi, Patricia Elung'ata, John K. Otsola, and Yazoumé Yé. 2011. 'Monitoring of Health and Demographic Outcomes in Poor Urban Settlements: Evidence from the Nairobi Urban Health and Demographic Surveillance System'. *Journal of Urban Health: Bulletin of the New York Academy of Medicine* 88, Suppl. 2 (June): 200–18. https://doi.org/10.1007/s11524-011-9594-1.

Englund, Harri. 1999. 'The Self in Self-Interest: Land, Labour and Temporalities in Malawi's Agrarian Change'. *Africa: Journal of the International African Institute* 69(1): 139–59. https://doi.org/10.2307/1161080.

——. 2002. 'The Village in the City, the City in the Village: Migrants in Lilongwe'. *Journal of Southern African Studies* 28(1): 137–54. https://doi.org/10.1080/0305707 0120117015.

——. 2006. *Prisoners of Freedom: Human Rights and the African Poor*. Berkeley; Los Angeles; London: University of California Press.

——. 2008. 'Extreme Poverty and Existential Obligations: Beyond Morality in the Anthropology of Africa?' *Social Analysis* 52: 33–50. https://doi.org/10.3167/sa.2008.520302.

——. 2011. 'Anthropologist and His Poor'. In *Forces of Compassion: Humanitarianism Between Ethics and Politics*, edited by Erica Bornstein and Peter Redfield, pp. 71–93. Santa Fe, NM: SAR Press.

European Commission. 2013. 'The Use of Cash and Vouchers in Humanitarian Crises: DG ECHO Funding Guidelines'. Ares(2013)317021-11/03/2013. Brussels: European Commission.

Evans-Pritchard, E.E. 1987 [1940]. *The Nuer: A Description of the Modes of Livelihood and Political Institutions of a Nilotic People*. New edn. New York: OUP USA.

Fassin, Didier. 2007. *When Bodies Remember: Experiences and Politics of AIDS in South Africa*. Berkeley, CA: University of California Press.

——. 2009. 'Another Politics of Life Is Possible'. *Theory, Culture & Society* 26(5): 44–60. https://doi.org/10.1177/0263276409106349.

Fejerskov, Adam Moe. 2017. 'The New Technopolitics of Development and the Global South as a Laboratory of Technological Experimentation'. *Science, Technology, & Human Values* 42(5): 947–68. https://doi.org/10.1177/0162243917709934.

Feldman, Gregory. 2011. 'If Ethnography Is More than Participant-Observation, Then Relations Are More than Connections: The Case for Nonlocal Ethnography in a World of Apparatuses'. *Anthropological Theory*, December. https://doi.org/10.1177/1463499611429904.

Feldman, Ilana. 2008. *Governing Gaza: Bureaucracy, Authority, and the Work of Rule, 1917–1967*. Durham, NC: Duke University Press.

——. 2012. 'The Humanitarian Condition: Palestinian Refugees and the Politics of Living'. *Humanity: An International Journal of Human Rights, Humanitarianism, and Development* 3(2): 155–72. https://doi.org/10.1353/hum.2012.0017.

Ferguson, James. 1992. 'The Country and the City on the Copperbelt'. *Cultural Anthropology* 7(1): 80–92. https://doi.org/10.2307/656522.

——. 1994. *The Anti-Politics Machine: Development, Depoliticization and Bureaucratic Power in Lesotho*. Minneapolis, MN: University of Minnesota Press.

——. 1999. *Expectations of Modernity*. Berkeley, CA: University of California Press.

——. 2010. 'The Uses of Neoliberalism'. *Antipode* 41: 166–84. https://doi.org/10.1111/j.1467-8330.2009.00721.x.

——. 2015. *Give a Man a Fish: Reflections on the New Politics of Distribution*. Durham NC: Duke University Press.

Ferguson, James, and Akhil Gupta. 2002. 'Spatialising States: Towards an Ethnography of Neoliberal Governmentality'. *American Ethnologist* 29(4): 981–1002.

Fortes, Meyer. 1949. *The Web of Kinship among the Tallensi*. London: Oxford University Press.

——. 1961. 'Pietas in Ancestor Worship'. *Journal of the Royal Anthropological Institute of Great Britain and Ireland* 91(2): 166–91. https://doi.org/10.2307/2844412.

Foucault, Michel. 1979. *The History of Sexuality*, vol. 1, trans. Robert Hurley. London: Penguin.

——. 1990. 'Social Security'. In *Politics, Philosophy, Culture: Interviews and Other Writings, 1977–1984*, edited by Lawrence Kritzman, pp. 160–77. New York: Routledge.

——. 1991. *Discipline and Punish: The Birth of the Prison*, trans. Alan Sheridan. Harmondsworth: Penguin.

——. 2008. *The Birth of Biopolitics: Lectures at the Collège de France, 1978–1979*, trans. Graham Burchell. Basingstoke: Palgrave Macmillan.

——. 2009. *Security, Territory, Population*. Basingstoke; New York: Palgrave Macmillan.

Fox, Roddy. 1996. 'Bleak Future for Multi-Party Elections in Kenya'. *Journal of Modern African Studies* 34(4): 597–607. https://doi.org/10.1017/S0022278X00055786.

Francis, Elizabeth. 2002. 'Gender, Migration and Multiple Livelihoods: Cases from Eastern and Southern Africa'. *Journal of Development Studies* 38(5): 167–90. https://doi.org/10.1080/00220380412331322551.

Fraser, Nancy, and Linda Gordon. 1994. 'A Genealogy of Dependency: Tracing a Keyword of the U.S. Welfare State'. *Signs* 19(2): 309–36. https://doi.org/10.2307/3174801.

Fukuyama, Francis. 1996. *Trust: The Social Virtues and The Creation of Prosperity*. New York: Free Press.

Gambetta, Diego. 1988. 'Afterword: Can We Trust Trust?' In *Trust: Making and Breaking Cooperative Relations*, edited by Diego Gambetta. Oxford: Basil Blackwell.

Garcia, Angela. 2010. *The Pastoral Clinic: Addiction and Dispossession Along the Rio Grande*. Berkeley, CA: University of California Press.

Geissler, Wenzel, and Ruth Jane Prince. 2010. *The Land Is Dying: Contingency, Creativity and Conflict in Western Kenya*. New York; Oxford: Berghahn Books.

Geller, Pamela L., and Miranda K. Stockett. 2006. *Feminist Anthropology: Past, Present, and Future*. Philadelphia, PA: University of Pennsylvania Press.

Gilligan, Carol. 1982. *In a Different Voice: Psychological Theory and Women's Development*. Cambridge, MA: Harvard University Press.

Gluckman, M. 1973. *The Judicial Process among the Barotse of Northern Rhodesia (Zambia)*. Manchester: Manchester University Press (for the Institute of African Studies, University of Zambia).

Goldstein, Donna M. 2003. *Laughter Out of Place: Race, Class, Violence, and Sexuality in a Rio Shantytown*. Berkeley, CA: University of California Press.

Goodell, Grace E. 1985. 'Paternalism, Patronage, and Potlatch: The Dynamics of Giving and Being Given To', and Comments and Reply. *Current Anthropology* 26(2): 247–66.

Graeber, David. 2011. *Debt: The First 5,000 Years*. New York: Melville House.

——. 2018. *Bullshit Jobs: A Theory*. New York: Penguin Books/Allen Lane.

Green, Maia. 2012. 'Anticipatory Development: Mobilizing Civil Society in Tanzania'. *Critique of Anthropology* 32(3): 309–33. https://doi.org/10.1177/0308275X12449107.

Gudeman, Stephen. 2001. *The Anthropology of Economy: Community, Market and Culture*. Malden, MA: Wiley-Blackwell.

Gupta, Akhil. 2012. *Red Tape: Bureaucracy, Structural Violence, and Poverty in India*. Durham, NC: Duke University Press.

Guyer, Jane I. 1987. *Feeding African Cities: Studies in Regional Social History*. Bloomington, IN: Indiana University Press.

——. 1993. 'Wealth in People and Self-Realization in Equatorial Africa'. *Man*, New Series, 28(2): 243–65. https://doi.org/10.2307/2803412.

——. 2004. *Marginal Gains: Monetary Transactions in Atlantic Africa*. Chicago; London: University of Chicago Press.

Hake, Andrew. 1977. *African Metropolis: Nairobi's Self-Help City*. London: Published for Sussex University Press by Chatto & Windus.

Han, Clara. 2012. *Life in Debt: Times of Care and Violence in Neoliberal Chile*. Berkeley; Los Angeles; London: University of California Press.

Hanlon, Joseph, Armando Barrientos, and David Hulme. 2010. *Just Give Money to the Poor: The Development Revolution from the Global South.* Sterling, VA: Kumarian Press.

Haraway, Donna. 1988. 'Situated Knowledges: The Science Question in Feminism and the Privilege of Partial Perspective'. *Feminist Studies* 14(3): 575–99. https://doi.org/10.2307/3178066.

Hardin, Garrett. 1974. 'Lifeboat Ethics: The Case Against Helping the Poor'. *Psychology Today* 8 (September): 38–43.

Hardin, Russell. 2006. *Trust.* Cambridge: Polity Press.

Hart, Keith. 1973. 'Informal Income Opportunities and Urban Employment in Ghana'. *Journal of Modern African Studies* 11(1): 61–89.

——. 2009. 'On the Informal Economy: The Political History of an Ethnographic Concept'. Working Papers CEB 09-042.RS, ULB – Université Libre de Bruxelles. https://ideas.repec.org/p/sol/wpaper/09-042.html.

Hart, Keith, and Chris Hann. 2011. *Economic Anthropology.* Cambridge; Malden, MA: Polity.

Harvey, David. 1989. *The Urban Experience.* Baltimore, MD: Johns Hopkins University Press.

Harvey, Penelope, and Hannah Knox. 2015. *Roads: An Anthropology of Infrastructure and Expertise.* Ithaca, NY; London: Cornell University Press.

Hayek, Friedrich A. 2011 [1944]. *The Constitution of Liberty.* Chicago: University of Chicago Press.

Haynes, Naomi. 2012. 'Pentecostalism and the Morality of Money: Prosperity, Inequality, and Religious Sociality on the Zambian Copperbelt'. *Journal of the Royal Anthropological Institute* 18(1): 123–39. https://doi.org/10.1111/j.1467-9655.2011.01734.x.

Heckscher, Charles C., and Anne Donnellon. 1994. *The Post-Bureaucratic Organization: New Perspectives on Organizational Change.* Thousand Oaks, CA: Sage Publications.

Held, Virginia. 2006. *The Ethics of Care: Personal, Political, Global.* New York: Oxford University Press.

Herzfeld, Michael. 1993. *The Social Production of Indifference.* Chicago; London: University of Chicago Press.

Hickey, Sam. 2008. 'Conceptualising the Politics of Social Protection in Africa'. In *Social Protection for the Poor and the Poorest: Concepts, Policies and Politics*, edited by Armando Barrientos and David Hulme, pp. 247–63. London: Palgrave Macmillan.

Hickey, Samuel, and Giles Mohan. 2004. *Participation, from Tyranny to Transformation? Exploring New Approaches to Participation in Development.* London; New York; New York: Zed Books.

HiiL. 2018. 'Justice Needs and Satisfaction in Kenya 2017'. The Hague Institute for Innovation of Law.

Hilhorst, Thea. 2003. *The Real World of NGOs: Discourses, Diversity, and Development.* London; New York: Zed Books.

Hobart, Mark. 1993. *An Anthropological Critique of Development: The Growth of Ignorance.* London; New York: Routledge.

Holston, James. 2007. *Insurgent Citizenship: Disjunctions of Democracy and Modernity in Brazil.* Princeton, NJ: Princeton University Press.

Hornsby, Charles. 2013. *Kenya: A History since Independence.* London: I.B. Tauris.

Hull, Matthew. 2012. *Government of Paper: The Materiality of Bureaucracy in Urban Pakistan.* Berkeley, CA: University of California Press.

Ikels, Charlotte. 2004. *Filial Piety: Practice and Discourse in Contemporary East Asia.* Stanford, CA: Stanford University Press.

Ikiara, Gerrishon. 2009. 'Political Economy of Cash Transfers In Kenya'. Report prepared for the Overseas Development Institute. London: ODI.

Iliffe, John. 1987. *The African Poor: A History.* Cambridge: Cambridge University Press.

ILO. 1972. *Employment, Incomes and Equality: Strategy for Increasing Productive Employment in Kenya.* Geneva: International Labour Office.

James, Deborah. 2014. *Money from Nothing.* Stanford, CA: Stanford University Press.

Jiménez, Alberto Corsín. 2011. 'Trust in Anthropology'. *Anthropological Theory* 11(2): 177–96. https://doi.org/10.1177/1463499611407392.

K'Akumu, O.A. 2013. 'The Production of Artisanal Dimension Stone in Nairobi: A Factor Analytic Study'. *Journal of Urban Technology* 20(4): 99–118. https://doi.org/10.1080/10630732.2013.855510.

Kelsall, Tim. 2011. 'Going with the Grain in African Development?' *Development Policy Review* 29: s223–51. https://doi.org/10.1111/j.1467-7679.2011.00527.x.

Kimani, Njoroge. 2007. 'Environmental Pollution and Impacts on Public Health: Implications of the Dandora Municipal Dumping Site in Nairobi, Kenya'. Nairobi: United Nations Environment Programme.

Kusimba, Sibel. 2021. *Reimagining Money: Kenya in the Digital Finance Revolution.* Stanford, CA: Stanford University Press.

Laidlaw, James. 2000. 'A Free Gift Makes No Friends'. *Journal of the Royal Anthropological Institute* 6(4): 617–34. https://doi.org/10.1111/1467-9655.00036.

——. 2013. *The Subject of Virtue.* Kindle Edition. Cambridge: Cambridge University Press.

Lavinas, Lena. 2013. '21st-century Welfare'. *New Left Review* 84 (Nov./Dec.): 5–40.

Lazar, Sian. 2004. 'Education for Credit Development as Citizenship Project in Bolivia'. *Critique of Anthropology* 24(3): 301–19. https://doi.org/10.1177/0308275X04045423.

——. 2017. *The Social Life of Politics: Ethics, Kinship, and Union Activism in Argentina.* Stanford, CA: Stanford University Press.

Lee-Smith, Diana. 1990. 'Squatter Landlords in Nairobi: A Case Study of Korogocho'. In *Housing. Africa's Urban Poor,* edited by Philip Amis and P. Lloyd. Manchester: Manchester University Press.

Levine, Robert A. 2008. *Child Care and Culture: Lessons from Africa.* Cambridge: Cambridge University Press.

Lewis, Joanna. 2000. *Empire State-Building: War and Welfare in Kenya, 1925–52.* Columbus, OH: Ohio State University Press.

Lienhardt, Godfrey. 1989. 'Self: Public, Private. Some African Representations'. In *The Category of the Person: Anthropology, Philosophy, History,* edited by Michael Carrithers, Steven Collins and Steven Lukes, pp. 141–55. Cambridge: Cambridge University Press.

Lipsky, Michael. 1980. *Street-Level Bureaucracy: Dilemmas of the Individual in Public Services.* New York: Russell Sage Foundation.

Lloyd-Sherlock, Peter, João Saboia and Baruch Ramírez-Rodríguez. 2012. 'Cash Transfers and the Well-Being of Older People in Brazil'. *Development and Change* 43(5): 1049–72. https://doi.org/10.1111/j.1467-7660.2012.01790.x.

Loeckx, A., and B. Githua. 2010. 'Sites and Services in Nairobi, 1973–1987'. In *Human Settlements: Formulations and (Re)Calibrations,* edited by V. d'Auria, B. De Meulder and K. Shannon, pp. 82–91. Amsterdam: SUN Academia.

Lonsdale, John. 1994. 'Moral Ethnicity and Political Tribalism'. In *Inventions and Boundaries: Historical and Anthropological Approaches to the Study of Ethnicity and Nationalism*, edited by Preben Kaarsholm and Jan Hultin, pp. 131–50. Roskilde, Denmark: International Development Studies, Roskilde University.

——. 2008. 'Soil, Work, Civilisation, and Citizenship in Kenya'. *Journal of Eastern African Studies* 2(2): 305. https://doi.org/10.1080/17531050802058450.

Lucchi, Elena. 2012. 'Moving from the "Why" to the "How": Reflections on Humanitarian Response in Urban Settings'. *Disasters* 36: S87–104. https://doi.org/10.1111/j.1467-7717.2012.01283.x.

Madise, Nyovani J., Abdhalah K. Ziraba, Joseph Inungu, Samoel A. Khamadi, Alex Ezeh, Eliya M. Zulu, John Kebaso, Vincent Okoth, and Matilu Mwau. 2012. 'Are Slum Dwellers at Heightened Risk of HIV Infection than Other Urban Residents? Evidence from Population-Based HIV Prevalence Surveys in Kenya'. *Health & Place* 18(5): 1144–52. https://doi.org/10.1016/j.healthplace.2012.04.003.

Mains, Daniel. 2007. 'Neoliberal Times: Progress, Boredom, and Shame among Young Men in Urban Ethiopia'. *American Ethnologist* 34(4): 659–73. https://doi.org/10.1525/ae.2007.34.4.659.

Mair, Jonathan. 2015. 'Ignorance and the Ethics of Detachment among Mongolian Tibetan Buddhists in Inner Mongolia, China'. In *Detachment: Essays on the Limits of Relational Thinking*, edited by Matei Candea, Jo Cook, Catherine Trundle, and Thomas Yarrow, pp. 236–55. Manchester: Manchester University Press.

Malkki, Liisa H. 1996. 'Speechless Emissaries: Refugees, Humanitarianism, and Dehistoricization'. *Cultural Anthropology* 11(3): 377–404.

Marsland, Rebecca, and Ruth Prince. 2012. 'What Is Life Worth? Exploring Biomedical Interventions, Survival, and the Politics of Life'. *Medical Anthropology Quarterly* 26(4): 453–69. https://doi.org/10.1111/maq.12001.

Masquelier, Adeline. 2013. 'Teatime: Boredom and the Temporalities of Young Men in Niger'. *Africa* 83(3): 470–91. https://doi.org/10.1017/S0001972013000272.

Mathur, Nayanika. 2015. *Paper Tiger: Law, Bureaucracy and the Developmental State in Himalayan India*. Cambridge: Cambridge University Press.

Mattingly, Cheryl. 2014. *Moral Laboratories: Family Peril and the Struggle for a Good Life*. Oakland, CA: University of California Press.

Maurer, Bill. 2006. 'The Anthropology of Money'. *Annual Review of Anthropology* 35(1): 15–36. https://doi.org/10.1146/annurev.anthro.35.081705.123127.

Maurer, Bill. 2012. 'Mobile Money: Communication, Consumption and Change in the Payments Space'. *Journal of Development Studies* 48(5): 589–604. https://doi.org/10.1080/00220388.2011.621944.

Mauss, Marcel. 2002 [1925]. *The Gift: The Form and Reason for Exchange in Archaic Societies*. Translated by W.D. Halls. Abingdon: Routledge.

Mayer, Philip, and Iona Mayer. 1961. *Townsmen or Tribesmen: Conservatism and the Process of Urbanization in a South African City*. Cape Town, South Africa: Oxford University Press.

Mbithi, Philip M., and Rasmus Rasmusson. 1977. *Self-Reliance in Kenya: The Case of Harambee*. Uppsala, Sweden: Nordic Africa Institute.

Mbui, Damaris, Emily Chebet, Geoffrey Kamau and Joshua Kibet. 2016. 'The State of Water Quality in Nairobi River, Kenya'. *Asian Journal of Research in Chemistry* 9(11): 579–86. https://doi.org/10.5958/0974-4150.2016.00078.X.

Merry, Sally Engle. 2011. 'Measuring the World'. *Current Anthropology* 52(S3): S83–95. https://doi.org/10.1086/657241.

Metcalf, Peter. 2001. *They Lie, We Lie: Getting on with Anthropology*. Abingdon: Routledge.

Miller, Peter, and Nikolas Rose. 1990. 'Governing Economic Life'. *Economy and Society* 19(1): 1–31. https://doi.org/10.1080/03085149000000001.

Mkawale, Steve. 2015. '"Ghost NGOs" in Kenya Received Sh35m to Fight HIV Spread'. *The Standard*, 29 July. https://www.standardmedia.co.ke/worldcup/article/2000170759/ghost-ngos-in-kenya-received-sh35m-to-fight-hiv-spread.

Mol, Annemarie. 2008. *The Logic of Care: Health and the Problem of Patient Choice*. Abingdon: Routledge.

Molyneux, Maxine. 2007. *Change and Continuity in Social Protection in Latin America: Mothers at the Service of the State?* Gender and Development Programme Paper 1. Switzerland: UNRISD.

Moodie, Megan. 2008. 'Enter Microcredit: A New Culture of Women's Empowerment in Rajasthan?' *American Ethnologist* 35(3): 454–65. https://doi.org/10.1111/j.1548-1425.2008.00046.x.

Moore, Henrietta L., and Megan Vaughan. 1993. *Cutting Down Trees: Gender, Nutrition, and Agricultural Change in the Northern Province of Zambia, 1980–1990*. Portsmouth, NH: Heinemann.

Morton, Gregory Duff. 2015. 'Managing Transience: Bolsa Família and Its Subjects in an MST Landless Settlement'. *Journal of Peasant Studies* 42(6): 1283–1305. https://doi.org/10.1080/03066150.2014.978298.

Mosse, David. 2005. *Cultivating Development an Ethnography of Aid Policy and Practice*. London; Ann Arbor, MI: Pluto Press.

Muinde, Jacinta Victoria Syombua. 2018. *An Economy of (Dis)Affections: Women-Headed Households, Cash Transfers and Matrilineal Relations in Kenya South Coast*. PhD dissertation, University of Cambridge.

Murimi, Peter, Joel Gunter and Tom Watson. 2020. 'The Baby Stealers'. *BBC News*, 15 November. https://www.bbc.com/news/world-africa-54892564.

Mutongi, Kenda. 2006. 'Thugs or Entrepreneurs? Perceptions of Matatu Operators in Nairobi, 1970 to the Present'. *Africa: Journal of the International African Institute* 76(4): 549–68.

———. 2017. *Matatu: A History of Popular Transportation in Nairobi*. Chicago: University of Chicago Press.

Mwangi, Monicah. 2018. 'Police Ruined My Life, Cries Mother of Three Slain Sons'. *The Star*, 16 January. https://www.the-star.co.ke/news/big-read/2018-01-15-police-ruined-my-life-cries-mother-of-three-slain-sons/

NACC and NASCOP. 2012. *The Kenya AIDS Epidemic Update 2011*. Nairobi, Kenya: NACC and NASCOP.

Neuwirth, Robert. 2006. *Shadow Cities*. Abingdon: Routledge.

Neves, David, and Andries du Toit. 2012. 'Money and Sociality in South Africa's Informal Economy'. Special Issue, *Africa* 82(1): 131–49. https://doi.org/10.1017/S0001972011000763.

Nguyen, Vinh-Kim. 2009. 'Government-by-Exception: Enrolment and Experimentality in Mass HIV Treatment Programmes in Africa'. *Social Theory & Health* 7(3): 196–217. https://doi.org/10.1057/sth.2009.12.

———. 2010. *The Republic of Therapy: Triage and Sovereignty in West Africa's Time of AIDS*. Durham, NC: Duke University Press.

Okello Weda, John, and Anne Wambui Mwangi. 2015. 'Human Factors and Child's Safety: A Review of Charitable Children's Institutions in Kisumu Municipal-

ity, Kenya'. *Humanities and Social Sciences* 3(1): 47. https://doi.org/10.11648/j.
hss.20150301.16.

Okeyo Pala, Achola. 1980. 'Daughters of the Lakes and Rivers: Colonization and the
Land Rights of Luo Women'. In *Women and Colonization: Anthropological Perspec-
tives*, edited by Mona Etienne and Eleanor Burke Leacock, pp. 186–213. New York:
Praeger.

Olivier de Sardan, Jean-Pierre, and Emmanuelle Piccoli, eds. 2018. *Cash Transfers in
Context: An Anthropological Perspective*. New York: Berghahn Books.

Onyango-Obbo, Charles. 2010. 'Kenya's "UnEast African" Constitution and Why
It Took So Long'. *The East African* 9 August. www.theeastafrican.co.ke/news/-
/2558/972908/-/pbijvxz/-/index.html

Oriedo, Michael. 2010. 'Transformer Oil Stolen to Fry Food'. *The Standard*, 3 March.
www.standardmedia.co.ke/the-standard/article/2000004652/transformer-
oil-stolen-to-fry-food+&cd=1&hl=en&ct=clnk&gl=no

Orora, John H.O., and Hans B.C. Spiegel. 1980. 'Harambee: Self-Help Development
Projects in Kenya'. *International Journal of Comparative Sociology* 21(3–4): 243–53.
https://doi.org/10.1163/156854280X00182.

Ortner, Sherry B. 2016. 'Dark Anthropology and Its Others: Theory Since the
Eighties'. *HAU: Journal of Ethnographic Theory* 6(1): 47–73. https://doi.org/10.14318/
hau6.1.004.

Paine, Thomas. 2000. 'Agrarian Justice'. In *The Origins of Left-Libertarianism: An
Anthology of Historical Writings*, edited by Hillel Steiner and Peter Vallentyne,
pp. 83–97. Basingstoke: Palgrave.

Parker, Melissa, Tommy Matthew Hanson, Ahmed Vandi, Lawrence Sao Babawo
and Tim Allen. 2019. 'Ebola and Public Authority: Saving Loved Ones in Sierra
Leone'. *Medical Anthropology* 38(5): 440–54. https://doi.org/10.1080/01459740.
2019.1609472.

Parkin, David. 1969. *Neighbours and Nationals in an African City Ward*. London: Routledge and Kegan Paul.

——. 1978. *The Cultural Definition of Political Response: Lineal Destiny among the Luo*.
London: Academic Press.

Parry, Jonathan, and Maurice Bloch. 1989. *Money and the Morality of Exchange*. Cambridge: Cambridge University Press.

Paul, L.A. 2014. *Transformative Experience*. Oxford: Oxford University Press.

Penglase, Ben. 2009. 'States of Insecurity: Everyday Emergencies, Public Secrets,
and Drug Trafficker Power in a Brazilian Favela'. *PoLAR: Political and Legal Anthropology Review* 32(1): 47–63. https://doi.org/10.1111/j.1555-2934.2009.01023.x.

Petryna, Adriana. 2002. *Life Exposed: Biological Citizens after Chernobyl*. Princeton,
NJ: Princeton University Press.

Pietila, Tuulikki. 2007. *Gossip, Markets, and Gender: How Dialogue Constructs Moral
Value in Post-Socialist Kilimanjaro*. Madison, WI: University of Wisconsin Press.

Pogge, Thomas Winfried Menko. 2007. *Freedom from Poverty as a Human Right: Who
Owes What to the Very Poor?* Paris; Oxford; New York: United Nations Educational,
Scientific, and Cultural Organization; Oxford University Press.

Poggiali, Lisa. 2016. 'Seeing (from) Digital Peripheries: Technology and Transparency in Kenya's Silicon Savannah'. *Cultural Anthropology* 31(3): 387–411. https://
doi.org/10.14506/ca31.3.07.

Polanyi, Karl. 2001. *The Great Transformation: The Political and Economic Origins of
Our Time*. 2nd edn. Boston, MA: Beacon Press.

Prince, Ruth. 2012. 'HIV and the Moral Economy of Survival in an East African City'. *Medical Anthropology Quarterly* 26(4): 534–56. https://doi.org/10.1111/maq.12006.

Prince, Ruth. 2022. 'Beyond Failure: Bureaucratic Labour and the Will to Improve in Kenya's Experiments with Universal Health Care'. *Social Anthropology/ Anthropologie Sociale* 30(2): 56–80. https://doi.org/10.3167/saas.2022.300205.

Prince, Ruth, and Hannah Brown, eds. 2016. *Volunteer Economies: The Politics and Ethics of Voluntary Labour in Africa.*. Woodbridge, Suffolk: James Currey.

Prince, Ruth, and Tom Neumark. 2022. 'Curious Utopias: Dreaming Big Again in the Twenty-First Century?' *Social Anthropology/Anthropologie Sociale* 30(2): 1–15. https://doi.org/10.3167/saas.2022.300202.

Procupez, Valeria. 2012. 'Inhabiting the Temporary: Patience and Uncertainty among Urban Squatters in Buenos Aires'. In *The Anthropology of Ignorance: An Ethnographic Approach*, edited by Casey High, Ann Kelly, and Jonathan Mair, pp. 163–88. New York: Palgrave Macmillan.

Rajak, Dinah. 2008. '"Uplift and Empower": The Market, Morality and Corporate Responsibility on South Africa's Platinum Belt'. In *Hidden Hands in the Market: Ethnographies of Fair Trade, Ethical Consumption and Corporate Social Responsibility*, edited by Geert de Neve. Bingley: Emerald Group Publishing.

Rancière, Jacques. 2003. *The Philosopher and His Poor*, trans. John Drury, Corrine Oster and Andrew Parker, edited by Andrew Parker. Durham, NC: Duke University Press.

——. 2012. *Proletarian Nights: The Workers' Dream in Nineteenth-Century France*. London; New York: Verso.

Redfield, Peter. 2005. 'Doctors, Borders, and Life in Crisis'. *Cultural Anthropology* 20(3): 328–61. https://doi.org/10.1525/can.2005.20.3.328.

Riles, Annelise. 2001. *The Network inside Out*. Ann Arbor, MI: University of Michigan Press.

——. 2004. 'Real Time: Unwinding Technocratic and Anthropological Knowledge'. *American Ethnologist* 31(3): 392–405. https://doi.org/10.1525/ae.2004.31.3.392.

Robbins, Joel. 2004. *Becoming Sinners: Christianity and Moral Torment in a Papua New Guinea Society*. Berkeley; Los Angeles; London: University of California Press.

——. 2013. 'Beyond the Suffering Subject: Toward an Anthropology of the Good'. *Journal of the Royal Anthropological Institute* 19(3): 447–62. https://doi.org/10.1111/1467-9655.12044.

Roberts, Dan. 2013. 'Extreme Poverty Could Be Wiped out by 2030, World Bank Estimates Show'. *The Guardian*, 2 April. http://www.theguardian.com/business/2013/apr/02/global-poverty-wiped-out-world-bank

Robertson, Claire Cone. 1997. *Trouble Showed the Way: Women, Men, and Trade in the Nairobi Area, 1890–1990*. Bloomington, IN: Indiana University Press.

Robins, Steven. 2009. 'Humanitarian Aid beyond "Bare Survival": Social Movement Responses to Xenophobic Violence in South Africa'. *American Ethnologist* 36(4): 637–50. https://doi.org/10.1111/j.1548-1425.2009.01200.x.

Rodima-Taylor, Daivi. 2014. 'Passageways of Cooperation: Mutuality in Post-Socialist Tanzania'. *Africa* 84(4): 553–75. https://doi.org/10.1017/S0001972014000497.

Rodima-Taylor, Daivi, and Erik Bähre. 2014. 'Introduction: Mutual Help in an Era of Uncertainty'. *Africa* 84(4): 507–9. https://doi.org/10.1017/S0001972014000461.

Ross, Fiona C. 2010. *Raw Life, New Hope Decency, Housing and Everyday Life in a Post-Apartheid Community*. Claremont, South Africa: UCT Press.

Roy, Ananya. 2010. *Poverty Capital: Microfinance and the Making of Development*. New York: Routledge.

Ruchman, Samuel G. 2017. 'Colonial Construction: Labor Practices and Precedents along the Uganda Railway, 1893–1903'. *International Journal of African Historical Studies* 50(2): 251–73.

Sahlins, Marshall. 2011a. 'What Kinship Is (Part One)'. *Journal of the Royal Anthropological Institute* 17(1): 2–19. https://doi.org/10.1111/j.1467-9655.2010.01666.x.

——. 2011b. 'What Kinship Is (Part Two)'. *Journal of the Royal Anthropological Institute* 17(2): 227–42. https://doi.org/10.1111/j.1467-9655.2011.01677.x.

Sandel, Michael. 1982. *Liberalism and the Limits of Justice*. Cambridge: Cambridge University Press.

Scheper-Hughes, Nancy. 1993. *Death without Weeping: The Violence of Everyday Life in Brazil*. Berkeley; Los Angeles; London: University of California Press.

——. 1995. 'The Primacy of the Ethical: Propositions for a Militant Anthropology'. *Current Anthropology* 36(3): 409–40.

Scherz, China. 2014. *Having People, Having Heart: Charity, Sustainable Development, and Problems of Dependence in Central Uganda*. Chicago: University of Chicago Press.

Schreiner, Mark. 2015. 'A Comparison of Two Simple, Low-Cost Ways for Local, Pro-Poor Organizations to Measure the Poverty of Their Participants'. *Social Indicators Research* 124(2): 537–69. https://doi.org/10.1007/s11205-014-0789-1.

Schuller, Mark. 2009. 'Gluing Globalization: NGOs as Intermediaries in Haiti'. *PoLAR: Political and Legal Anthropology Review* 32(1): 84–104. https://doi.org/10.1111/j.1555-2934.2009.01025.x.

Sealander, Judith. 2003. 'Curing Evils at Their Source: The Arrival of Scientific Giving'. In *Charity, Philanthropy, and Civility in American History*, edited by Lawrence J. Friedman and Mark D. McGarvie, pp. 217–40. Cambridge: Cambridge University Press.

Seeley, Janet. 1987. 'Social Welfare in a Kenyan Town: Policy and Practice, 1902–1985'. *African Affairs* 86(345): 541–66.

Seligman, Adam B. 2000. *The Problem of Trust*. Princeton, NJ: Princeton University Press.

Sen, Amartya. 1982. *Poverty and Famines: An Essay on Entitlement and Deprivation*. Oxford; New York: Clarendon Press; Oxford University Press.

——. 2001. *Development as Freedom*. Oxford; New York: Oxford Paperbacks.

Shack/Slum Dwellers International. 2001. *Korogocho Informal Settlements Enumeration Report*. Nairobi.

Shipton, Parker. 2007. *The Nature of Entrustment: Intimacy, Exchange, and the Sacred in Africa*. New Haven, CT: Yale University Press.

——. 2014. 'Topics and Tangents for Mutual Help in Uncertainty'. *Africa* 84(4): 510–29. https://doi.org/10.1017/S0001972014000473.

Silberschmidt, Margrethe. 1992. 'Have Men Become the Weaker Sex? Changing Life Situations in Kisii District, Kenya'. *Journal of Modern African Studies* 30(2): 237–53.

Sillitoe, Paul. 2010. 'Trust in Development: Some Implications of Knowing in Indigenous Knowledge'. *Journal of the Royal Anthropological Institute* 16(1): 12–30. https://doi.org/10.1111/j.1467-9655.2009.01594.x.

Simmel, Georg. 2011. *The Philosophy of Money*. Abingdon, Oxon; New York: Routledge.

Simon, Vendelin Tarmo. 2015. *Ageing, Health and Care in Rural Tanzania*. PhD, University of Basel.

Simone, AbdouMaliq. 2004a. 'People as Infrastructure: Intersecting Fragments in Johannesburg'. *Public Culture* 16(3): 407–29.

———. 2004b. *For the City Yet to Come: Changing African Life in Four Cities*. Durham, NC: Duke University Press.

———. 2005. 'Urban Circulation and the Everyday Politics of African Urban Youth: The Case of Douala, Cameroon'. *International Journal of Urban and Regional Research* 29(3): 516–32. https://doi.org/10.1111/j.1468-2427.2005.00603.x.

Smith, Daniel Jordan. 2010. 'Promiscuous Girls, Good Wives, and Cheating Husbands: Gender Inequality, Transitions to Marriage, and Infidelity in Southeastern Nigeria'. *Anthropological Quarterly* 83(1): 123–52. https://doi.org/10.1353/anq.0.0118.

Stambach, Amy. 2000. *Lessons from Mount Kilimanjaro: Schooling, Community, and Gender in East Africa*. Routledge.

Stasch, Rupert. 2009. *Society of Others: Kinship and Mourning in a West Papuan Place*. Berkeley, CA: University of California Press.

Stirrat, R.L., and Heiko Henkel. 1997. 'The Development Gift: The Problem of Reciprocity in the NGO World'. *Annals of the American Academy of Political and Social Science* 554: 66–80.

Strathern, Marilyn. 1990. *The Gender of the Gift*. Berkeley; Los Angeles; London: University of California Press.

———. 1996. 'Cutting the Network'. *Journal of the Royal Anthropological Institute* 2(3): 517–35. https://doi.org/10.2307/3034901.

———. 1999. *Property, Substance and Effect: Anthropological Essays on Persons and Things*. London; New Brunswick, NJ: Athlone Press.

———. ed. 2000. *Audit Cultures: Anthropological Studies in Accountability, Ethics and the Academy*. London; New York: Routledge.

Tanner, Nancy. 1974. 'Matrifocality in Indonesia, in Africa and among Black Americans'. In *Woman, Culture, and Society*, edited by Michelle Zimbalist Rosaldo and Louise Lamphere, pp. 129–56. Stanford, CA: Stanford University Press.

Tendler, Judith. 2005. 'Why Social Policy Is Condemned to a Residual Category of Safety Nets and What to Do about It'. In *Social Policy in a Development Context*, edited by P. Thandika Mkandawire, pp. 119–42. Houndmills, Hampshire; New York: Palgrave Macmillan.

Therborn, Göran. 2007. 'After Dialectics: Radical Social Theory in a Post-Communist World'. *New Left Review* 43: 63–114.

Thieme, Tatiana A. 2013. 'The "Hustle" amongst Youth Entrepreneurs in Mathare's Informal Waste Economy'. *Journal of Eastern African Studies* 7(3): 389–412. https://doi.org/10.1080/17531055.2013.770678.

Thomas, Lynn M. 2003. *Politics of the Womb*. Berkeley, CA: University of California Press.

Thornton White, L.W., L. Silberman and P.R. Anderson. 1948. *Nairobi: Master Plan for a Colonial Capital*. Report Prepared for the Municipal Council of Nairobi (London: HMSO).

Ticktin, Miriam. 2011. *Casualties of Care: Immigration and the Politics of Humanitarianism in France*. Berkeley, CA: University of California Press.

Trapp, Micah M. 2016. 'You-Will-Kill-Me Beans: Taste and the Politics of Necessity in Humanitarian Aid'. *Cultural Anthropology* 31(3): 412–37. https://doi.org/10.14506/ca31.3.08.

Tronto, Joan C. 1993. *Moral Boundaries: A Political Argument for an Ethic of Care*. London: Routledge.

Vaughan, Megan. 1987. *The Story of an African Famine: Gender and Famine in Twentieth-century Malawi*. Cambridge: Cambridge University Press.

Venkatesan, Soumhya, and Thomas Yarrow. 2012. *Differentiating Development: Beyond an Anthropology of Critique*. New York: Berghahn Books.

Warren, Mark E. 1999. *Democracy and Trust*. Cambridge: Cambridge University Press.

Weber, Max. 2001 [1930]. *The Protestant Ethic and the Spirit of Capitalism*. London; New York: Routledge.

Weiss, Brad. 2002. 'Thug Realism: Inhabiting Fantasy in Urban Tanzania'. *Cultural Anthropology* 17(1): 93–124.

——. 2009. *Street Dreams and Hip Hop Barbershops: Global Fantasy in Urban Tanzania*. Bloomington, IN: Indiana University Press.

Welker, Marina. 2012. 'The Green Revolution's Ghost: Unruly Subjects of Participatory Development in Rural Indonesia'. *American Ethnologist* 39(2): 389–406. https://doi.org/10.1111/j.1548-1425.2012.01371.x.

Weru, Jane. 2004. 'Community Federations and City Upgrading: The Work of Pamoja Trust and Muungano in Kenya'. *Environment and Urbanization* 16(1): 47–62. https://doi.org/10.1177/095624780401600105.

White, Luise. 1990. *The Comforts of Home: Prostitution in Colonial Nairobi*. Chicago: University of Chicago Press. http://hdl.handle.net/2027/heb.02671.

Whyte, Susan R., Michael A. Whyte, Lotte Meinert, and Jenipher Twebaze. 2013. 'Therapeutic Clientship'. In *When People Come First: Critical Studies in Global Health*, edited by João Biehl and Adriana Petryna. Princeton, NJ: Princeton University Press.

Wilkis, Ariel. 2017. *The Moral Power of Money: Morality and Economy in the Life of the Poor*. Stanford, CA: Stanford University Press.

Williams, Raymond. 1976. *Keywords: A Vocabulary of Culture and Society*. Oxford: Oxford University Press.

Wilson, Richard Ashby, and Richard D. Brown, eds. 2008. *Humanitarianism and Suffering: The Mobilization of Empathy*. Cambridge: Cambridge University Press.

World Bank. 1990. *World Development Report 1990: Poverty*. Washington, DC: World Bank. https://doi.org/10.1596/0-1952-0851-X.

——. 2012. *Managing Risk, Promoting Growth: Developing Systems of Social Protection for Africa. The World Bank's Africa Social Protection Strategy 2012–2022*. Washington, DC: World Bank.

Zelizer, Viviana A. 1994. *Pricing the Priceless Child: The Changing Social Value of Children*. Princeton, NJ: Princeton University Press.

Zigon, Jarrett. 2014. 'Attunement and Fidelity: Two Ontological Conditions for Morally Being-in-the-World'. *Ethos* 42(1): 16–30. https://doi.org/10.1111/etho.12036.

Zigon, Jarrett, and C. Jason Throop. 2014. 'Moral Experience: Introduction'. *Ethos* 42(1): 1–15. https://doi.org/10.1111/etho.12035.

Index

n refers to a note

acquisitiveness 142
Actor-Network-Theory 100
Africa 9, 11–13, 118–9
African Development Bank 9
African Population and Health Research
    Center 4, 37–8, 87, 93, 118,
    184–5*n*4
*African Socialism and its Application to
    Planning in Kenya* (1965) 63
agricultural schemes 51
Ahero 51, 53
airline industry waste 61
algorithms 94–6
AMREF Health Africa 84–5
Anderson, David 42
anthropology 2, 4, 7–8, 16, 21–2, 105
    Africanist anthropology 21
    of care 137, 181–2
    of development 16–17, 101, 117–8,
        123, 179
    economic anthropology 11–13, 21, 142
    of ethics and morality 7, 23–4, 132–3,
        148
    of humanitarianism 74, 157
    fieldwork in 5, 25–7
Appadurai, Arjun 77
Arid and Semi-Arid Lands (ASAL) 77–9
Ariès, Philippe 166
Awori, Moody 76

Bähre, Erik 18, 129–30
Baier, Annette 110
Ballard, Richard 18–19
Bayart, Jean-François 49
Bloch, Maurice 105
Boma Rescue rehabilitation centre
    155–6
Bornstein, Erica and Peter Redfield 10
Bowker, Geoffrey and Susan Leigh Star
    Sorting Things Out 94

Brand, Russell 3
Brazil 4, 157
    Bolsa Família (Family Allowance)
        system 15, 20
Britain
    and Universal Basic Income 177
    welfare state in 62, 71
British colonialism 41–3
bureaucracy 105–8, 113–4, 129–30
    see also ghetto-level bureaucracy

care and caring 1, 6–8, 20, 24–5, 137,
        182
    ethics of 23
    failure of 6, 10–11
CARE International 64
Carsten, Janet 163
cartographic knowledge 37
cash grants 1–3, 4–6, 7, 8–13, 18–19,
        75–7, 179–81
    conditionality of 15–17, 26
    dependency on 107–8, 117, 123–4,
        142–3
    enabling freedom of choice 13, 110,
        121
    evaluation of 116–7, 162
    interviews for 89–90, 92
    refusal of 68–9
    regulation of 106–8, 114–6, 121,
        126–7
    selection process for 86–7, 98
    see also child grants; unconditional
        grants; urban grants
Cash Transfer Learning Partnership 16,
        17, 185*n*8
Chant, Sylvia 88
charity 98–9, 112–3, 119
Chiefs 47, 184*n*3
    role in dispute resolution 83–4
child grant 5, 30, 40, 72–3, 79, 98–9,
        127, 128
    evaluation of 117–8

child mortality 38
childhood 166
children 75, 151, 158–62, 175
    and crime 161, 163
    disappearance of 68–9, 188n1
    'rogue' children 56
    see also mother-child relationship
Comaroff, Jean and John 178
Community Development Fund (CDF)
    64, 65, 66
community workers 80–2, 84–6, 113,
    116
Covid-19 pandemic 9, 177

Daily Nation 99
Dandora 3, 44
Darfur famine (1984-5) 156
Das, Veena 16
Davis, Mike xi
    Planet of the Slums 77
de Soto, Hernando 187n4
de Waal, Alex 156–7
debt 48, 68, 144, 179
    see also microloans
Demographic Surveillance Survey 4,
    37–8, 87, 93
Department of Approved Schools 163
Department for International Develop-
    ment (UK) 9
devil worship 68–9
Di Nunzio, Marco 52
dispute resolution 83–4
domestic work 59–60, 164
du Gay, Paul 17, 107

Eastlands 41, 42, 43, 46–7
education 72, 163, 172–4
El Niño flood (1997) 39
electricity supplies 39
Englund, Harri 170
entrepreneurship 123, 124–5, 138–9
ethnicity 83, 86, 88–91
European Commission
    'Use of Cash and Vouchers in
        Humanitarian Crises' 14

families 150, 153, 163
    and filial piety 169–72
    structure of 61–2

famines 156
Fassin, Didier 70
Ferguson, James 17, 19–20, 26, 73, 101,
    118, 179
food aid 65, 78–9
food price controls 58–9, 65, 79
Fortes, Meyer 153, 170
Foucault, Michel 17, 26
Friedman, Milton 17

General Service Unit (GSU) 47, 188n5
Ghana 11, 170
ghetto-level bureaucracy 31, 80–2,
    106–7, 108–9, 112–4, 121, 125,
    128–9
ghettoes 4, 35–9, 49, 77, 79, 151, 184n1
Gilligan, Carol 23
girls 159–60, 162
Gitathuru 45
GiveDirectly (organisation) 9, 19, 109,
    111, 177
giving and gifts 131, 141–5, 146–7, 174
GIZ (Germany) 9
Global Acute Malnutrition Rate 78
Global Relief Foundation 78, 82–3, 84,
    86–91, 94–5, 96–7, 116
gorogoro 191n1
Graeber, David 107, 142, 177, 181–2
Green, Maia 117–8
Grogan xi–xii, 45

Hagen people 174
Han, Clara 137, 172, 182
Hann, Chris 21
Haraway, Donna 83
Hardin, Garrett 157
Hart, Keith 11, 21
Harvey, Penny and Hannah Knox 70,
    101
Hayek, Friedrich 14–15
Held, Virginia 23
HIV/AIDS 1, 21, 28, 36, 38, 55, 58, 65,
    70, 97, 157
    social impact of 57, 74–5, 79, 116
Holston, James 187n4
Horn of Africa 73, 79, 152
households 55–6, 61–2
housing 37, 39, 43, 45–6, 90–1, 151

humanitarian assistance 50–1, 78–9, 96–7

Imperial British East Africa Company 41
individual, the 22–3, 138
informal economy xi, 11–12, 52
internally displaced persons (IDP) 127, 128
International Development Coopera-tion Agency (Sweden) 9, 79
International Labour Organization 10–11, 13, 45, 52
International Monetary Fund 51, 59

Jaffer, Murtaza 47
Japan 26
Johannesburg 49–50
Johnson, Peter 110
Just Give Money to the Poor (Hanlon et al.) 95, 122

Kalenjin people 51
Kalomo Cash Transfer Scheme 76
Kamau, Joyce 110
Kamba people 42
Kano Plain 51
Kenya
    attempted military coup (1982) 46, 51
    colonial era 41–3, 61–3
    Constitution (2010) 178
    Declaration of Emergency (1952) 42–3
    election (2007) 72
    fertility rate in 166–7
    independence of (1963) 43–4
    post-colonial era 45, 63, 178
    welfare systems in 19, 62–5, 71–3
    for other topics relating to Kenya, *see* the topic, e.g. HIV/AIDS
Kenyatta, Jomo 44, 46, 51, 63–4, 65, 71, 128
Kenyatta, Uhuru 72
Keynes, John Maynard 43
Kibaki, Mwai 65, 71–2, 75, 76
Kibera 37, 97, 189n11
Kikuyu people 40, 41, 42–3, 46, 62, 91
kinship relationships 57–8, 76, 132–3, 135–6, 140, 166, 171

Kituo cha Sheria (legal aid organisation) 47
Koch FM radio station 36
Korogocho x –xiii, 5, 37, 186n16
    mapping of 35–6
    for other topics relating to Korogocho *see* the topic, e.g. ghettoes
Korogocho Owners Welfare Associaton (KOWA) 47–8
    legal case against Pamoja Trust 48–9
Korogocho Slum Upgrading Programme 48
Korowai people 137–8
kwashiorkor 88, 189n10

landfill 4, 155–6
landless proletariat 40
Latin America 11, 18, 88
Lewis, Joanna 62
Lipsky, Michael 81
Living Faith Community Church 82, 83, 88–9, 93, 115–6, 117, 120
Local Authority Transfer Fund (LATF) 65, 66
Lonsdale, John 86
Luo people 42, 51, 91, 139, 188n7
    family structure of 55–6
    marriage customs of 52, 58

Maasai people 40, 75–6
Madaraka Day (1963) 63
Mair, Jonathan 148
Maize and Produce Board 59
malnutrition 78, 79, 84, 86–9, 151, 189n10
marasmus 88, 189n10
Marcus, George 5
market economy 13, 14–15
marriage customs 54, 167
Masquelier, Adeline 52
Master Plan for a Colonial Capital (White et al., 1948) 43
Mattingly, Cheryl 7
Mau Mau resistance movement 42
Maurer, Bill 13
Mauss, Marcel 131, 146
Médicins Sans Frontières 36, 97
Melanesian people 22, 23

men and women, roles of 28, 55–6, 62, 134, 145–7
microfinance 89
microloans 2, 3, 15, 68, 89, 179
Middle East Youth Initiative 52
mobile money x, 68, 73, 81–2, 189n7
Moi, Daniel arap 47, 51, 65, 71–2, 74
Molyneux, Maxine 18
moral philosophy 22–4
Morton, Gregory Duff 20
Mosse, David 179
mother-child relationship 24, 32, 76, 150–65, 167–9
    detachment in 153, 162–3
mothers 165–9
    single mothers 166, 167
Musk, Elon 177
Mutiso Menezes International 46
Mutunga, Willy 47

Nairobi 3, 10, 39–44, 139–40
    Europeans in 41
    migration to 42, 53
Nairobi River 44
National Safety Net Programme 5, 72
National Social Security Fund 63
neighbourly relationships 131–2, 141
neoliberalism 9, 10
Neuwirth, Robert *Shadow Cities* 77
Neves, David and Andries du Toit 125
NGOs (non-governmental organisa-tions) 5, 64–6, 77, 118, 126
    'ghost' NGOs 164
Nguyen, Vinh-Kim 26, 157

Official Development Assistance Debt 48
Ogiek people 40
Operation Anvil 42
Orange telecommunications company 100
Ortner, Sherry 4
Oxfam 64, 77–8

Paine, Thomas 129
Pamoja Trust 47–8
Papua New Guinea 4, 174
parenthood 28–9, 32
Parkin, David 56

Parry, Jonathan and Maurice Bloch 142
Parsons, Talcott 129–30
paternalism 16–17
Paul, Laurie Ann 29
Penglase, Ben 157
personhood and self 22–4, 132–4, 167, 172
    moral personhood 167, 172
Pogge, Thomas 19
Polanyi, Karl 10, 124
political philosophy 22–3
poor people 122–3
    attitudes to 14–17
    trust in 108–11, 115
President's Emergency Plan for AIDS Relief (PEPFAR) 65
Provide Health Centre 82, 84

railway workers 41–2
Rancière, Jacques 122
Rawls, John 23
Redfield, Peter 96
rich people 135, 140
rickets 151
Riles, Annelise 26
Robbins, Joel 4
Robertson, Claire Cone 62
Rongo 52, 53
Ross, Fiona 141

Sahlins, Marshall 133, 163
Sandel, Michael 23
Scheper-Hughes, Nancy 4, 157, 174
Schreiner, Mark 87
schools 163–4
secure shelter movement 120
Sen, Amartya *Poverty and Famines* 156
Shakespeare, William *Hamlet* 24
Shipton, Parker 139
Silberschmidt, Margrethe 55
Simmel, Georg 13
Simone, AbdouMaliq 49–50
slums *see* ghettoes
social problems 73, 74
Social Protection Floor (ILO) 13
social relationships 21, 22–5, 100–1, 131–3, 135–9, 148–9, 182–3, 186n13
    detachment in 31–2, 132, 136–8, 145, 147–9
South Africa 9, 18, 19–20, 26, 70, 125

Speenhamland welfare system 124
squatter settlements 45
Stasch, Rupert 137, 148
Strathern, Marilyn 22, 100, 105, 174

Tallensi people 170
technocratic knowledge 16, 26, 31, 37,
    71, 80, 114
Therborn, Göran 19
Throop, Jason 23–4
Tronto, Joan 23
trust and mistrust 108–12, 115, 132
Turner, Victor 133

unconditional grants 1, 2–3, 15–17, 26,
    89, 111, 126, 179–80
UNICEF 5, 9, 64, 75, 76, 77, 79, 96
United Nations 119
United States Agency for International
    Development (USAID) 64, 84
Universal Basic Income (UBI) 19,
    107–8, 177, 185–6n11
Universal Declaration of Human Rights
    178
urban grant 5, 18, 30, 73, 77, 79
    registration for 92–6, 105–6
    selection process for 81–3, 86–7
urban poor 187n4

Village Elders 80, 83, 85, 89–90, 91,
    95, 98
Vision 2030 development programme
    11, 84
Voluntarily Unemployed Persons
    Ordinance 128
vulnerability 72, 75, 87

waste materials, sale of 60–1
water resources 39
Weber, Max 129–30
Weiner, James 100
Weru, Jane 47
Wilkis, Ariel 99, 108
Williams, Raymond *Keywords* 119
women xiii, 2, 18, 28, 41, 123, 134–6,
    138
    as heads of households 55–6, 88
    and income earning 59–60
    and maternal mortality 38
    single women 55, 116
    widows 58, 134, 135
Women Enterprise Development Fund
    123
World Bank 5, 9, 11–12, 21–2, 30, 40,
    45–6, 66, 72, 76, 119, 185n10
    designation of poverty line by 61
World Development Report (1990) 9
World Food Programme 9, 36, 65, 85,
    150, 154
World Health Organization (WHO)
    36, 119
World Vision (organisation) 36
World War II 62

young people 49–50, 52, 59, 188n6
Youth Enterprise Development Fund
    123

Zambia 76
Zanotelli, Father Alex 46–7
Zeliger, Viviana 166
Zigon, Jarrett 23–4, 133, 148
Zuckerberg, Mark 177